MORE PRAISE FOR KRISTIN HAHN'S
In Search of Grace

"*In Search of Grace* is a fascinating and moving story about one woman's spiritual journey, full of anecdotes and insights regarding the nature of mind and reality, as well as the various teachers, teachings, and practices she encounters along the way. I recommend it to anyone who is likewise striving to find their own way amidst the many offerings available in the world of contemporary spirituality."   —LAMA SURYA DAS

"Kristin Hahn has an acute ear, a deft pen, and a keen mind. As one of those who is profiled in this book, I found her insights illuminating even of my own religious journey. That she has so accurately rendered such a rich variety of pilgrimages makes a reading of *In Search of Grace* a gracious experience in and of itself."
    —REVEREND WILLIAM F. SCHULZ, president, Unitarian Universalist
Association of Congregations (1985-93);
executive director, Amnesty International USA

Michael Sanville

About the Author

KRISTIN HAHN grew up in New Mexico, then moved to Los Angeles, where she spent a decade working in the television and film industry. With Shainee Gabel, Hahn wrote, produced, and filmed the acclaimed independent documentary *Anthem* and wrote the book based on the film. She lives in California with her husband and son.

ALSO BY KRISTIN HAHN

Anthem: An American Road Story

A JOURNEY ACROSS AMERICA'S

LANDSCAPE OF FAITH

IN SEARCH OF

GRACE

Kristin Hahn

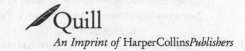

Quill

An Imprint of HarperCollins*Publishers*

The publisher wishes to thank Hampton Roads Publishing Company, Inc., for the use of "The Lord's Prayer" from *Conversations with God—An Uncommon Dialogue, Book 3*.

A hardcover edition of this book was published in 2002 by William Morrow, an imprint of HarperCollins Publishers.

HarperCollins books may be purchased for educational, business, or sales promotional use. For information please write: Special Markets Department, HarperCollins Publishers Inc., 10 East 53rd Street, New York, NY 10022.

First Quill edition published 2003.

Designed by Nicola Ferguson

The Library of Congress has catalogued the hardcover edition as follows:
Hahn, Kristin.
In search of grace : a religious outsider's journey across
America's landscape of faith / by Kristin Hahn.
p.   cm.
Includes bibliographical references.
ISBN 0-380-97701-X
1. United States—Religion—1960-. 2. Hahn, Kristin—
Journeys—United States. 3. United States. I. Title.
BL2525 .H34 2002
200'.973'090511—dc21   2001044765

ISBN 0-380-80271-6 (pbk.)

03 04 05 06 07 ❖/RRD 10 9 8 7 6 5 4 3 2 1

To Charlie—my muse, my mirror,
my best friend

Contents

Judaism

Islam

Buddhism

Hinduism

Sikhism

The New Age

Self-Help

Neopaganism

Acknowledgments

First and foremost, I would like to thank the many individuals who opened their homes and sanctuaries to share with me their most intimate expressions of faith.

To Maxine and Hillary for speaking the right words at the right time; to Huston Smith for digging my letter out of his garbage can; and to Shainee and Nick for never tiring of reading rough drafts—your encouragement and contributions kept me on track.

A special thank-you to Lotus for her illuminative guidance and her humor about all things spiritual.

And to my agent and friend, Jennifer Rudolph Walsh—there is no greater super-heroine to have on your side.

This book would have remained only in my imagination were it not for my editor, Jennifer Hershey, who fearlessly went the distance with this self-taught writer, earning through every step of the process my admiration and respect.

To those who gave their time and patience to my fact-finding—and -checking—missions, I am indebted to each of you. I of course assume full responsibility for the application of those many suggestions.

My gratitude goes out to my very small family for their very big support, and a particularly hearty squeeze to my grandfather for very intentionally planting in me the instinct to explore.

And to my old friends whom I adore—your faith in me is my ongoing revival.

For anchoring what follows, I'd like to single out Gene Begay, whose lighthearted wisdom has taught me many things, not the least of which is the deeper meaning of "going home."

Introduction

I once braved a ride at a state fair, a ride that was shaped like a giant angel food cake pan. I and other scrawny youngsters just tall enough to make the cut were strapped to its curved walls by a bearded carny. Having secured us to his satisfaction, the man sauntered over to a control panel and with the casual flip of a switch set the cake pan spinning, centrifugal force throwing each of us off our feet and pinning us against its cold steel sides. Then the ride began to buck wildly like a mechanical bull. Our collective howls of thrill soon turned to terror, our pleas to stop drowned out by bass-heavy Top 40 hits reverberating from blown-out speakers. Traumatized by this hunk of metal, I vowed in midwhirl that if I survived this version of "fun," I would never again choose—and especially not pay—to repeat it.

Some twenty years later, my self-preserving vow began to haunt me when I realized my adult life in Los Angeles had begun to simulate that ride. What had indeed been fun at the start was changing, Hollywood's grind of performance and pretense pressing and stretching me out of my natural shape, as if the town's switch were being manned by a dozing carny. I knew it was time to get off.

At the age of twenty-nine, I'd spent ten years working long hours in television, theater, and film. During that time I perfected the art of distraction, doing all the multitasking things we do that keep us from seeing clearly what is right in front of us, or confronting what lurks just below the surface of ourselves. Parts of me that I had ignored and neglected were shouting to be heard—internal howls overwhelmed by my own bass-heavy busyness. Like many Los Angelenos—and countless other overstimulated, overworked, but adequately fed, clothed, and sheltered Americans—I had developed a host of remedies to quiet my acutely preoccupied mind, soothe my exhaustion and anxiety, and submerge the inconvenient feelings I didn't have time for. I had my aura, chart, palm, and coffee grounds read; I was acupunctured, acupressured, and hypnotically regressed; I was depolarized, magnetized, and analyzed; I regrouped by way of the occasional "spiritual" workshop, and was always reassured by New Age bestsellers that my life was happening this way for a *reason*.

But I grew tired of hiring people to make me feel better. I aspired to thrive, not simply survive on the laurels of others' experiences and insights, many of which eased my symptoms, though with an effectiveness that tended to last about as long as the time-release of an over-the-counter cold tablet. It was becoming increasingly apparent how easily secondhand clarity or comfort can be misplaced or forgotten. I longed for something more enduring, more tangible and direct, something *I* could do to instigate perspective, stability, generosity, and peace when my head started to buck and spin like that state fair ride.

Instinctively drawn to ritual, I turned my attention to the myriad ways others find and *sustain* the balance I longed for. The realms of traditional devotion were almost completely unknown to me as the offspring of an irreligious family. I wanted to learn more about how Americans' religious and spiritual practices satisfy our shared human needs: to belong, feel "whole" and part of a "people"; to succeed and earn second chances; to equalize anger, fear, self-doubt, guilt, love, and forgiveness; to celebrate life's passages and mourn its losses; to sense the sacred and feel renewed; to create purpose and meaning; to be guided; to assure justice and equity; to temper excessiveness; to earn a legacy; and, for some, to secure immortality.

So in a torrential downpour, I left Los Angeles. For the next few years, I settled here and there, seeking out people of faith everywhere I went. My desire wasn't to "try on" each religion in the hope of finding myself a good fit; rather, I was compelled to understand—firsthand—how and why people practice what they preach. For this informal investigation, I focused on those for whom religion is not merely an affiliation—an identity worn like a name tag at a convention—but a daily effort, an integrated *way of life*. I witnessed—and sometimes participated in—the intentional and disciplined gestures that people make in observance of their beliefs. I wanted to illuminate the impact, real or perceived, those acts of devotion had on the questions that preoccupied me: how we develop and maintain our character, overcome our personal struggles, experience life more completely and fully, and enhance the quality of other people's lives.

Born at the end of the 1960s—part of an age group generically termed "generation X"—my peers and I have at our disposal a staggering number of options, whether in the market for underarm deodorant or inner solace. No longer must one travel the world to find and explore diversity. We live in the Noah's Ark of countries, where a sampling of the globe's multitudes, including religious peoples, have come to call a single vessel of land "home." Since its founding, America has been one nation under many notions of God—a place where differing ideas about creation and the Creator coexist. Having so many religions concentrated in my own country both contained my mission and complicated it.

In organizing my intentionally unscientific journey into America's world of faith, I divided the topic categorically. I began where our country began, with a sampling of this land's oldest known practice, as embodied in one indigenous medicine man. I devoted the most time and energy to Christianity, as the faith statistically embraced by about 80 percent of our nation's population. I also allotted chapters to other world religions generally acknowledged as "primary": Judaism, Islam, Buddhism, and Hinduism. In addition, I dedicated time to examples of practices that originated in America, such as Scientology and one that evolved from the book-driven "pop-guru" movement, as well as three modern outgrowths of ancient traditions: Spiritualism, 3HO Sikhism, and Neopaganism. Unfortunately, because of limitations imposed by page counts and publishing deadlines, and by the inherent difficulties of breaching people's sacred time and space, dozens of sects, schools of thought, and entire faiths fell from my itinerary.

A lifetime or more could undoubtedly be spent probing the subtleties of any *one* of the traditions treated in these pages. What I've compiled is not a comprehensive resource of comparative religion, but an account of a very personal journey—an up-close chronicle of Americans caught in the act of faith. Many strangers granted me permission to participate in their private rituals, and shared with me their most intimate thoughts about their beliefs and daily practices. The thrust of each chapter is shaped by both my own impressions and the words and deeds of those willing accomplices.

I did not set out to validate or invalidate any one religion or individual. Rather, my aim was to attempt to understand the highest intentions that inform people of faith in their search for truth, ideals, inspiration, comfort, quietude, and—ultimately—happiness. Along the way, with different faiths lined up side by side, I came to see not only what is unique to each, but also what is common among them.

Dr. Elisabeth Kübler-Ross—a self-inducted expert on faith and the first person I spoke to after embarking on this journey—provided useful orientation for what follows. In her heavy Swiss accent, she insisted that I distinguish between the concepts of the religious and the spiritual. The seventy-something psychiatrist chided me for thoughtlessly interchanging the two words during our conversation at her ranch home in the Arizona desert.

Being religious, she argued, entails *belief* in doctrine too often driven by fear of eternal consequences. There is another approach—one she would consider spiritual—that emphasizes direct *experience* over doctrine. The feisty Kübler-Ross was adamant that I adopt her distinction between the passive compliance of religious belief and the unimpeded engagement of spiritual experience. So much so, in fact, that she threatened to "karate-chop" me with her "good arm" if I failed to do so, even as she lay in bed convalescing from a stroke. I hastily clarified to the agitated doctor, as I more casually do for you now, that my plan was indeed to focus on *the doing,* seeking out what Kübler-Ross would consider the spiritual element underlying each of the traditions I explore.

For the sake of continuity, I refer to "the doing" as a "practice." This I loosely define as acts of holy reverence or worship, exercises that lessen afflictive emotion and the tyranny of ego, rituals that evoke a sense of the sacred, and experiences that connect an individual to something regarded as divine. I've tried to convey a little bit of the doctrine of each belief system simply to show how it motivates the practice. For this purpose, each chapter begins with a brief overview of that faith's genesis and its intersection with the American continent, as well as the most current available estimates of constituency.

It is my hope that the following pages will pass along to you at least some of what has been given to me: a greater knowledge of, and appreciation for, the religious and spiritual "tools" available to anyone in search of a practice, and a deeper self-understanding by way of intimate exposure to people who use them. But perhaps even more significant is the bigger picture the words in this book point to: the layer upon layer of contributions that are each day made by so many different traditions to ignite one nation's vibrant declaration of faith.

Native American Beliefs

Chapter One

There are more than five hundred Native American tribes officially recognized by the U.S. government, and hundreds more lost in the annals of American history. The religious practices belonging to the multitude of tribes were, until recently, actively and forcefully subverted by Christian churches and the U.S. government. It was not until 1978 that native practices were officially recognized as worthy of protection under the Native American Religious Freedom Act. This act of Congress, coming after centuries of repression, has not, however, been a panacea for Native Americans struggling to protect and revitalize their spiritual heritage. In 1988 the U.S. Supreme Court declared that sacred land central to Native American religious practices—land whose pristine quality is so essential that the practice becomes extinct without it—is not protected against federal development and desecration. In this opinion, the Court rendered the 1978 act a toothless expression of political goodwill.

Meanwhile, tribes and individual American Indians continue efforts to resuscitate their spiritual traditions and preserve sacred sites. Among the most active on this front are what many Native Americans refer to as "medicine people." As a leader within the community, a medicine person's role ranges from treating physical ailments, to overseeing rites of passage such as birth, marriage, and death, to guiding people, if only by example, along a spiritual path *rooted in centuries of oral tradition. To these ends, medicine people call upon the supernatural assistance of spirits who work in concert with the Creator—an omniscient, omnipresent entity also addressed as "Spirit" and "God."*

Though each tribe and reservation is unique, of the twenty-eight hundred Ojibwe Native Americans populating the Lac Courte Oreilles reservation in Hayward, Wisconsin, only about one-fourth incorporate traditional spiritual practices into their lives. Even fewer would be considered strict practitioners who are fully knowledgeable about the spiritual and historical meaning behind practices that are quickly disappearing.[1]

Communing with a Medicine Man

One fall day in the eighth year of my life, my mother came into my bedroom and announced that she and I would be moving from our house in Omaha, Nebraska. Our new city would be a place whose name I could not spell, in the faraway southwestern state of New Mexico. My mother rested her forehead against mine as if to brace us both and confided that we would leave in a matter of days. Pulling a piece of paper from her pocket, she unfolded a Realtor's listing, which described in shrunken print and abbreviated terms the dimensions of our new life: its square footage, its conditions and features, and how many miles it stood from the school I would attend. Hovering in a corner was a miniature black-and-white, overly xeroxed photograph of the home my mother promised we would love, bordering the yards of new friends I would make, sheltering under its roof the fun she and I would have. In the worn creases of this one page portrait of our future was her need for this all to be true.

People tell me I'm adaptable. Perhaps my high tolerance for change is a genetic inheritance. Or maybe it was an added feature—along with the new appliances and view of the Sandia Mountains—that came with that first of many desert homes. Whatever the case, I promptly accepted my new New Mexican identity, memorizing the correct, staccato spelling of Albuquerque. While my mother unpacked, I ceremoniously sheared off my long hair to mark into my own invisible calendar yet another beginning.

Little by little, our modest shell of a home was transformed into an Anglo's vision of a hacienda—Spanish décor accented by Native American tchotchkes, ornamental leather goods, patterned rugs and blankets, portraits of Indian women in long skirts, and our own small tribe of Hopi kachina dolls. Along with our accessorizing came an awareness that we shared our desert paradise with the Apaches, the Navajos, and the Hopis, among other pueblos and tribes—that the place we now called home had once been their own exclusive land of enchantment.

Whether motivated by intrigue, guilt, homage, or an unspoken yearning for something deeper and more authentic than anything her own past could offer her, my mother crowded our lives with emblems of our Native American neighbors. I was most drawn, out of both fear and wonder, to the vibrantly colored and mysteriously masked kachina dolls. Each foot-high wooden carving of a Hopi man in full regalia contorted its body toward the ground or sky, one knee raised in midstomp, mouth rounded in silent song. To the Hopis, the figures, however necessary they've become for tourist revenue, first and foremost represent their most sacred practice of communing with nature, guardian spirits, and the Creator. To my mother—perhaps unconsciously—these unmistakably indigenous objects provided reflections of something culturally rich, something with history and tradition, something spiritual. Things we did not, on our own, possess. Like many Americans, purchasing had become our religion, a practice of accumulation we believed could make us feel whole.

In my compact, mixed family of mostly European descent, no one spoke much of homelands, cultural identity, tradition, or religion, as if somehow such things had been washed away by the tides our ancestors crossed to reach the new land of opportunity. So, instead of crosses hung on our walls, or Testaments resting on our shelves, I came of age surrounded by an earlier, distinctly Native America. It required little of us in return, for unlike some non-Indians who experiment with and, in some cases, adopt Native American spiritual practices, my mother kept a reverential distance from the nativism she exposed us to. Perhaps in her mind, trying on rituals that didn't belong to her was the equivalent of shoplifting the totems and baskets and turquoise necklaces she had always paid, or traded something, for.

In time, my mother's attraction to Native America extended beyond the interior of our home, as we ventured out on weekends to attend public powwows—occasional tribal enactments of prayers that are otherwise private. Holding hands, we'd eat Indian fry bread while watching an unabashed communion between a people and their Creator. In this way pueblos and tribes offered non-Indians an education in their traditional "ways," hoping to dispel the prejudice that their practices were nothing more than primitive idolatry.

Eventually, a deeper desire burgeoned in me. I wanted to understand what was behind the wood, weavings, and sandstone that had decorated the walls and mantels of my childhood home. So while exploring the Great Lakes at the age of twenty-nine, I approached Gene Begay, a medicine man from one of several Ojibwe tribes in northern Wisconsin. Gene and I spent days together talking about his religious practices and the challenges he faced as one of his people's last living vestiges of its tradition.

"My uncle Pipe Mustache always told me," said Gene, as we sat in the lobby of his reservation's casino, "that to be a medicine man, to be a spiritual chief—an *oh-get-che-dah,* as my people say—is an unfortunate thing to have happen to you. 'I'm really sorry I had to pick you,' my uncle often said to me." Gene laughed gutturally; he has understood only in hindsight the complexities inherent in his uncle's apology. Gene's uncle Pipe was an "elder" medicine man who entrusted his trove of secret medicine teachings and sacred songs to the nephew he selected as his successor. In accepting his appointment, Gene inherited a huge responsibility: the physical, emotional, and spiritual well-being of his people.

I struggled to reconcile this traditional, ancient-looking man with our noisy, neon surroundings. He spoke of "the medicine, the Creator, and the spirits" over the shrill sound of machines gulping coins emblazoned with the busts of presidents who had expanded the new America until little remained of its original inhabitants. Gene was unfazed by the paradox, and as our time together unfolded, I came to see how his life as a Native medicine man in a postmodern America had prepared him for such scenes of incongruity.

"Most of my people are Christian converts," he stated matter-of-factly. Though there is a growing movement today among certain denominations to respect and even support Native spirituality, the consequences of centuries of aggressive missionary work is as evident on the reservation as the aftermath of a pileup.

"When the Christian church showed up and taught us how to talk to Jesus, my people said, 'Great!—another way to commune with the Creator—thanks.'" Gene shrugged. "But it wasn't that simple in the minds of the missionaries," he continued, less jovially. "My people were forced to choose between Christianity and the ways of their own people, our traditional practices labeled 'the work of the devil.' Spiritual artifacts and traditional garb were burned at the persuasion of priests and nuns as many of my people finally gave up what had been a long struggle for cultural and physical survival." His words and the silence that followed them left behind a residue of sadness. "Linguists say that if your children don't use the language, it and its social structures are as good as dead. Today, my people know they are Ojibwe, but they do not know what that *means*."

Gene offered an example of the widespread ignorance of ancient spiritual practices. Historically, the Ojibwes had their own New Year's Eve. "A month before spring equinox, men had a 'period'—just like women do, only symbolically," Gene recalled. "We'd spend a month going within, being introspective. We'd fast and do special prayers in anticipation of the new life that was coming. And then we'd have a big ceremony for the day of the new year, when the birds' song was heard again.

"Today, my people don't even know this existed," he said, shaking his head. "They think the new year is the turning of midnight on December thirty-first, when there is snow on the ground and champagne in their hand." Tiny puffs of ironic laughter escaped from his rounded belly.

The epidemic of cultural amnesia among Gene's people has forced him to redefine what it means to be a practicing spiritual leader when so few are interested in being led. "One of my greatest competitors is television," Gene lamented, the revolving door behind him revealing rows of blinking poker screens. I asked Gene whether he'd considered trying to preserve his tradition in print or on video for those who one day might want to unearth their obscured ancestry. He reminded me that his beliefs and practices—and the complex stories that encompass them—are strictly oral teachings. The act of verbal initiation and mentorship is itself an integral and dynamic aspect of the practice. "Passing the songs and stories down requires intensive commitment, time, and sacrifice," said Gene, adding with what seemed like hard-won acceptance: "Even my own kids—they live modern lives—aren't interested in learning them."

"Why do you keep doing it," I asked, "when this fire you're stoking will likely die with you?"

"I keep doing it," Gene bellowed back, "because I trust God with certainty, not happenstance. I keep going because it is my *responsibility,* and because no one promised me this way of life would be easy.

"Plus," he added, as a more hopeful aside, "I believe there's going to be a revival of Ojibwe spirituality. Everything that has happened was foretold in our ancient prophecy, including the coming of the white race to this continent. Our way of life and our customs have changed as a result of that arrival, but our ability to change has also been one of our sources of strength." Gene said he'd recently witnessed young people from his tribe indoctrinating themselves in a kind of pan-Indian ritual practice. He's relieved to see the interest, regardless of its tribal origin or orthodoxy of practice. "It is like the new sunrise which I face every morning. . . . One way or another," Gene pronounced, "people come full circle, they go home."

Gene spoke from experience, having made his own circular journey back to his literal home. Born to a Navajo father and an Ojibwe mother, Gene followed the matriarchal custom of identifying with his mother's tribe, and was raised in his grandmother's home. A medicine woman, his grandmother often took Gene with her as she—"guided by Spirit"—gathered medicinal resources from her reservation's trees, plants, lakes, and soil. But as a teenager, Gene shrugged off his grandmother's legacy. "When I moved off the reservation, I lived a typical American life," Gene said, remembering the relocation that he and his wife, Bernice, made from their families' homes in Wisconsin to the suburbs of New Jersey. "I was just a regular guy, working, trying to raise my family and be a good husband." And along with the "typical American life," Gene admits, came a fair share of "partying and distraction," and an absence of all things spiritual.

But Gene's life took a turn when, at the age of forty-five, he had a dream—a haunting vision of an owl—that remained as vivid in his waking hours as it had been in the dark of night. "The owl attacked me in the dream, and the interpretation given to me was it was time to come home," Gene recounted. Though he couldn't recognize it at the time, the owl eventually afforded Gene a bird's-eye view of the contradiction in which his people seemed caught: the competing pulls of individualism and community, the secular and the spiritual, the manufactured and the handmade.

A few years after Gene's return to the reservation, a visit from a tribal elder he hardly knew gave him direction. "I was sitting on my front porch with my wife when an old car pulled into the driveway," Gene recalled. "It was just getting dark, but I could make out the figure of a man, Jim Funmaker, who comes from the Winnebago tribe (also Ojibwe) about a hundred and thirty-five miles south of here. Jim Funmaker has been around awhile—he's about a hundred now—but at the time, I didn't even know him, except for seeing him at powwows. I used to go up to him and shake his hand because he's a big-time spiritual leader, this guy, a healer. But he certainly had no reason to know who I was."

The unexpected visitor sat down on the porch next to Gene and Bernice. He took a can from his pocket and opened it up, holding it out to Gene. "This is real Indian tobacco, not store-bought," he said. Gene asked him why it was being offered to him. "Because I've come to say something to you, something sacred, something important," Funmaker declared.

Among Ojibwes, the practice of offering tobacco has long and varied meanings. When one comes to speak of sacred things, or seek spiritual assistance, the gesture of presenting tobacco is made out of respect and gratitude for all that is unseen and for that which will come to pass. There are conflicting legends about when the custom began, and why tobacco, in particular, is assigned such import. But among most tribes today, the gifting of raw tobacco remains "partially to appease, and partially to acknowledge a presence."[2] "*Real* Indian tobacco," as Jim Funmaker had called his, is consecrated, having been blessed by Spirit through tribal elders in ceremony.

"So I accepted his offering and we talked all night long," continued Gene. "And I was fascinated by his visit, honored that he would come and see me." During their starry meeting, Funmaker explained the impetus for his visit—a dream he'd had about Gene, the details of which Gene would not divulge to me. All he'd say was that the dream and the encounter resulted in the promise of a gift: a medicine pipe.

To craft a medicine pipe for someone is more than a sacrifice of time; it is an act of midwifery for another's spiritual birth. In contemporary American culture, if someone decides to become a religious leader or a healer, whether conventional or alternative, it is a decision commonly arrived at independently. The custom among many Indian tribes, however, has always been a ritual of unsolicited recognition by one's community or a credentialed elder, a system under which individual preference is secondary to collective need.

As Gene continued peeling back the layered story of how his pipe—the central ritual object of his practice—came to be, I marveled at the attention to signs and dreams he and Jim Funmaker had demonstrated. I thought of the many times I had dreamed of an acquaintance, and how it never occurred to me to decipher meaning from these nocturnal visits, much less travel a hundred and thirty miles to announce the coming of a dream-inspired gift. But in the view of many American Indians, an individual's personal spiritual progress is a matter of public interest, one you're expected to go out of your way to facilitate.

Gene's circuitous route to spiritual awakening made me consider my own newly christened quest. I knew I would have to come to terms with the possibility that what I was seeking might, in one sense, have to find its way to me. And yet, from our first encounter, I had also learned from Gene's example that receptivity is as active as it is passive; one must cultivate preparedness for whatever lies ahead.

After Jim Funmaker had followed the signs to Gene's door, Gene began a process of self-purification. A year later, the two met again. In a private six-hour ceremony, Funmaker presented the pipe he had made for Gene. "This pipe came from the Creator," Funmaker said, holding its two pieces in his hands. "The pipe is not yours; it belongs to all the Ojibwe people. You are its caretaker, a *keeper* of the pipe," he instructed. A medicine pipe is intended to crystallize a holy bond between an individual and his or her Creator. In Gene's case, the transfer of the carved instrument was an anointment to diagnose and heal people, to become a medicine man.

It was shortly after his induction with Jim Funmaker that Gene's uncle Pipe Mustache approached him, commencing a fifteen-year apprenticeship that would fill his pipe with potent medicine. Along with sacred songs, prayers, and stories, Pipe Mustache introduced his chosen successor to the four totem spirits—buffalo, turtle, bear, and wolf—who have appeared in both physical and spirit form among the Ojibwe people for thousands of years.

Considered agents of protection, guidance, and change, as well as guardians of the outer doors of human perception, totem spirits are revered by Native traditionalists. They are a pipeline to the Creator in the way saints, angels, and prophets are for people of other faiths. "Most of us experience life with the five senses," Gene said. "Some can use the sixth and beyond. Jesus was an example of this kind of person, as are medicine people. I actually see the spirits. They talk to me, *literally* talk to me. When someone comes to me for a healing, I know right away if I can help them, because the spirits tell me."

Gene does not know how his healings work, nor does he seek to, reflecting a respect for life's inherent mystery. "It's not necessary that we understand the mechanics. As medicine people, we just need to show up and let the spirits work through us," Gene said. Humility is as vital to his practice as the pipe he carries. "Even though people around me might assume that being a doctor of Indian medicine, a spiritual person, means that I have some special dispensation of the Creator—that I'm unique in some way—I don't and I'm not," Gene said emphatically, pulling a Marlboro from his pack and groping in his shirt pocket for a light. While Gene's commitment to physical purification has, since his visit from Jim Funmaker, included abstention from all substances that alter perception, such as alcohol and drugs, he allows himself two indulgences: greasy, overprocessed food and store-bought cigarettes.

But Gene's humanness—even his *own* need to be healed—does not, in his eyes or in those of the people he helps, diminish his competence as a spiritual teacher and healer. In fact, most medicine people speak of having endured a serious illness—even a self-inflicted one—before being endowed with healing power, as if the empathy resulting from suffering prepared them for their role. Though Gene has had plenty of physical challenges, he's more concerned with the kind of psychological maladies that strike the mind and heart. "I'm a human being, and as such, susceptible to faults and mistakes during any given day," he said, inhaling deeply from his cigarette. "So when I wake up in the morning, the first thing I deal with is myself. Sometimes I wake up with resentments, anger, confusion, conflict in my life—like everybody else does. But when I roll out of bed, I don't drop down on my knees and fold my hands and ask the Creator for forgiveness. Ojibwe people don't practice shame or guilt," he said, drawing a distinction between his faith and traditional Christianity.

"I take a shower and get out bare naked, and before I put on my clothes, I sing songs, and I burn sage, and I smudge my whole body with that medicine to purify. In that act I'm getting rid of anger, resentment, conflict, confusion—emotional distractions that can undermine my ability to diagnose and heal." Relaying an ancient Ojibwe saying that has distinctly modern echoes, Gene says: "You cannot truly love anyone or anything else until you first love and accept yourself."

"My uncle Pipe warned me that the gift of healing is something that is given by Spirit and can just as easily be taken away," Gene said. "So, being human is a hazard to Native American doctors. But what's most important in everything we do, believe, and practice as spiritual people," he said, raising his voice to overpower the heckling of a bustling casino, "is to live *namajeen*—the good life."

It would be months before Gene would elaborate. But given the patience by which his faith is framed, it seemed fitting that I would have to wait—and wait—for him to complete his thought.

A full season later, one dark, snowy mid-January evening, I arrived at the Begay home in northern Wisconsin at the agreed-upon time of 5:30 P.M. The house was dark, my knocks went unanswered, and I found no note taped to the door. I waited, paced, speculated, and—given the snow accumulating on the ground, the dropping temperature, and the remoteness of the house—I tried the door handle. It turned easily. Peering down the entranceway, I spied only the shadow of a cat leading my eye to where a tiny lamp splashed a dim cast of yellow over a cluttered kitchen table. After calling out into an eerie silence, I quelled my feelings of trespass and sat down at the table to wait.

As time glided past my island of Formica, I pondered what was behind the many closed doors and cupboards. Driven by both boredom and hunger, I pried open the kitchen pantry. Greeted by rows of popular snack foods, I poached a few crackers, and returned to my post. Inventing an I Spy game, I inventoried every square inch within my sight line, including the kitchen and two adjoining rooms, all of which were in the throes of remodeling. I scanned numerous framed photographs of family members hung on an enormous wall—a collage of extended kinship—and thought about how bare, in comparison, mine would be. And I spent considerable time contemplating one gigantic tub of federally issued peanut butter. The stuff was a sticky reminder of the origin of the reservation, the type of generic commodity the U.S. government had given in exchange for the most precious and prodigious parcels of Native American land.

Sometime after the kitchen clock struck eleven, my games exhausted themselves, and my head came to rest on the table. Startled from sleep, I heard the sound of car doors slamming. Gene's wife, Bernice, threw open the front door and stomped the snow from her boots, unsurprised, it seemed, by the sight of a stranger at her kitchen table. "Hello. How long have you been waiting?" she inquired, hoisting heavy bags onto the already crowded counter.

"Since about five-thirty," I answered honestly.

"Oh good, you haven't been waiting long, then," she reckoned, mumbling something about "Indian time" and getting stuck in Duluth buying tiles for the bathroom.

Gene shuffled in with his elderly mother's arm folded over his. He braced her passage to her bedroom next to the kitchen, then, with a sigh of relief, returned and plunked himself down in the chair across from me. Bypassing greetings and small talk, Gene resumed—as if only momentarily interrupted—the conversation we had begun several months earlier.

"*Namajeen* is the highest level of existence," he began. "It is the *good* life: to be honorable, dignified, and carry respect in all that you do and say, to have great respect and honor for all the people of the world. That's what my people have always aspired to." Whereas followers of many other religions aspire to kindness and charity to earn admittance to heaven, Ojibwe tradition holds that *all* people—no matter what their beliefs or earthly actions—are admitted to heaven, or "home."

Around midnight, Gene suggested we all get some sleep and meet again for his early-morning ritual, which he agreed to perform at the kitchen table—the axis around which all important household happenings seemed to turn. Lying in one of his granddaughters' beds, drifting in and out of sleep, I revisited Gene's explanation of "the good life"—a phrase that for most of us has come to connote the spoils of success, like speedboats, second houses, and martinis. I thought about how, for Gene, to live the good life meant an intimacy and authenticity with his Creator, a code of honor that called for him to respect others as well as—and as much as—himself.

A few short hours later, hearing the rustling of feet, I lunged out of bed, not wanting to oversleep and miss my chance to experience Gene's practice. I found Bernice alone in the kitchen making coffee, a ritual so familiar to her that no light was necessary to perform it. I was grateful for the concentrated source of heat and the energy that our steaming cups offered, as we sat huddled over them—me in my pajamas, Bernice in her zip-up fuzzy peach robe.

Gene traipsed loudly down the stairs toting a black nylon duffel bag. He joined us, striking up a cigarette but no conversation. It was as if Gene believed that salutations like good morning, good night, and good-bye unnecessarily disrupted the intended continuum of life.

After adjusting to his extraction from the womb of bed, Gene stubbed out his cigarette with purpose. He dipped into the bag, removing a square of red cloth, which he began to unfold. "Has the sun shown itself yet?" he asked no one in particular. Indeed, its glow had just crowned the horizon, as Bernice lifted her ashtray into the air allowing Gene to drape his cloth over the table, smoothing the ripples with his large hands. Gene pulled objects, one by one, from his bag: three eagle feathers, a bundle of sage sticks, two rattles—one made from a turtle's shell, another of bronze—a pouch of tobacco, a jar of something sallow and mushy, and an exquisitely beaded leather bag. He laid each object onto the cloth, precisely spaced, from his right to his left.

Gene raised his eyes to me. "What I'm going to share with you is not secret," he said as he loosened the ties of the leather bag, gently removing its contents: the head and body of the sacred medicine pipe Jim Funmaker had made for him. Gene held the two sections, one in each hand. "When the Europeans came to this continent a long time ago, our practices went underground for fear of oppression. I openly share this ceremony with you now, because they were never intended to be secretive." With that, he mated the hand-carved torso to its black bowl.

Gene turned to Bernice, who set down her cigarette to take hold of a large ceramic bowl Gene had filled with dried sage—a substance, like raw tobacco, many Native Americans consider sacred and purifying. Gene lit the sage and rallied it with his breath. Without words, he and Bernice stood, taking turns bathing each other from head to toe in the gray, sweet-smelling twists of smoke rising from the bowl. Gene handed the sage back to Bernice, who traced me in a ghostly pattern that spread and mingled with the lingering haze of their own.

We returned to our seats, now bound together in ceremony. Gene filled the mouth of his pipe with tobacco he'd been given by someone seeking his prayers in return. "I'm waking up the Creator to tell him I'm going to pray to Him," Gene narrated for my benefit. He pulled a deep breath from the sacred pipe in recognition of the spirits of the east, the first of four directions he would acknowledge. His cheeks ballooned like Dizzy Gillespie's, his teeth chewing the tiny captured cloud as if to sink deeply into the prayer it held before allowing its escape. With closed eyes he honored the remaining directions, speaking in his native tongue an invitation to the "guardian spirits" to join us. As the last bit of smoke was exhaled, Gene opened his eyes to follow its trail heavenward.

The outline of Gene's mother, Lucy, emerged from the hallway's shadows. Her steps seemed an exercise in mindfulness, each lift and placement of a foot requiring her full attention as she steadied herself against her cane. With the clear intent of joining us—as if the smell of sage had beckoned her—she lowered herself onto the stair leading to the kitchen, an arm's length away from our uneven circle. Incorporating her into his flow, Gene handed the pipe to his mother, whose hands, crooked with time, supported its neck and back as she drew her smoke, connecting herself to her son and to the spirit world. Bernice was next, her eyes closing as her lips tasted tobacco that was not "store-bought," an inhalation intended to *awaken* the senses. She returned the pipe to Gene, who then passed it to me, decreeing my formal introduction to the spirits. "The spirits are here now, they smoke the pipe along with us," he said as I puffed, feeling the tobacco offer itself to me, and I to it. "With the smoking of the pipe, the medicine—the tobacco which was once alive—is being sacrificed."

Gene lifted the bronze rattle with his right hand, and began to shake it. "I don't say prayers, I sing them," he said, seeming to drift away from us. I watched the thick fingers of his left hand curl inward to form a fist on the table, as if to keep at least half of him anchored to earth. His voice followed the rattle's lead, wrapping a melody around us with an unexpected silky perfection. Comprehending not one of its foreign words, I felt the prayers instead. Gene's cadence began to slow. *"Nee-kana-gah-nah,"* he repeated three times as he stilled the rattle, a punctuation akin to *Amen*. "That prayer was for you, and for your long journey," he said in English, directing his opening eyes toward me.

As Gene resumed his native language, his fist reconnected with the table, and he began a new song. Again it appeared as if he had left his body, transcending the confines of the kitchen nook to explore an ethereal, more expansive turf. When the song-filled odyssey was complete, his arms jerked, as if abruptly reintroduced to gravity, and the rattle stopped. *"Nee-kana-gah-nah,"* he repeated again three times. "That prayer was for my people, that they may know God. Not believe, but *know*," he emphasized, raising his fist into the air. "There is so much frustration in belief. Belief breeds doubt; we must *know* God and the spirits."

Gene dedicated his third song to spiritual leaders of every faith "who are also singing this morning," he said, extending his pointer finger toward the sun. "May they see clearly the road. May they see clearly that there is a God; that we all come from one place and return there; that there are spirits; that there is healing; that as life fills us with distractions, we never forget these truths." Exchanging the bronze rattle for the one of turtle, Gene pleaded his prayer like a well-prepared counselor, drawing in the jury of spirits with his lilting words of conviction.

"I pray now for everyone who is taking my medicine, for their healing to continue," he translated. "I'm not going to speak for them; I'm going to sing on their behalf—this healing song." At the song's close, Gene bent down and knocked his rattle on the ground four times. *"Nee-kana-gah-nah,"* we all repeated in unison.

Gene laid the rattle back in its place, taking up the bundle of sage sticks, which he rested above his upper lip like a twiggy mustache. He inhaled deeply four times, binding the physical healing of his songs with the purity of the raw sage. "Breathe in as deeply as you can," he encouraged, handing the sticks around.

"If I were by myself, I would now sit quietly and just listen," Gene said. Though his tradition is oral, its signs of divine guidance are often discerned, and understood, in silence. "It takes time to be silent, but when I reach that place, that's when the spirits talk to me, tell me how to help people, explain mysteries of life. Sometimes spirits talk to me in my mind, sometimes audibly, sometimes through an animal," Gene elaborated, citing for me a recent morning when he awoke to find a wolf staring at him from the glass door of his bedroom's second-story balcony. By the time he roused Bernice, the animal had disappeared, leaving Gene with a message as personal as his sighting had been fleeting. Like his relationship to the spirits, Gene's connection to animals is one of kinship, a collage of relatives as real and extended as the one displayed on his kitchen wall.

Gene's practice has trained him to wait for meaning to emerge from his surroundings and encounters. I admired, even envied, how much he trusted this process, how relaxed and accepting he was in his pursuit of betterment and understanding.

We all sat quietly for a while around the kitchen-table-turned-altar, steeped in our own thoughts and private prayers. Gene picked up an eagle wing feather—the emblem of healing—its tip wrapped in dark red string, as if dipped in ink of blood. He twirled it between his fingers and fanned something that was invisible to me. "My purpose in prayer is not to ask God for favors but to give thanks, and to ask that I be shown the truth," he said. "If I say a prayer on my own behalf it's simply to ask the Creator to keep one eye on me, to not turn His back to me."

Gene raised the medicine pipe above his head and, after a reverential pause, dismantled it. "The ceremony is broken," he said, signaling that it was now okay to return to real time, idle chat, and store-bought tobacco. "Thank the spirits, not me, for any good that comes from having shared this ceremony together," he insisted, carefully packing away his ritual objects. As he did, I couldn't help but ask what was in the rusting jar. "Bear grease, bear medicine," he said offhandedly.

"Where did you *get* it?" I pressed.

"It was given to me. Medicine usually *comes* to medicine people; Spirit brings it," he said. "A few years ago, a woman came to me for help with severe headaches," he offered as an example. "I was in Canada for some business, and I went out to a creek at sunrise and sang songs on behalf of this woman, for her healing. A man who was a caretaker for a property nearby came down to the water—apparently I had woken him up. We talked for a while, and then, without having told him why I was there at that stream, he said to me, 'I have something I want to give to you that I no longer have use for. Wait here.' He came back with a bundle of black mushrooms and said that a medicine man had given them to him for severe headaches, and that he no longer suffered from them. Then he relayed to me how to administer the medicine, because the substance itself is not medicine unless you know how to properly apply it. Within a week of administering these mushrooms, which had been passed along to me, the woman I'd been praying for was free from her pain."

Gene said the bear medicine had come to him similarly, one more addition to his ever-expanding apothecary. "Every affliction has a specific medicine and approach, and as medicine people we specialize and give referrals, just like Western doctors," said Gene. His specialty is illnesses that have mental origins, whether physically or emotionally manifested.

I asked Gene if his diagnoses and treatments were reserved solely for Native Americans. He said he administers his medicine to anyone who comes to him, if Spirit instructs him to do so, and as long as the patient believes in the treatment's—that is, the Creator's—power. However, he is cautious when combining spirit medicine with "white man's medicine," and as a rule he does not treat people who've been formally baptized unless and until they submit to a process of renunciation.

I was surprised by what seemed like an uncharacteristic hang-up. Gene defended his position on the basis of concern that "split beliefs" resulted in a kind of schizophrenia of the soul. "You have to make room for the medicine," he said. Every belief system is like a language with a unique set of symbols and intonations all its own, he explained. Prayers of healing are most effective when the language of faith being spoken is mutually understood.

"The only difference between us and other believers is the *way* we worship," he said. "A lot of my own people who've converted to the Christian faith have called me 'pagan.' But when we as traditionalists look at nature and the environment, we don't worship trees, we don't *worship* animals; we come to them with respect—a deep, respectful acknowledgment for the Creator who is in everything. When I go out and talk to the bones of my ancestors—those trees—I put my tobacco down. 'You've been here much longer than I have,' I say to them. But people misinterpret that; they think we're worshiping or idolizing nature. We're not, we just have a different way of talking to the Creator."

In the sun-drenched morning, I asked Gene one final question about his teacher, Uncle Pipe Mustache, of whom he'd told me many stories. I asked about his death—his journey to "the other half of the totality of life," as Gene had described it.

"I answered the phone one day and there was my uncle's voice," remembered Gene. "'You know which song to sing as I take my last breath—to send me home?' my uncle asked me." Gene did. He had sacrificed much so that, in that moment, he was able to recite the ancestral song that would both celebrate his uncle's life and usher it home.

Sitting at the Begay's kitchen table, surrounded by the disarray of construction—a home in transition—I marveled at the fact that not once did anyone apologize "for the mess." My hosts were at ease with their home as a work-in-progress. No one seemed anxious to finish the framing of the new addition, though a heavy snow bowed its plastic roofing; no one was in a rush to cover the bare shower walls with the newly purchased tile, or empty the dining room of the dozens of items it was temporarily storing. In bold defiance of a hurried America, Bernice and Gene were satisfied that the job—their vision—would get done in due time.

I suspect they feel similarly about the remodeling of their people's traditions. While Gene openly mourns the dearth of willing successors, he doesn't worry too much about who among his tribe will sing the ancestral song when he takes *his* last breath. Perhaps he trusts that his spirit guides will fill the void, on call to howl, bellow, and growl their Creator's most ancient lullaby.

"Should we go for a buffet breakfast at the casino?" Gene suggested, putting out his cigarette.

"Sure, why not," I agreed, rising up with a stretch. The time for such things as pancakes and eggs and brash, blinking machines was undeniably upon us.

Chapter Two

The Native American Church is the largest spiritual coalition of American Indians from around the country, observing an eclectic blend of Christian and Native beliefs and practices. One of those practices—the peyote rite—combines prayer with the ingestion of a nonaddictive "spiritual medicine" extracted from a spineless cactus called peyote, which grows wild around parts of Texas and New Mexico and along the Rio Grande. For thousands of years, indigenous peoples of North America have gathered the peyote plant as the centerpiece of a communal ceremony.

Regarded as sacred flesh the way the Catholic Church regards sanctified bread, peyote is experienced by Native peoples as a sacrament, as "God's special gift to the Indians," the effects of which are equated with the workings of the divine Spirit.[1] For some Native practitioners, the peyote ceremony is a principal and—as of 1994—legally protected spiritual rite that instigates direct access to the presence and the will of God, and provides a forum for the elevation of human consciousness.

Some in the Native American Church have stirred controversy by sharing the sacred peyote rite with non-Indians, and even initiating some as ceremony facilitators. These individuals are then empowered with the autonomy and expertise to indoctrinate other non-Natives who have no formal affiliation to the pan-Indian church.

Appropriating with Non-Indians

I arrived at my host's remote southwestern home in the early afternoon, just in time to help clean and prepare the medicine for that night's ceremony. Sitting outside around a card table, a small group of us shared pocketknives to chip away short tufts of silky fiber from the craggy surface of the shriveled peyote "buttons." Though bone-dry and barely the size of potato chips, the buttons felt large and alive—almost frighteningly so. I imagined swallowing the bald medallions and their resuscitation inside of me like the waking of a wild animal from hibernation. Working the plant's crevices, I reminded myself that what I held in my hands was considered a *medicine*—a kind of spiritual antibiotic—and a portal to the unseen world Gene Begay entered through his sacred pipe and ancient songs. I wanted to understand the purpose of this Native practice, to distinguish a drug from a medicine, to experience the difference between a joyride and a vision quest.

Since I'd grown up in the region of the peyote plant, its legend was not entirely new to me. As a teenager I often heard stories about shamans gathering atop mesas around bonfires, shape-shifting into animals that leaped with supernatural power from this dimension to the next. These tales grew even taller in my mind as I scalped the plant of its hair. Looking around the card table at our intimate gathering, which had expanded to about twenty, I felt my uneasy anticipation escalate at the sight of so many non-Indian faces, for whom this tribal rite was borrowed. Each of us was about to take that appropriating plunge my mother had refused. I sympathized with her reluctance to help herself casually to another's practices without any sort of formal context or commitment. I worried that I was no different from certain youthful travelers who pay big bucks for adventure vacation treks through remote lands, hoping their stories and slides will make them seem more courageous and interesting back home in the workaday world.

Gene had spoken of how Native traditionalists generally feel about the appropriation of their rituals. Some are comfortable and even encourage it, he said, if participants are properly tutored and approach the ceremony honorably and responsibly. Others are bluntly opposed to the idea. And the rest treat it with bemused tolerance. Gene seemed to fall into the last camp, though he spoke respectfully about a few non-Natives who had dedicated years to learning the language of his tribe and the rituals that accompany it. "We've adopted some of these white people into our tribe, and most of them even live on the reservation," he had said. "If you closed your eyes and listened to them speak," he added with a marveling wonder, "you wouldn't know they weren't *born* Ojibwe."

But among our assembled group, there didn't seem to be anyone who fit the definition of *near-Indian* that Gene had laid out. We were, instead, an assortment of Jews, Christians, Buddhists, agnostics, neopagans, and a few, like myself, undeclared. Throughout the afternoon, we all listened carefully to our resident teacher—a middle-aged woman with honey-colored hair and blue eyes—who prepared us for what lay ahead, though more than half of those present were already veterans, having attended her biannual ritual a number of times. She described medicine circles as an act of "retribalizing." Rather than an act of borrowing, she deemed it a *burrowing* into "the collective experience" of being human, a route of "direct communication" with the Creator.

She explained that just before sunset, we would ingest the peyote and begin to sing, taking turns offering improvised melodies and lyrical prayers, and continue through the night until sunrise. My heart raced at the thought of mixing a mind-altering (however sacred) substance with the assignment of singing a cappella in front of an audience of strangers. Just hearing the preview, I was paralyzed by a sweat-producing flashback to the fourth grade when, during a packed assembly, I stood on a stage and humiliated myself with a solo rendition of "The Impossible Dream" from *Man of La Mancha*. Unfortunately, I had not, with only ten years under my belt, foreseen the irony each off-key note would produce.

A woman from San Francisco—one of the veterans of this peyote rite—calmed my egocentric fears when she proclaimed for the benefit of all newcomers: "I don't come here all the way from California to *perform;* I come here to sing my prayers to God." Her words grounded me in my experience with Gene. I focused my mind on his infectious clarity of intention and his knowing trust, easing myself into the idea that I would soon be the one holding the rattle and dictating the prayers.

In the bend between afternoon and evening, we all gathered up ritual supplies and carried them down a sagebrush path to a circular clearing. From our vantage point nothing of human civilization could be seen or heard. We filed in, filling the edge of the circle until it was complete. Next to me sat "the keeper of the fire"—a gracefully lanky black man with dreadlocks dangling past his waist, who'd accepted the responsibility of feeding the flames that anchored the center of our giant human wheel.

Once everyone had settled, legs covered with blankets, backs braced with pillows, the circle was officially "opened." The four directions of the compass were ceremonially acknowledged as Gene had done at his kitchen table. Setting the tone and our intention, our guide led us in group songs to the beat of a Native American drum she braced between her legs. Bite-size pieces of the freshly cut peyote plant and a distilled tea made of its dehydrated buttons were passed and imbibed in clockwise rotation. Our guide had brought live peyote plants into the circle as well, placing their terracotta pots next to her as if seating honored guests. She addressed the plants as "grandparents" and watered them with a sip of the broth made of their brethren before she took a sip herself.

A whittled wooden staff referred to as a "talking stick" and "the staff of life" was placed in the circle, and our first round began. A brave soul volunteered to start us off, planting the stick into the bare ground with one hand, holding the rattle in the other, as he inaugurated our solstice meeting with impromptu, unrhymed lyrics spoken in our shared English tongue. His song acknowledged the journey upon which we were about to embark, hoping that all of us—some old friends to him, some strangers—received whatever it was we were seeking. Thanking "the spirits" with a final shake of the rattle, he passed it to the person on his left, and we continued this way as darkness fell. Some of the songs that followed were melancholic and emotional, some were forced and silly, others were poignant and lyrical—all ranging in length from about three to ten minutes. Some songs were not easy to decipher, coded in personal allusion, while others were simply put: a father wishing his teenage son a safe passage into adulthood; a soft-spoken woman praying for courage and physical healing; a tearful mother finding some forgiveness for her abusive father; a man in his sixties wishing everyone in the world a little more peace, love, and understanding; and others offering prayers on behalf of a family member or friend who was ailing, or had recently died. As refrains developed, postures relaxed, and the peyote took hold, more people joined in, humming someone else's melody along with them, or replying to a call-and-response that seemed to emerge naturally from certain prayers.

At first I was caught up in others' songs as the stick inched its way around the circle toward me. Its sudden proximity flooded my head with distracting, defeating thoughts. "Stop trying to intellectualize spirituality," I could hear Gene calling out over the din of slot machines. "Stop trying to intellectualize your concept of God. Understand yourself and your destiny outside of condemnation, and you will find your place within the perfect balance that exists." As I watched the faces and body language of those around me who would also soon have to sing, it was apparent I was not alone in my dread. Apparently, singing backup for other people's prayers was, for many of us, a more comfortable role to play. Our guide had said earlier in the day that we could expect the peyote to sharpen our senses, allowing us to see, hear, feel, and know more than we tend to outside of these kinds of ceremonies. Perhaps it was the power of suggestion, but I did feel as if I could see, in an X-ray sort of way, insecurity and shame underneath the skin of many of the people sitting around me. We were told that "the medicine" would work to rid us of—or at least help us "better understand"—our illnesses, whether they were emotional, psychological, or physical.

The wooden staff was placed in my hand, and my mind contracted, as if breathing thoughts in, uncertain which one to exhale. Finally a few shaky, off-pitch words—at first so soft they were hardly audible—toppled out of me, feelings escaping of their own accord to form a spoken word poem about letting go. Each of us had brought into the circle our individual life events, relationships, crises, disappointments, thankfulness, and visions for the future. I had come in mourning, reeling from my recent move away from the place I had called home for twelve years and from my familylike circle of friends to venture out on a mission that was still unclear and abstract. I was homesick and struggling to adapt to my new, untethered life.

As I sang, the peyote seemed to settle deeper into me. Rather than providing momentary escape from my sadness and discombobulation, it intensified my sense of no longer having a center of gravity. I had left Los

Angeles four months earlier, and I was beginning to accept that it would be a long time—if ever—before I would return. In my silence, as well as in my song, I rode out emotional swells, acknowledging the past with gratitude while trying to release attachments to it.

Over the many hours that followed, I fought to keep my mind from slipping too far down any one rabbit hole of my psyche, an exercise made easier by my giving undivided attention to the songs of others whenever I wasn't holding the stick and rattle. My efforts were reinforced by our guide, who at intervals advised us to "stay on the road," reminding us that we were individuals praying as *one*. And slowly her vision came to fruition as our songs became a unified chorus that reflected an unending prayer we shared and understood.

As the night wore on with the passing of more bitter tea and fleshy nuggets of peyote, I shed something, becoming lucid, bare, and vulnerable. I felt like a turtle whose shell had been sent out for cleaning. This sensation of nakedness felt like breaking a taboo; accustomed to built-in mechanisms for deflection and anonymity, I wasn't prepared for such open terrain, where one can expose one's insides without the usual self-editing. The boundaries that had earlier defined and controlled everything—my self, the surrounding space, and other people—seemed to dissolve.

Gazing up at the moon patrolling above this body of people, I watched the fire's streams of smoke rise into the luminous night, our collection of prayers ascending with them. I saw merit in this uninhibited communication being directed upward toward the unseen world—toward the spirits and God. But I found myself imagining an even greater value in such openness staying earthbound, directed at this world and those living in it. I imagined what it would look like if these ritualized experiences—not of blissed-out escape, but of acute awakeness, expansiveness, and connectedness—were to become commonplace in our society. I pictured families, friends, colleagues, and neighbors "circling" together—without the aid of hallucinogens and shamans—to discover their own "way," as Gene had defined spiritual practice.

In the middle of the fourth round my jaw began to clench. I swore I could hear the arms of time rust and slow, and wondered if it was this sound we hear when we die. I wasn't sure how much more of the medicine I could stomach. Tilting my head back, I was relieved to see the darkness receding. A rooster launched its throaty call over the mesa, and the contained light of our fire slowly blended into the light of day. When we had completed our final loop of prayers, our guide "parted" the circle, allowing a few designees to slip out momentarily while the rest of us stretched our legs and arched our backs from where we sat. The intent for coming together had been largely completed, but the circle hadn't yet been formally broken, as Gene had done when he separated his pipe's black bowl from its stem. We remained, suspended in time and space, together.

Soon, those who had disappeared returned, carrying bowls, baskets, and platters. Serenaded by the tunes of waking birds, our guide ended our ceremony with a prayer of thanksgiving over an enormous basin of rose-petaled water, plates of turkey, beef, and salmon jerky, loaves of home-made bread, chunks of dark and milk chocolate, and chilled ripe strawberries. After replenishing our bodies, something began to bubble up in us. Perhaps it was simply the result of collective relief, having made it to sunrise and overcome parts of ourselves that we never thought we would. Simultaneously and suddenly, uncontrollable laughter overcame all of us.

It was as if we were each making up for the times in life we should have laughed but didn't—an uproarious debt demanding payment in full. Over an hour later, when the collective outburst began to subside into sighs and people started to meander back to the nearby house for much-needed rest, I continued to be driven by a laughter that only accelerated. Joyfully out of control, I felt liberated not only of my intellectualization of God but of myself as well. Heading in the opposite direction of our host's house, I found a nearby pond into which I plunged and swam until finally corralling deep, measured breaths. At last, I floated peacefully and fearlessly under the sun's expanding warmth.

I moseyed back toward the house and sat in a patch of grass speckled with people quiet and reclined. I thought about how many rituals of all religions are now accessible to anyone. And I thought about Gene and how he had said that (spiritual) medicine means nothing unless you understand how it is administered. It seemed this shrinking distance between the for-mally indoctrinated and the layperson could either result in widespread revelation, or an incurable psychic plague, depending on who was doing the administering. As a peyote novice, I had no doubt missed subtler shades of the experience reserved for those more intimately acquainted with the medicinal properties of the desert plant, not to mention a cultural context for its reverence.

And while a mere twenty-four hours earlier, appropriating a Native

American practice such as this one seemed a frightening and even sacrile-
gious act, I suddenly saw the universal relevance in our prayerful communion, among total strangers. Tucked in the cool grass as I closed my eyes to
sleep, I felt an integral part of two things: the budding of spring, and a band
of retribalized urbanites. And I felt I'd been reminded that, like the turtle,
my home, at least for now, could travel with me.

Christianity

Chapter Three

The origin of the Amish people and their practices can be traced back to the Reformation of sixteenth-century Europe. There, Swiss-born followers of Jesus Christ who became known as "Anabaptists" (or "rebaptizers") boldly seceded from the reigning Catholic Church. In a time when compulsory infant baptism was the law of the land, these dissenting believers insisted that the rite be conferred only upon adults who voluntarily and publicly chose a life of radical obedience to the teachings and simplified lifestyle of Christ. Even more sweeping, the Anabaptists rejected the claim of infallibility held by the Roman Catholic Church and its papacy, redirecting the power of ultimate authority to their biblical scripture and the example of Christ.

A period of secretiveness and hiding was forced upon the Anabaptists as civil and religious authorities commissioned hunters to "torture, brand, burn, drown, imprison, dismember, and harass [these] religious heretics."[1] At the end of the seventeenth century, a bitter disagreement among the Anabaptists over the scriptural interpretation of shunning (excommunication of a member for noncompliance) splintered them into multiple groups, which today include the Church of the Brethren, Brethren in Christ, the Hutterites, the Mennonites, and the Amish. Like other persecuted religious peoples of that time, many among the various factions of the Anabaptists eventually fled their homelands to seek refuge in North America. At the invitation of a Quaker named

William Penn, some of them, including the Amish—whose name is derived from an early Anabaptist leader named Jacob Ammann—emigrated to what is now Pennsylvania. Throughout the eighteenth century, the Amish homesteaded the state's rich farmlands.[2]

While the Amish are now extinct in their European homelands, they continue to thrive in Canada, Central America, and North America, with most of their total population concentrated in Ohio, Indiana, Pennsylvania, Minnesota, and Wisconsin. Of the many autonomous communities—each emulating varying degrees of austerity—the "Old Order" Amish, with approximately eighty thousand members, are considered the sole custodians of orthodox Amish culture and practice.

Yielding with the Amish

Having no access to any of the seemingly impenetrable Amish communities around the country, I took a time-honored route: I joined a steady stream of tourists and paid to get in.

During my travels around the Great Lakes, I had heard of a small town on the southern edge of Minnesota called Harmony, home to more than one hundred Old Order Amish families. I was interested in visiting Harmony for two reasons: to satisfy my curiosity about whether a town could live up to such a name; and more pointedly, to see if those living a distinctly Amish life were at all approachable.

From St. Paul, I wound my way through the less prophetically named towns of Marion and Preston until I met up with the extrawide one-lane Main Street of Harmony, Minnesota. I spotted three different businesses boasting signs that advertised AMISH TOURS, and stopped at the one nearest a gas station. Inside this shop, which seemed to expand as I moved through it, were rows and rows—and then more rows—of arts and crafts portraying Amish life. The scene reminded me of my home growing up—different culture, same fascination: foot-tall dolls in black bonnets, country quilts, framed drawings of Amish women at work, and many creations handcrafted in wood, from sensibly designed toys to reproductions of old-fashioned sewing spools, rocking chairs, and baby bassinets. Two vacationers in shorts and costume-jeweled T-shirts stood next to me, inspecting the handiwork and choosing tokens of their visit small enough to fit into the trunk of their car. Perhaps they hoped the objects might somehow bring them closer to the simpler time and purer life that Amish culture represents to most Americans.

Wandering back to the front of the store, I inquired about a tour. I was quickly appointed a private guide, Merlin, an eighty-year-old retired local grocer and a seasoned escort. Merlin sat shotgun in my car like a driver's ed instructor, guiding my turns down dusty back roads, leading us deeper into what he called "Amish country." He pointed to farmhouses along the way belonging to Amish families, nearly every one with an empty wooden swing hanging from a sturdy tree. Merlin navigated us to the one-room schoolhouse where—thanks to a decision by the U.S. Supreme Court— Amish children are allowed to study a uniquely Amish curriculum with a member of their own community. No further formal education is required after the equivalent of the eighth grade, at which point children join their family's workforce. In some less strict Amish communities, a child might receive spare supplemental home schooling during nonworking hours. Each child is given enough academic instruction to speak English as well as their faith's primary German dialect, understand their biblical Scripture, and calculate basic math. Segregated from their non-Amish peers, Amish children come of age with little or no exposure to anything that is not carefully filtered through rigid doctrine.

Merlin and I scooted past small tribes of young boys harvesting neatly cropped fields, enduring the summer heat under wide-brimmed straw hats identical to those worn by their fathers who worked alongside them. Through my car window, it appeared that nowhere in America could one find a generational Xerox machine as faithful to the original—exact length of hair, dress, and physical gesture indistinguishable from boy to boy and man to man. I wondered if this phenomenon wasn't the Amish community's most seminal religious practice, so precise in its countywide enactment. By the time Amish children would normally feel the urge for independence, they are already so conditioned as to need no further example but their own. They've become the next generation's master print from which future reproductions can be made.

Obedience and pragmatism are the most valued virtues among the Amish, and consequently a strict hierarchy exists, descending from God, to local bishop, to community, to parent, to child—every earthly act having its realm of accountability and authority. While the basic values and philosophy of Amish culture are universal, exactly how the conformity and practicality are expressed varies from community to community. These differences are primarily determined by each church district's *two* bishops, who together are elected for life to collectively monitor the socioreligious practices of some twenty to twenty-five families. Under the supervision and direction of these men, each community negotiates the delicate balance of tradition and change, preserving a time without modern conveniences like electricity and most machinery, without articles of vanity like mirrors and makeup, and without superfluous decor, like ornate moldings and frilly curtains. The lines surrounding an Amish life are straight and clearly drawn; the objects filling it, upright and functional. The occasional need to compromise usually arises from economic necessity, as when Amish farmers and craftspeople are forced to compete with the modernism that pulses along the periphery of their pastures.

Offering an example of compromise, Merlin spoke of the invention of the telephone. Under certain bishops, he explained, phones might be permissible, but only if used *outside* of the home, as in the case of a nearby pay phone, or the borrowing of a line from a non-Amish neighbor. Or a family furniture business might be allowed one handheld calculator or a gas-powered saw to keep up with customer orders. But outside pockets on clothing are strictly forbidden as too "handy"—a small yet measurable reminder of the austere character of Amish life and faith. And while some decorative landscaping might be acceptable, Merlin added, pointing to a finely manicured lawn, the *hiring* of professional landscapers would be a clear case of money too frivolously spent. To the unaffiliated, these sanctions and limitations can seem contradictory and arbitrary. But their effectiveness in keeping a community intact cannot be denied. The sense of belonging and conforming that holds these people together appeared as powerful and persuasive as the freedom of individual choice that binds most Americans.

As Merlin and I drove toward two Amish men on foot, he pointed out their lack of buttons—another accessory the Amish have branded as overly ostentatious; they use hooks and eyes to fasten their clothes instead. Catching myself slowing down to get a closer look at these men, I suddenly felt guilty for invading their privacy. Hermetically sealed in a dust-stirring glass and metal capsule, Merlin and I buzzed and darted through their quiet lives, unashamedly ogling.

To Merlin there was nothing unusual about his daily voyeuristic ritual, his bread and butter. He had lived in Harmony all his life, owning and operating a corner store frequented by local Amish families whose children loved the shopkeeper's handouts of candy and gum. Those children now have children of their own, which explained the waves, however reticent, as we drove by.

No longer the store's keeper, Merlin kept himself close to the Amish by offering them an occasional car ride, which most are permitted to accept from the "English" (as they refer to the non-Amish) in the case of doctors' appointments or emergencies. His relationship with the community was a complex one. Formerly the purveyor of ice and flour, he was now both public educator and professional exploiter. It was easy to tell who was happy to see Merlin and who was not. I imagined that being a character in a live-action museum must feel like a high price to pay for a lift to the dentist.

Vans belonging to competing tour companies passed us on the road, eliciting polite waves from Merlin. At one stop sign, I watched the day-trippers through their van's windows, cameras poised. I was just as intrigued as they were. More successful at staving off the kind of cultural infiltration that has threatened the Ojibwe tribal tradition, Amish communities exist as a more self-sufficient and timeless world within a world.

Merlin and I pulled up to a farmhouse advertising (in modest small print) BAKED GOODS. The afternoon was rolling in, bringing with it a heat wave that only a tall lemonade and a peach turnover could cure. We opened the door to the establishment and found two people aflutter in flour: one pink-cheeked, pear-shaped woman of about forty in a black smock overlaying a simple ankle-length dress, stockings, black shoes, and matching bonnet; and a girl of about nine, a slimmer replica of her mother. The temperature in the room of wood-fired ovens was higher than it was outside, but you would not have known it from the pace of the two women, save for the tiny beads of sweat collecting around their brows and above their lips.

Merlin made small talk about the weather with the mother. She seemed to appreciate his delivery of a customer, but was otherwise guarded. I watched as her shy daughter finished mixing a batch of cookies, spacing them perfectly on a metal sheet in measured spoonfuls, while her mother observed from the corner of her eye. This kind of apprenticeship was how this girl's life would be shaped. In a kind of communion, Amish youth ingest an attentiveness to religious obligation in the shadow of their parents' movements.

No matter what our faith or culture, we all, as young children, emulate our parents to some degree. Growing up, I looked to my mother as this girl did to hers, as my sovereign, my constant keeper, my protector and idol. As far back as I can remember—at least until I reached my self-righteous teens—I could only hope to imitate my busy, professional single mother, who managed our lives with the dexterity of one of those circus-trained plate spinners, simultaneously juggling countless responsibilities. As an only child I spent untold hours play-acting the scenarios I imagined my mother lived out in the "real world." I'd dress up in her navy blue suits and silk blouses, fashion myself an executive office and take calls on my speakerphone, dictate letters, give presentations, run board meetings, and fill my briefcase with work to bring home.

It was after one of those long days mimicking my mother's daytime ritual that I first tried my own hand at baking. While my baby-sitter sat on the phone entranced by the voice of her boyfriend on the other end, I rolled up my silky sleeves, pulled the Betty Crocker cookbook from the shelf, found the visual of a cookie, and began an improvisation of orchestral proportions. I began with a base of flour, dollops of vanilla ice cream, and a dash of hot cocoa mix, adding water to the unruly powdered mound until a kind of batter could be spooned onto a metal sheet, which I placed in the oven on its highest setting for a good and tedious few minutes. While my third batch was in the oven I was struck with culinary genius and added jelly beans and coconut shavings to each of the concaved doughy centers.

I divided my bounty into servings and packaged them, still warm, in tin foil "boats" I molded with my own two very capable hands, as I'd seen done in fancy restaurants for leftovers. Going door-to-door, I made deliveries, cheerfully explaining that my mom and I had baked for our favorite neighbors. My offerings were met with various expressions of curiosity. New in town, with a full-time job and a kid to raise, my mother had hardly had the chance to introduce herself, much less form a bond with those living around us. When she came home that night, I poured her an iced tea and shared my success—our success. After all, I had managed something on my own in her likeness, this goddess of mine, and had, I was confident, made her proud. Presenting her with a trophy cookie—a gooey brooch with an emerald, ruby, and sapphire setting—I watched her take a nibble from its translucent edge. She said only, "And you told everyone *we* baked these?"

I smiled to myself, remembering my baking experiment as I watched the Amish girl remove a perfectly browned batch of sugar cookies from the oversized oven. Unlike my unfortunate one-of-a-kind cookies, the Amish girl's would come out looking and tasting just like her mother's. Observing the mother's quick inspection, it was clear that her understudy was all but ready to take over her role as an exact protégée. It was so unlike my child-hood, in which the more I grew, the more I outgrew the idea of following in my mother's footsteps.

From their first breath, Amish children are tutored in every detail of *Ordnung*—the mandatory law of Amish "right conduct." However, the formal commitment to the faith, marked by baptism, is regarded as an inde-pendent decision, one that should be contemplated by each youth when he or she "comes of age"—normally between the ages of sixteen and twenty-one. Statistically, about four out of five Amish make the choice to faithfully follow their parents' treaded path.[3] But for a few, conformity is eventually usurped by a primal need for individualism and the wider world. When a young adult chooses a non-Amish life, they are shunned, and contact of any kind with any member of the family or community from that day for-ward is forbidden. Only if the individual returns and submits to an involved repentance process—and once again dutifully observes the faith and its practices—is he or she acknowledged and welcomed back into the fold.

Ultimately I had no luck penetrating Harmony's Amish community beyond distant waves and the polite exchange of money for tasty pastries, but I did happen upon one of its outcasts. Stopping in a small wood-worker's shop on my way out of town, I struck up a conversation with its proprietor, a man of about thirty who introduced himself as Jake Junior. After we talked awhile, he confided that he had been raised Amish, but at age twenty decided he could no longer abide by what he saw as petty judg-ment and hypocrisy among his community and from his father, a bishop.

"I was a curious child," he confessed. "I questioned my community's man-made rules, not to try and change them but just to understand their purpose. But that was the wrong thing to do in my parents' eyes. They believe that in order to be accepted through 'the gates' [of heaven] we have to live close to our fathers' beliefs—that that alone will save us. Amish kids are so brainwashed, they think if they touch something their dad didn't touch, they're going straight to hell. I once asked my dad why we had to wear black socks in the summer," Jake Junior added, recalling a childhood visit to the county doctor, who told Jake Senior his son needed to wear *white* socks in the unbearable summer heat. "But my dad said no, because it's always been black."

I knew where Jake Junior's family lived; Merlin had pointed out "Bishop Jake's home" on our drive-by tour—a small compound set on a bluff no more than two miles from his excommunicated son's storefront. I asked Jake Junior if he ever saw his family, which included his parents, nine brothers, and four sisters. He paused, peering out his front window overlooking Harmony's Main Street. "Sometimes my father drives by in his buggy," he said with hardened mournfulness. His father will not even acknowledge him with a wave or hello. "My mother did send me a card about a year ago," he added. But her correspondence failed to profess any of the love, understanding, and forgiveness she studied so often in her book of faith—"the *first* teachings of Christ," as Jake Junior pointed out. And yet if defectors were spared the harsh punishment of ostracism, he acknowledged in afterthought, there would be less incentive for Amish youths to commit fully to their faith's—and their bishop's—terms of devotion.

Leaving home is as American as apple pie. The incredible fact that this passage is all but bypassed by most Amish youths (or manifested in some less obvious manner) provoked me to delve deeper into the nuances of Amish practice. I was fascinated by the institutionalized pressure to conform, which certainly exists in all faiths and cultures, but rarely to such an extreme extent or with such effectiveness. After my twenty-five-dollar tour of the Amish in Harmony, I tracked down a friend of a friend near Lancaster, Pennsylvania—the first North American region to be settled by Mennonite and Amish families in the eighteenth century. There, I was introduced to an *unshunned* Amish person willing to talk to me about his faith and way of life.

John, age sixty-five, lives with his wife in a blink of a Pennsylvania farming town, surrounded by the homes of other conservative Old Order Amish—the oldest and largest Amish group in North America with common beliefs and practices.[4] As John and I went to shake hands through the frame of his front door, our palms missed each other by a good six inches. John has been blind ever since a construction accident some ten years ago. Otherwise strong and healthy-looking, he has broad shoulders, a ready smile, and rough hands, one of which I guided to mine for the completion of our awkward greeting.

He invited me in, and we sat together at his kitchen table. His wife was visiting her mother down the road, so the house was empty and much more quiet than most homes, with an absence of all things mechanical that tend to emit noise. My friend had told me little about John's life except for his blindness. One of eighteen children raised in a traditional Old Order home,

John described his upbringing as "particularly strict" given that his father, like Jake Junior's, was his town's bishop. Although his father had passed away, John's ninety-two-year-old mother and all of his seventeen siblings were still alive. With six children of his own, John had a small brood by Amish standards, and all were grown with families of their own. After my experience in Minnesota, I was pleasantly surprised by John's instant and jovial friendliness, his willingness to open a window onto his life.

"We the people have an obligation and a right to understand each other," he declared, as if delivering a proposed amendment to the Bill of Rights. "Many Amish are opposed to the giving of opinions to outsiders, but there would be much more peace in the world if we'd just try to know and understand each other. Even if the person has different opinions, it doesn't mean he's wrong. Accept the good, reject the bad. If people don't interfere with my rights, they're my friend."

A natural and curious conversationalist, John was one of those people who under "normal" circumstances would probably have many diverse friends. But since he was a member of a society that pointedly denies individual freedoms in favor of the welfare of the community, I wondered how many people he knew who didn't interfere with his rights, and whom he thus could call friend. From his appearance, John seemed to conform completely, in his buttonless, collared shirt, pocketless home-sewn trousers, and suspenders. He wore the prescribed uncut beard, a silvering gray, and the same shaggy helmet of hair I'd seen all over Harmony, a kind of early Ringo Starr, cropped precisely at the earlobe. His blue eyes were all his own, though, and they locked onto those of the person he addressed. It was almost eerie, actually, the way he stared so intently into my eyes as we spoke; I kept forgetting that he couldn't see me. When I later gathered the courage to ask him how he maintained such accurate eye contact, he said that his physical therapist had taught him that "trick," training his eye muscles to hone in on the source of a sound.

Throughout our day together, John asked me as many questions as I asked him. "Can you describe yourself to me?" was his first request.

"I'm five feet two, twenty-nine years old," I began, "of Irish-French descent. I have a roundish face, a 'pug' nose, as my mom has always called it, almond-shaped brown eyes, and dark hair prematurely graying at the temples." I watched him compute an image in his mind.

"Do you burn in the sun?" he asked.

"Usually," I replied, filling in his picture.

Taking turns with our questions, I asked John about his childhood, one spent working tirelessly on a farm. "We never got a break on the farm, which wasn't right of my father—he was a slave driver," said John. "I don't want to condemn him; just explaining, not complaining. But he taught us the work ethic—stick to it till it's done, no matter how hard it is. The farm is still the best way to raise a family. A hard day's work has never killed anybody, but people do pass away from lack of exercise, from *sitting still*."

For many centuries it was nearly impossible to separate Amish faith from Amish farms, the land itself serving as a link to God and a receptacle for sacrifice and obedience. But the increasing scarcity of land and the growing unprofitableness of farming has begun to force the Amish in Lancaster County, and those of other American regions, off the fields and into other lines of work. "It's almost impossible for young men now to buy livestock and equipment and a farm; you just can't do it, unless you have a rich uncle or father," John explained. "So that leaves forming a business that relies upon tourism." This shift undermines the very core of Amish life, making a once-independent people dependent upon secular society.

Though the origin of Amish tourism dates back to the 1930s,[5] John doesn't remember spotting his first tourist until the 1950s. "I was a farmer at that time, and I thought, *Man*, these dumb people—why don't they stay home and save their money? Our parents grew up in the Depression, we were taught to save, we didn't have extra money. And here are these people wasting all this gas to come from New York to see these Amish people—what's the matter with them?" Eventually, recognizing there was nothing they could do to stop the tour companies from invading their privacy, some Amish invented ways to work the inevitable to their advantage.

Today, about five million tourists visit Lancaster County annually, spending over four hundred million dollars.[6] Though they encourage their congregants to pursue the agrarian work that has long been their mainstay, bishops tend to allow tourist-oriented vocations if they prove more economically viable, so long as the effort involved, such as crafting chairs or sewing quilts, is "useful."

"It's going to be harder to teach Amish values without the farm," John lamented. "Amish people are now starting to have too much money and too much free time working these other kinds of jobs." He didn't mention the question of contamination from people who do not sound, look, or think the way the Amish do.

Loathing idleness as "the devil's workshop," the Amish have historically embraced physical labor as the preeminent teacher of discipline, simplicity, collectivism, and faith. To apply this viewpoint to one's worship, relationships, dress, and personal values is to live *Gelassenheit*—a German term roughly translated to mean "submission." As a worldview, the posture of *Gelassenheit* "discourages high school education, abstract thinking, competition, professional occupations, and scientific pursuits, which lead to conceit and arrogance."[7]

"Beware lest any man spoil you through philosophy and vain deceit after the rudiments of the world and not after Christ,"[8] their holy book warns, and the Amish heed.

Though exposure to the "outside" through tourism doesn't seem to have markedly changed John's community, he says it is reshaping religious rituals, particularly that of baptism. "More and more young Amish, especially males, are leaving their communities for a period of time," he said. It is a sojourn allowed among most Amish settlements. Most of the young people return by choice to be baptized into an adulthood of faith. "Amish youth don't always know why they come back," John said, posing the simple theory that "when they see what's out there, there's just something that propels them back into the fold.

"When I was younger," he said, "I didn't go through a 'wild phase'; back then, everyone mostly accepted what was in front of them. For me, it wasn't a question, because my father was so strict. But when I got older, I thought I'd have to leave my community because of the hypocrisy I saw in the practicing and living of the faith, in the lack of genuine Christianity in some of the people around here. I thought, Man, our people are *wrong*! But that's where I was wrong—judging others.

"During that time, I secretly visited many churches 'outside,'" he confided, "and when I saw what was out there, I knew that if I went to any one of those churches, I'd eventually disagree with some things there too, and see hypocrisy among *them*. So I chose the Amish lifestyle for myself and my family. Not that the Amish are better than other kinds of people. There are a lot of hindrances in the Amish faith, a lot of brainwashing, but there's a lot of hindrances and brainwashing in other faiths, and other kinds of lives, too. Everybody's brainwashed to an extent, even if only by the TV. I see a lack of faith in God everywhere."

John went on to say that though change is slow in coming, more Amish bishops are placing a greater emphasis on their charges' spiritual development and individual expression. In some cases, they are even relaxing the unforgiving scrutiny of social constructs—a shift John sees as hopeful for future generations. But even Amish communities seemingly more concerned with conformity than an intimate relationship with God are still, in John's opinion, a better place to raise a family than a non-Amish environment. "When I became aware of how much crime, drug addiction, suicide, and divorce there is on the outside," John said, "even among people who call themselves religious, that got my attention. My cousin's daughter left the Amish community for reasons of genuinely wanting deeper spiritual development and fewer commandments of man. Even with good intentions, she was the first person from our community to be divorced. That was a lesson for me," he said, reflecting the prevailing Amish belief that there is something divisive lurking below the gloss of modernity that slowly corrodes character and morality, tearing people and families apart.

"You know, you have to set limits to live a happy life," John said emphatically. "*Things* don't bring happiness. The more things we accept into our lives, the more hectic and out of control our lives become. The Amish know this." The Amish do not condemn pleasure, or material objects. But they are apprehensive about what human conceit, selfishness, and over-indulgence can make of them if their pursuit is unrestricted. For John, the stability and happiness of his traditional family has always been his priority, so he stifled his doubts and remained loyal to the faith he knew best.

Although each Amish community is virtually segregated, collectively they manage to stay current with one another's lives through a national newspaper called *The Budget,* which I subscribed to after my visit to Harmony. The thick weekly paper includes column entries submitted by Amish and Mennonite communities in an effort to keep the Anabaptist "family," as a whole, informed. A typical entry:

We're having ideal butchering weather with lows going down in the teens. Brother Jacob plans to do his 3 porkies tomorrow. Our church last Sun. was at Raymond J. R. Schwartzes, and to be at Jake D. Eicher Jrs. on March 7. Visitors were Min. Ernest B. Girods, David S. Schwartz and Edith M. Schwartz. Simon, 4-year-old son of Ernest L. Girod, had the misfortune of falling down their cellar stairs and broke his arm. Jake M. and Mary Wickey are first-time parents since the arrival of Levi. He was named after Grandpa Girod.

Week after week, I found myself drawn to the pen-pal-like newspaper, fascinated by the fact that this religious subculture—spread out all across the country—avidly exchanges information that most of us would consider too mundane or too personal to commit to print. *The Budget*'s subscribers read about whose cow has given birth, who is planting what crop, who has endured hardship from drought, who has hosted out-of-town visitors, whose elders are bedridden, who is canning peaches, and who is picking peas—no matter that most readers are strangers to one another and will probably never meet.

"People here no longer have roots, do they?" John asked me, like an anthropologist new to our continent. "You don't, do you?" he speculated, quite astutely. John spoke from the experience—the opposite of mine—of still living in the town in which he was born, surrounded by every member of his extended family, who recently gathered for a reunion of "immediate relatives" totaling *four hundred* identically dressed men, women, and children. "Once you pull your roots," he declared, "you can't establish them any other place—did you know that? When that root is pulled out, it is permanently gone."

Having roots—having a legacy of place and identity—has a nice ring to this wayward child of the new millennium. And yet the maternal, watchful eye of a tight-knit community—in the case of the Amish, constructed to ensure religious obedience and social welfare—can turn squinty and oppressive. As in any enclave, gossip can serve as a useful electric fence, but according to John, its abuses can be more like a jolt of harsh and jealous judgment. "Amish life can be cruel," he admitted. "Traditions and 'commandments of man' [the bishop's mandates] come first. And because of that, everybody's minding everybody else's business. If you don't do everything just so, you're likely to become an outcast. But Jesus forbade the traditions and commandments of man," John noted, quoting a biblical injunction that is particularly paradoxical for the Amish: *Be ye not conformed to the world.*[9]

John's reflective, questioning nature is the exception and not the rule among the Amish; some of his words and actions directly negate his community's code, including his willingness to talk to an outsider. In fact, when I asked John more about his wife, expressing a hope to meet her, he shuffled his feet and said I probably wouldn't. "She doesn't really approve of me talking to you," he admitted, "and she wouldn't want to have to answer any questions, so she'll stay away until your car is gone." But defending his own maverick spirit, John says that occasionally challenging his people's—including his wife's—boundaries has strengthened his decision to remain Amish, not weakened it. Before going blind, John worked for a local welding company, which once sent him to New York City for a three-day training seminar. "The evenings by yourself can be long with nothing to do," he said. "After a few days, I couldn't sit in the hotel alone again. I looked across the street and saw a movie sign that said *Woodstock*. We're not supposed to go to movies," John acknowledged as an aside, "but most things I'll try once."

"*Woodstock,* the film about the concert?" I asked. I tried to wrap my mind around the idea that a topless, in-depth look at America's 1960s counterculture was the *one* movie this Amish person had seen in his lifetime.

"Yeah!" he exclaimed. "I'm glad I saw it. Now I understand young people better." Launching into a synopsis of the film, he marveled at the "rock guys who slung their long, sweaty hair around, making noise with guitars while the crowd danced, sang, and slid in the mud." John closed his eyes, momentarily transported.

"That must have been an education," I ventured.

"It was," he agreed. "That was a time of rebellion for the young people, rebelling against 'the system.'"

"And seeing *Woodstock* didn't seduce you, didn't change your commitment to being Amish, or even pique your interest in a 'free love' world where it's normal to dance naked in public?" I asked.

"No, it didn't corrupt me; it informed me."

"Do you have any regrets about having chosen an Amish life, knowing what you know now?" I asked.

"Yes, and not at all," John said, calling both sides of the coin in the air. "You could say that about your own life, too, I bet," he added. "You probably regret leaving your roots, but you also don't because of the experiences you've had, the going forth in life that you have been able to do because you *didn't* stay. I still cherish being Amish. I wish you could see what happens when someone is sick, when we have a funeral, when there's a barn raising, if there's a tragedy among the Amish—the support that is there. If a person starts to fall away, people are encouraging, some in a nice way, some not tactful—but *caring* that you might get lost."

After we had talked for a few hours, my stomach began to grumble. I scanned John's countertops for a sign of food, but his kitchen, so bare and ordered, promised nothing but water from a faucet. I asked John if I could take him to lunch, hoping that if he said no, he'd at least offer me whatever was behind cabinet number one. He thanked me for the offer, graciously declining, and left it at that. "But you *must* be hungry," I projected.

"No, I didn't work hard enough this morning to be hungry," he countered. "I should be capable of doing things myself, I'm such a burden," he said, referring to his blindness.

Forgetting my hunger pains, I asked John if his sight loss had affected his faith.

"Do you really want to know?" he asked, hesitating. "It wasn't as much my blindness," he said, finally. "I've learned to cope with my blindness. But another part of me is very bitter and has changed my faith in God." And then, as if someone were holding a gun to his head, he unleashed the following, literally without a pause for punctuation, let alone breath: "We had a son who chose not to marry and lived at home with us here after I lost my sight we became very dependent on him he worked as a construction worker he was very good at his work and he done a lot of work in this house it was an older house and he repaired it like the cabinets that you see five years ago he fell at a construction site and died." John gulped, fighting back tears.

Absorbing John's tragedy, I immediately thought of Jake Junior, a split screen in my mind of two sets of Amish fathers and sons, a thousand miles apart. One father felt he had affirmed—even safeguarded—his faith in the act of disowning his son. Another father has seen his faith profoundly tested by the fact that his son was taken away from him. "I don't want to put my burdens on you," John interjected in the room's stillness. I did my best to convince him that he wasn't.

"I met another father once who lost a son," John said, accepting the latitude to continue. "The father said he didn't think there was anything harder than losing an adult son. That's what God asked Abraham to lose. The Bible says that when we suffer, God suffers with us, he grieves with us. But I can't figure out why he would permit this to happen to this selfless, handsome man, my boy," John said, pausing. "My family and I sat in the hospital waiting room for twenty-two hours. The doctor came into the room, put his hand on my shoulder, and said, 'John, your son is no longer with us.' I said, 'Where'd you take him?' Then it hit me. The doctor didn't say any more."

Among the Amish, John explained, faith and community are supposed to be all one needs to endure any crisis. To seek help on the "outside," like professional therapy, is considered feeble and self-indulgent. "I just heard a book on tape recently about the loss of a child, and how most people cannot cope on their own, that they need professional help. But with my people, you're not supposed to show weakness, because that weakness is a reflection of your faith. 'If you had faith, you'd accept that loss and go on with life,' they say. So what happens to a lot of Amish," he summated, "is a kind of numbing out."

I asked John if he still prayed. "Yes, I do," he said with some hesitation. "I need something to hold on to, we all do." I asked him if he prayed more than before his son died. "No, it doesn't have the strength it once did," he said.

I asked him, "Though God might not have taken your pain away, has having a life patterned by religious practice, overall, given your life more meaning?"

John described his practice of fifteen years earlier, when his children were still living in the house, a time he remembers fondly, when his spiritual life was more representative of a typical Amish person. In addition to biweekly group worship, John and his family prayed throughout the day and studied Scripture, and attended biannual communion services to ceremonially renew their faith. He spoke of ritualized foot washing among his community congregation, an Amish practice in accordance with Christ's command to stoop and wash the feet of a brother or sister, a sign of voluntary submission and humility. But the practice John seems to have encouraged the most in his children was an alternative to traditional silent and rote prayer. "I taught my children to pray aloud so they would know how to teach *their* children. We prayed out loud from our *heart*," John said.

I wondered if John still attended the Sunday services. "Oh yes, I go. I'm in hiding, I'm 'in the closet,'" he bluntly admitted. "I go and everyone thinks everything is fine. But I'm a hypocrite. I'm pretending to be something I'm not, to have a faith I don't right now. There's a lot of that in the world, isn't there? We all do it to an extent."

I realized that living in America—a land that glorifies and epitomizes a spirit of rugged individualism—must be especially hard for this unusual man. But as we continued talking, he revealed a rather unexpected outlet he's found, allowing for at least the tiniest bit of creative self-expression. "I do a pig show in the summer for tourists," he blurted out with a good deal of pride. He asked if I might want to meet his four-legged leading ladies.

Guiding me outside, feeling his way with a cane, John reached for the door to a small barn. "I hope you're okay with animal smells," he warned as we entered. Inside, two fat mama pigs lounged with their squealing spot-ted litters. "They both just had babies," he said, talking to the pigs by name as he tapped his cane against their pen. "I used to train horses, horses that other people couldn't work with. I spoke gently to them, and most of them came around," he said. "And now I train pigs; if you use the right tech-nique, they're very intelligent." John reminisced about the part-time job he once had at a petting zoo, which is where he noticed people's general love of pigs. He decided to try his hand teaching a few pigs to slide down a chute, and the rest is his personal history. "Now I have sliding pigs, run-ning pigs, and kissing pigs," he boasted, *click-clacking* his way over to a big bag of pretzels, taking a few into his palm.

Handing me one, he suggested that if I held it between my lips and bent down, I would get a kiss. "Some of them are gentle, and some aggressive," he cautioned, as my nose touched Carmel's with the hope that she was one of the pacifists. The pretzel was gone in a flash, a trace of wetness on my cheek as evidence of her affection. I asked John how his bishop reacted to the pig show. "We're not supposed to go to *any* kind of shows or enter-tainment," he acknowledged.

"Much less *provide* the entertainment," I noted.

"But nobody has said anything to me, except for my wife, who wishes I wouldn't do this," he said. "But working with the pigs helps me make a living and helps me keep my mind—at least *partially*," he joked.

I suddenly realized that John's pig show was where he'd accumulated much of his experience with the "outside world," as he called it, retaining like flypaper ideas and phrases he overheard, such as *in the closet*. "I often wonder what got me to look outside of my little world, to be accepting and to want to learn more," John said thoughtfully, offering his words to the pigs as much as to me. "I want to do and see and try everything there is to do and see and try in this world. I'll probably never do it, but I *want* to."

When, sometime after meeting John, I transcribed our taped conversation, I compiled not only his answers to my questions, but my responses to his. In reviewing the tapes I could hear—and remember—how uncomfortable I sometimes felt from John's cross-examination. I was a captive resource for his desire to know and understand more about everything. His questions, fired like fastballs, covered the bases of my life—past, present, and future. He quizzed me about my childhood, about my family's (nonexistent) religious affiliations and beliefs, about my parents' divorce: "Did they remain friends?" he wondered. "Did they talk badly about each other to you? . . . How did your relationships change? . . . Did you ever feel abandoned?" He asked if I or my mother cried when I left home at seventeen, seeming relieved when I answered affirmatively. He asked if I'd ever received professional counseling, interested in what it was like and what kinds of things were discussed; he was curious to know if I volunteered time to "help people," whether I had ever participated in group meditation, how much television I watched, whether or not I intended to marry and have children, how much hard physical labor I had done, and whether or not I knew how to garden. What about my life would I change if I could? he wondered. What else did I hope to one day write? he asked, positing with his inquiry that "writers appear kind of crazy to most people, don't they?"

By the end of the day, I felt as if I'd filled out a stack of hospital forms for a family of ten, detailing all medical histories, allergies, and emotional and psychological conditions for a new internist. It had been a while since anyone had requested a top-to-bottom inventory of my life and psyche.

Listening to my choice of words in response to John's questions, I was reminded that I had, in places, conveniently remodeled my past and myself, giving a nip or a tuck here or there, altogether sidestepping some of the more troubling spots. John, as far as I could tell, had instead laid his puzzle pieces right on the table, even the faded ones with corners lopped off.

But as the day had wound down and I sensed our good-bye was imminent, and my hunger lessened my defenses, I had begun to feel bad that John had given of himself so willingly and I had not. Standing near his doorway, I blurted out that there had actually been *two* divorces in my childhood, not one, that I had more than just a few pulled roots, with three parents residing in three different states. I admitted that though I sometimes felt as if my life had been wrought with exhaustion and physical laboring, my hands, in fact, could not remember ever being callused. And I explained that besides the selfless service I had accounted for, I had volunteered equal amounts of time to being selfish, superficial, and vain. And I was no gardener, though I aspired to be someday, when I had a yard and more patience.

John didn't seem surprised by my shotgun footnotes, proving he understood more about human nature than most people who have the benefit of sight and unlimited access to the world. In his probing, he had held up a mirror to the person I had fought so hard to stake out in my adolescent process of individuating, and reminded me that the shadow self—the imperfect nonpublic self—cannot be separated out like a yolk from its white. I had experienced this truth in the medicine circle but seemed to have unconsciously filed it away as "protocol for ceremony" to be reserved for safe spaces where vulnerability is *the norm*. John widened the circle and my understanding that transparency and willing self-examination are the building blocks for any life of authenticity, religious or otherwise. And while John himself had not mastered these lessons in the company of his own community, he was at least having an ongoing dialogue about them, if only with a sympathetic audience of pigs. If reaching out to be a more honest person is integral to the daily business of holiness, then I learned that aspect of spiritual practice from a blind "in the closet" Amish man, who's trying the best way he can to get out.

As we approached our good-bye, I acknowledged how difficult it must have been for John to have struggled through such a crisis of faith in secrecy, for going on five years now.

"Most of the time I'm okay," he said, paused, then admitted, "Winters are difficult." It is during the icy months, with no pig show to keep him busy, that John is left to work things out inside his mind. A man racked with overthinking, he has examined everything in his life from dozens of angles, and in doing so has developed more than a few irreconcilable perspectives.

"All in all, do you still consider yourself an *Amish* man?" I asked, bringing our conversation full circle. John didn't answer. Instead, he smiled, looked me in the eye, and offered his open hand. I gave him mine in return, and we shook our good-bye more gracefully than our hello.

I pulled out of John's driveway near dusk, onto his narrow street, behind a passing Amish buggy. I followed the carriage until, together, we came to a stop at the intersection of a four-lane road filled with speeding cars. We sat there, the two of us, for a very long time, long enough for me to realize that the motionless man was merely practicing his faith, no different than if he were kneeling in prayer. For his practice was to yield—to observance, sacrifice, tradition, a collective identity, and yes, also to the increasing traffic of the world around him. Eventually, the horse did find a large enough opening, heaving the weight of his passenger into motion as I held my breath, watching as they clippity-clopped over the bright yellow lines to the other side of the intersection; to safety.

Chapter Four

Monasticism—a discipline of renunciation, contemplation, and solitude—is a way of life that dates back to the earliest annals of Eastern religion. Prebiblical Hindus wandered India in this state of existence, seeking union with the divine Absolute, followed by Buddhists who, centuries later, attempted to reach nirvana by segregating themselves in monasteries. Groups of celibate Jews withdrew into the desert to seek God "through a true conversion of heart and fraternal charity," living by the basic tenets of monasticism.[1]

Later, during the third century after Christ's death, Christians who were living in Egyptian desert caves under the guidance of Anthony the Abbot infused their own monastic way of life with an intense devotion to God. With great discipline they strove to achieve union with God "by withdrawing from the world and severing all associations with people and material attachments."[2] These early desert hermits were eventually joined by others who subscribed to a more communal configuration of monastic life called "cenobitism." While both forms of Christian monasticism flourished in various parts of the world, they managed only sporadic growth across Europe.

Around A.D. 480, a boy named Benedict was born to a distinguished Italian family of Catholic faith. As a young man, Benedict elected to forsake his home and wealth to follow a self-directed spiritual path of penitential solitude.

After sequestering himself in a remote cave for a number of years, Benedict con-cluded that religious life is, except in rare cases, best exercised not in solitude but in a domestic setting among a community of men or women who live, work, pray, and eat together. Hoping to bring some sense of unification to Western monasticism, Benedict wrote the Rule—the code of regulations governing the daily life of a "household" of monks or nuns. Drawing upon both Western and Eastern traditions, Benedict's time-tested framework for the quest for union with God emphasizes the virtues of obedience and stability as the most decisive for leading life as reflected in the Gospels.

By design, making solemn vows to become a Benedictine nun or monk is not a simple initiation. As Saint Benedict himself declared: "Admission to the religious life should not be made easy for newcomers."[3] While anyone who earnestly expresses interest in a monastic commitment is offered an intimate and friendly peek behind the abbey curtain, they are often discouraged from taking vows by those who have already done so, in a test of the pre-initiate's serious-ness and fortitude. Submitting to a multistep process, the individual passes through a probation period and into a trial extension until finally allowed the opportunity to express a formal commitment to a monastery.

This final ceremony is a symbolic offering of one's life to God for the sake of community and the world. In it, the initiate promises to remain loyal to the teachings of Christ and comply with the Rule of Saint Benedict, living and laboring as a monk or a nun for the rest of his or her days and nights.

Today, there are more than one hundred Benedictine monasteries and "mother houses" spread out all across America.

Congregating with Monks and Nuns

The closest I came to Catholicism during all my childhood years was Saturday-night sleep-overs at the house of my best friend, Maria. Maria belonged to a junior bowling league, and although I never had an affinity for the game, I liked to tag along with her on Sunday afternoons and keep score. Or maybe it was the cheap and cheesy nachos and video games that I liked. Whatever the case, part of our Sunday bowling ritual included a layover at High Mass. I never understood a lick of the Latin and Spanish sermons, but the candle-carrying choir sweeping by in slow procession, the ghostly figures escaping from the priest's swinging orbs, and the biblical stories depicted in tall panels of colored glass held my imagination enough to pass the time. As far as my friend and I were concerned, church was the toll we paid to spend the rest of the day at the bowling alley.

From the distant perspective afforded me by Maria's pew—and later in life by television and other Catholic acquaintances—nuns and monks seemed like strange folk. They either flew, kept company with lepers, or beat children's knuckles with wooden rulers. And then there was the indelible mark left on me by a kindly, devout Catholic woman in her midsixties who, over tea one day in a sleepy village in Ireland, referred to the nuns responsible for her childhood education as "fucking bitches." All in all, those in robes and habits were no more real to me than the statues of Saint Paul and Mother Mary found inside my friend's cathedral.

For most devoted Catholics, practice typically involves weekly attendance at Mass, baptism of infants, prayer and recitations of the rosary, and repentance at the requisite once-a-year confession. But what transforms Catholic faith into a full-time religious vocation is the making of solemn monastic vows. In exploring monasticism as a way of life, I couldn't help but wonder what would lead a person to the radical gesture of discarding individual striving, material consumption, and creature comforts in favor of collective living, public service, and self-denial. I was also curious about whether the founding Church's most disciplined practice—a fifteen-hundred-year-old monastic tradition—was, like Gene Begay's, waning in the face of modernism. To find answers to these questions, and to observe what a day in the life of a monk or a nun entails, I signed myself up for a weeklong conference on Catholic monasticism in the twenty-first century, an annual gathering intended for formally affiliated monks, nuns, and priests from all corners of America. My request to attend was unhesitatingly accepted by the monastery's facilitator.

Within minutes of arriving at Saint John's Abbey in Collegeville, Minnesota—the largest Benedictine monastery in the Western Church—I encountered my first monk. Introducing himself as Brother John, he asked why I had come. I briefly explained my explorations into daily spiritual practices and the book I hoped to write.

"Aren't you brave," he said.

"Why do you say that?" I asked.

He smiled, head tilted. "It's just that . . . well, I hope you do realize that when writing about Catholicism you're responsible for getting *every single* one of those words *right*. Your salvation depends upon it." He scanned the room, taking inventory of the arriving brothers and sisters. Then he added, "Personally, I wouldn't want to risk it."

Before I could be certain whether the monk was teasing or dead serious, he excused himself to greet the new arrivals. My eyes followed the back of his brown robe as he welcomed his colleagues to this virtual family reunion. I had read about the monastic "vow of stability"—a commitment that gives the initiates "spiritual roots" and a family to replace the one they renounce when they choose to "leave the world." For most of us, living as two is enough to try our saintliness; imagine cohabiting with two hundred brothers or sisters. Perhaps that is why Saint Benedict challenged his followers to see the perfection of Christ *particularly* in those they would normally find intolerable. As the gospel of John declares: "Those who do not love a brother or sister whom they have seen, cannot love God whom they have not seen."[4]

After my not-so-tender exchange with Brother John, I was abashed enough to loiter discreetly around the edges of the conference room, which now brimmed with predominantly gray–haired men and women. Some wore monastery attire—long robes for men, long skirts and buttoned-up blouses for women, all in the same drab colors—while others dressed in conservatively cut street clothes permitted for long-distance travel. Laughter percolated in intimate circles, everyone catching up on the news since their last assembly. Like those of a party crasher, my tentative attempts to penetrate any one of the circles were unsuccessful. As the only person with exposed clavicles, my outsider status was immediately apparent, and while I was eager to defend what I felt were my good intentions for being there, no one seemed eager to hear them.

The conference facilitator tapped the podium mike, interrupting conversation to introduce the inaugurating guest speaker: a Notre Dame theology professor. The forty-something scholar and father of four had been selected to give an "overview" of contemporary Catholic faith by depicting the three generations that currently define American culture. His focus, however, quickly turned to the generation he considered to be the real threat to Catholic identity: "generation X"—those roughly eighty million Americans born between 1962 and 1982—of which I am a part. The professor illustrated the unique spiritual challenges my generation presents to the Church, given our apparent lack of interest in it, especially in its monastic form. He attributed this "thinning of American Catholicism" to our adherence to the new "religions" of nihilism and the self. We indulge in a kind of narcissistic gnosticism that cobbles together bits and pieces from random philosophic fads to construct a revolving, self-tailored theology of "today's me." Thus this generation of aging youth is fraught with an "anxiety to commit," seeking short-term salvation through a privatized pursuit of happiness.

Glancing around the room, I noticed three other people my age, two twenty-something dark-haired nuns and a wide-eyed junior monk. They, too, were surveying the crowd, curious to see the older nuns' and monks' reaction to the speaker's words. The lined faces of the elders looked road weary, puzzled, and—in at least a few cases—alarmed. "No previous generation of American Catholics," the professor went on, "inherited so little of the content and sensibility of the faith from their parents as have today's Catholic youth." I later learned that this was not breaking news to the assembled. Though perhaps they had not yet fully accepted the implications of the professor's statistics, the elders were well aware that in their hundred-plus Benedictine monasteries, the average age of a resident is currently about sixty—the oldest average since 1846, when monasticism was first established in America.

I had to agree with the professor that this country's thirteenth generation of "settlers" seems less open to traditional religious dogma and not as driven by the promise of delayed gratification in heaven. It's easy to be hooked on the instant karma of the here and now, perhaps because we've been born into an ever-shifting world in which skepticism seems normal and healthy. While I clearly do not represent the proclivities of an entire generation, I can say that I personally feel less drawn to traditional expressions of faith whenever affiliation overshadows elucidation, when "group think" becomes an acceptable substitute for independent reason, inquiry, and emotion. From my observations and conversations with people my age, many seem to be seeking out their own less bureaucratic, less homogenized soulful outlet—one they're willing to work to uncover. As one Gallup poll reported, 81 percent of those asked agree that "one should arrive at his or her religious beliefs independent of a church or synagogue."[5]

Conscious of these competing influences, our visiting professor challenged the attendees to usher in "the new American Catholicism," a refurbished faith. "It wasn't expected to be a smooth ride, and it hasn't been," the professor said in acknowledgment of the period since the 1960s when the Catholic Church underwent a practical face-lift in an effort to update some of its centuries-old features. The outcome of this mandated evolution, called Vatican II, resulted in new practices ranging from the replacement of the Latin Mass with a more accessible English language version, to the redirection of the once-obscured priest who now *faces* the congregation he addresses. In general, the intent of Vatican II was to better engage and involve those sitting in the pews and those living in the monasteries. "And the job's not done yet," the professor declared.

As if given a "wrap it up" hand signal, the professor brought his overview to a sudden close, imploring the elders not to forsake the American youth who now, more than ever, needed them. Silently pondering this weighty assignment—one I presumed many of them were already attempting—the monks and nuns looked relieved when we were suddenly dismissed.

The next morning, church bells rang out promptly at six, rousing us all from our cots to dress and shuffle from our gender-specific dorms to the source of the clamor. As with most Catholic cathedrals, St. John's architecture is not modest. One would think that only intensely claustrophobic artisans were hired to design and construct these colossal spaces of worship. Many Catholics, monastic and otherwise, feel that all this grandeur—the ornate, lofty ceilings, saturated prism windows, impressive pillars, and marbleized saints—conjures a more spiritual state of mind. It signifies the distinction between that which belongs to the glory of God and the ordinary depravity just outside the cathedral's massive doors.

I followed a cluster of nuns as they silently made their way from the mundane to the sacred, through the monastery's portal. They passed empty rows to the front pews where their colleagues sat poised for the prayer of daybreak. I took my cues from them as best I could, using my peripheral vision to guide me to the correct hymnal page, through the proper ritual of pause and praise, trailing the rise and fall of the monastic body as its many arms and legs flexed in unison toward God, like a tide folding in and out of its sea. Rejecting the more spontaneous, improvised prayer popular among Protestant churches, Catholics communicate with and about God through "liturgy"—a scripted repertoire of adoration, thanksgiving, petition, and atonement. The intent of such repetitive prayer is to liberate worshipers from having to *think* about their praise, freeing them to simply *feel* the prayers they know by heart.

It wasn't until the third day of the conference that I began to viscerally experience why group prayer—called the Divine Office, and practiced five to seven times a day, seven days a week—is given a priority over all other Benedictine obligations. During those first few days, just as my busy mind would begin to eclipse the remembrance of the last service, the bell tower would bid a return to God's most inner domain where our minds would once again be cleansed, restored, and reoriented. A Catholic ritual of mindfulness, these cyclical prayers are like an IV that continuously drips Christ-consciousness into the vein of the believer.

As the routine of prayer became more familiar to me, as I retraced my steps to the pew again and again, I thought of Gene Begay's simple request to the Creator that he keep one eye on him at all times. Surrounded by the unceasing psalms of the monks and nuns, they had, it seemed, found *their* way of keeping their eye on God, hoping, like Gene, for the same in return.

———

After one morning's prayer service, I shared breakfast with the two twenty-something nuns I'd spied from across the room the first night. Over bowls of sugary cereal we talked about what it's like to be young and avowed, about what had compelled them to step outside of mainstream America in order to be of service to its communities. As would be the case with others I'd later meet from numerous religious traditions, the nuns felt drawn by an indescribable, almost involuntary pull. "My search for God brought me to the monastery," explained the younger of the two nuns, "but greater than mine was God's search for me." The smooth-faced, dark-haired girl went on to say that by most standards, she'd had a "full and complete life" for someone in her early twenties. "I had the college education, the great job, the good friends, an apartment I liked, the furniture, and the car, but something was missing, tugging at me," she said, dunking her spoon in the pool of milk.

At the time, the young woman was involved in her parish but did not personally know anyone who'd taken religious vows. "No one ever spoke of becoming a nun," she recalled, "at least not anyone from *my* generation." Intrigued by the idea of exploring monastic life, she attended a religious vocation fair, a kind of job fair where a variety of religious "professionals" provide information and answer questions. "I liked the Benedictine balance between prayer, work, and public service, and after spending some extended time at a monastery, I realized it could offer me something my secular life couldn't, something I wanted: a spiritual path with *pointed focus,* a way to grow in prayer in a communal setting." The youthful nuns had chosen God as their ideal life partner.

Both women insisted they didn't feel confined by their matrimonial vows to God, or limited by the demands of its daily discipline. Indeed, they reveled in the all-encompassing rigor of their lives. "Is there *anything* you find hard about being a nun?" I asked. "Not in practice," they said, but sometimes in theory, citing a few of their church's more polemical positions—ones more generally Catholic than specifically monastic—such as the refusal to ordain women or advocate any form of birth control.

While it was obvious these women were broad-minded and outspoken (one of them was even carrying around a book of Sufi poetry), I still wasn't prepared for their reaction to my next question. I asked if they had ever met their Pope in person. "No," one replied, "and I'm not that interested in meeting him either, though I'd give anything to meet the Dalai Lama." Nearly choking on a Lucky Charm, my eyes darted around the noisy cafeteria searching for undercover pope narcs. I found it perplexing that a person would renounce her independence under the auspices of a religious leader she wasn't even that interested in meeting.

"I think the Dalai Lama has remained close to his people," the nun elaborated. "He seems to know what's going on with them, not separating himself apart in an ivory tower. He's out there fighting for the Tibetans every day. I just think he's a true holy man."

The nun's words reminded me of Gene Begay's observation that every belief system is like a language with a unique set of symbols and intonations all its own. As a result, though these women may be drawn to other worldviews and teachers, the embedded Catholicism of their youth rendered the possibility of *practicing* a distinctly different religion, such as Buddhism or Sufism, unthinkable. They seemed willing to accept, though not quietly, the few aspects of Catholicism they were unable to conjugate in order to continue speaking their native dialect.

If America were scoured for poster children for the new millennium nun, these young "women religious"—liberated of habits and toting around mystical Indian poetry and a soft spot for exiled reincarnates—would be good casting. Approaching their religion with loyal commitment *and* independent criticism, the nuns balanced their own conscience and evolving virtue with all that they deferred to the Church.

When I asked what they felt was most essential to living the daily practice they were so vigorously committed to, the youngest of the two concisely proffered: "Dying to the self." The stark imagery slipped easily off her tongue, though it wasn't immediately clear to me what such a feat might entail. Televised magic tricks came to mind, like sawing the assistant in half—grand illusions performed with the caveat to "never try this at home." Expounding, the nun said that taking vows required the surrendering of one's own will to the will of God. "I was very self-centered when I first came to the monastery," she said. "Now, I still take care of my needs, but I also care for others' needs, while keeping my attention on God."

Under the surface of the disciple's selfless plunge, both women assured me, is something unexpectedly exquisite: a self refitted with more authentic love, integrity, humility, gratitude, and peace than was before possible. It's a monastic prescription for purposeful happiness called "the Christself." As the nuns' Scripture paradoxically promises: "Those who seek their own life will lose it, but those who give up their life will find it."[6] Over time, as they moved further away from the demands and desires of their ego-centered self—what they called the "false self"—the common sensations of feeling abandoned, stranded, divided, and misunderstood slowly dissipated. In their place emerged a greater capacity to sense the presence, and will, of God.

"Do you ever just wish you could take a long vacation, or go on a date?" I asked, shifting the direction of our conversation.

"Oh, on really bad days," one of them chuckled, "I think we both sometimes think: wouldn't it be great to find the right guy and get married and have kids. . . . But I always come back to my *deepest* desire to be in union with God—the greatest of all relationships, and one longer lasting than a two-week vacation."

I wondered if this sense of divine oneness could be attained without joining a monastery and without discarding all worldly possessions. Because if the nuns' path was the only way to this end, I knew I could never make such a steep climb. Talking with them about their intensive schedule of daily rituals, I realized just how attached I am to my sense of independence and feeling *in charge* of my own life. After all, our Founders fought—and died—to secure our independent freedoms. "I have sworn before the altar of God," wrote Thomas Jefferson, "eternal hostility against every form of tyranny over the mind of man." The idea of relinquishing one's own thoughts and free will has long been considered by the American psyche—and my own—as cowardly weakness, the crying of uncle while in the headlock of oppression.

Not so, said the nuns. And they're not alone in their assertion that to surrender can, depending on the circumstances, be an act of unparalleled courage. With further exploration in the days that followed, I came across a few book passages that shed light on the nuns' commitment to a self*less* life. As Richard J. Foster writes in *Celebration of Discipline:* "Most of us have been exposed to such a mutilated form of biblical submission that either we have embraced the deformity or we have rejected the discipline altogether." The nuns had assured me that their disciplined willingness to surrender to God's will was not a form of religious bondage—nor an annihilation of personality or identity—but an *expansion* of selfhood. By loving and trusting in God utterly, they had liberated themselves from needing to control all the unknowns that make up a life.

I heard more than one Benedictine characterize the impulse to "be in control" as a tragic human illusion, and even the source of Eden's "original sin," a futile attempt at "playing God." To come to terms with the limitations of humanness is to attain true wisdom, to "no longer act out of the fear of Hell," as Saint Benedict explains, "but for the love of Christ."[7] This, asserted the nuns, is a revelation of strength, not frailty.

After another long day of lectures, group discussions, and routine religious observance, an announcement was made that Brother Willie's Pub—an on-campus bar—would be open that night, and we were all invited to come.

Though I was aware of the long—and linguistically apropos—monastic tradition of *making spirits,* I wasn't expecting the likes of Willie's. Minnesota Vikings posters loomed over bar stools where robed monks palmed frothy steins, zippy commercials blasting loudly from the TV in the corner. The scene was startlingly contrary to the picture of monastic self-denial and unworldliness conjured by the proceedings of the days before. The monk who'd earlier advised me to get every word right raised his glass to me as I entered the bar. Handing me a glass of *root* beer, Brother John clinked it, toasting to my good health.

We wandered over to the noisiest table just in time for a joke: "Once there was a man who wanted to become a monk of the strictest kind," a nun began. "This particular order was so strict they never talked except every five years. After the first five years, the superior interrupted the monk's regimen of work and prayer to ask him how he liked it there so far. 'Well, sometimes the oatmeal is lumpy,' the monk acknowledged before returning to his chores. Five more years of silence go by, and the monk is again summoned by his superior to find out how things are going. 'Well, occasionally my room gets a little cold,' he replied. Five years later the superior asks, a little annoyed, 'And how are things *now*?' 'Well,' says the monk after his years of hard labor, 'my back aches some.' With a sigh of disappointment, the superior tells him, 'I'm sorry, we're going to have to let you go.' The monk, in disbelief, begs to know why. The superior says, 'In fifteen years you've done nothing but complain.'"

As the table's laughter lulled, everyone's attention turned my way. By this time, it was widely known that I was not a nun, nor was I entertaining the idea of becoming one. The joke-telling nun cajoled me to share whatever impressions of monks and nuns I might have had before coming to Saint John's. I reluctantly obliged, even including the Irishwoman's short review, which (thank God) produced more laughter around the table. The nun said it was one of her personal missions to help dispel both the cold and cruel *and* the romanticized images of a mother superior. She contended that she and her Benedictine colleagues have more in common with everyday people than one might think. "We wish people knew that we, too, struggle for the answers, the meaning, the purpose of our everyday lives—that it's an ongoing process for us as well," she said. "Just because we have the garb and choose to live in community doesn't mean we don't experience self-doubt and faith doubt."

I left Willie's around eleven—well before a few celibates more than twice my age in just-below-the-knee skirts and Hush Puppy slip-ons—forced to acknowledge that while our struggles might be similar, our stamina was not. And it was clear that one other thing separated me—and many other "everyday" people—from my bar mates: a daily attendance to faith. The joke-telling nun described it as "a bottomless Dixie cup of Gatorade that helps get me around those hard bends." As I followed the path cut through Saint John's campus thinking of the nun's words, I recalled something a Baptist minister had said to me a few weeks earlier: "The secret to religion is the fact that religious practice allows you to cope in the *absence* of religious experience. I think that's what the ancients understood; they weren't ecstatic at every step of the way; they said their prayers, burned the incense, did the job—that's what you do . . . in between moments of terrible despair and moments of deep ecstasy."[8]

Brushing my teeth in the communal bathroom, I contemplated meaning and purpose as an ongoing process, not a finite accomplishment, like the passing of a test. An older monk had told me, "Faith is an ongoing *attempt,* a brave attempt." To me, his humble words spoke to how ultimately hopeful it is to have faith, and how radically fearless it can be to remain so *publicly* hopeful in times and places that discourage, even degrade, such attempts.

Flopping onto my cot, I slept for what felt like ten minutes, awakened at dawn by the church bells, an ominous bellowing that Thomas Merton, a renowned monk of the twentieth century, said reminded him "that God alone is good, that we belong to Him, that we are not living for this world."[9] Staring at the ceiling, I thought that while it may be that God alone is good, a cup of coffee wouldn't be bad. I had overheard one nun complain that the morning prayers began before the cafeteria's coffee was brewed, and was relieved to know that I wasn't the only one distracted by the details of living, if not *for* this world, at least *in* it.

On the way to the chapel, I groggily walked alongside Anita and Rosetta, both about eighty years of age and second cousins. As we passed through the cathedral's enormous wooden doors, I watched Rosetta cross to the marble basin of holy water and dip her finger in as Anita and I stood next to each other speaking in hushed tones. I had given the holy water a try a few days earlier, but I felt too much like an imposter, so I'd decided to avoid the ritual altogether, especially in the company of professionals who would know if I accidentally crossed backward. As we all turned to proceed to the pews, I saw Rosetta's index finger reach out for Anita's, transferring with its touch a drop of water. With heads slightly bowed, the cousins each brought their fingertip to their forehead, chest, left, then right, shoulders. The shared gesture bound them together and to the greater body of their church.

As we prayed that day's prescribed psalm, I caught a glimpse of a few monks and nuns who seemed to be struggling with the "faith doubt" the nun in the bar had mentioned. Or else they were just momentarily overtaken by common boredom or accumulative exhaustion. They looked distinctly like people stuck at the end of a long line at the DMV. However, after attending dozens of services, I found this inattentiveness to be the exception and not the rule among people committed to perpetual "at-one-ment" with their God.

Following another afternoon of lectures envisioning the future role of monasticism, we were once again summoned by the bells, this time for the holiest of the seven Catholic sacraments: the Eucharist, or Holy Communion. And I again witnessed—amid all the emphasis on the oral authority of the clergy and on the ritual—a deeply personal and emotional engagement.

A kind of scaffolding for Catholicism's ceremonial dressing, the liturgy is recited by the congregation throughout the Eucharist as one echoing voice—a mass proclamation culminating in communion. At that moment, the devout make a minipilgrimage to their priest (considered the living extension of God's will on earth) to receive the "body and blood" of Christ, a symbolic reenactment of the Last Supper.

The priest purified the bread and wine, swinging the smoke of incense back and forth over the altar the way Gene Begay had smudged the medicine with the smoke of sage over his kitchen table. Having not been baptized in the Catholic faith, I remained an observer as the monks and nuns streamed toward their altar and priest. Many held their hands behind their back and kept their head bowed as they walked, arching them up at the last moment like baby birds eager for nourishment. In kneeling silence, each dissolved and digested the mysteries of Christ.

———

For our very own last supper, we all retreated to the cafeteria. Anita and Rosetta, the elderly cousins from Arkansas, invited me to join their table. After nearly six decades of godly service, the two were forever calling their monastery a *convent,* only to then correct themselves or each other, trying to keep up with the liberated times, in which the term has become obsolete. They were, together, a living record of the transformations that had taken place in the kinetic interplay between consciousness, tradition, and change—the topic relentlessly covered each day of the conference. Anita and Rosetta seemed relatively adjusted to the incongruity between the world they prayed for when they, on the very same day, entered the monastery some sixty years ago and the one they pray for today. But they had, in earlier conversations, wondered how much *more* change might be required of them.

Anita and Rosetta bowed their heads to give thanks to their Lord for the cafeteria-style Salisbury steak and green beans on our plastic trays. Noticing that they looked a little shaken, I asked if everything was okay. Hesitating with a glance in each other's direction, Anita and Rosetta relayed a faxed message they had just received from their "convent—I mean monastery." Three of their sisters at the abbey had passed away over the course of our week at Saint John's, each of whom they had known through decades of side-by-side devotion. With welled-up, disbelieving eyes, hands held across the table, Anita led us in a prayer for their friends, a loss that was as symbolic as it was personal. For the three empty places in their pew may not, like Gene Begay's place at his table, be filled by a fresh influx of believers willing to make the sacrifices necessary to carry the practice of Catholic monasticism into the future.

After dinner, Anita and Rosetta and I hugged good-bye. I told them how inspired I was by their fortitude in observing their religious vows. Their mournfulness gave way to schoolgirl giggles in response to what they considered undue flattery in my suggestion that they had actually *achieved* their vows. "Oh no," Anita said definitively, her proper silver curls rotating in concert with her cousin's. "We try to live them, but we'll die still only trying."

Early the next morning, the bells rang out right on cue. Father Eugene, a priest I had spoken to the first night, said that to him the bells invoked the voices of the saints. On that particular morning, however, the bell's ancestral invitation was not being met by the usual flow of worshipers, save for the monks who lived permanently at Saint John's. For their visiting brothers and sisters, it was time to return to their own monasteries, to focus not so much on the future, but on the everyday routine of house chores, volunteer work in their towns and cities, and religious study among their smaller "family" unit.

As I loaded my bags into my car, Brother I-hope-you-don't-burn-in-hell-for-being-a-writer mysteriously appeared, offering to say a prayer for my departure. I accepted, thanking him in advance as he placed one hand on the hood of my car, bowed his head, and asked that I be given a safe journey, protected and expedient. I suspected his prayer was intended metaphorically, that he hoped my *life's* journey would, without delay, guide me to the Catholic faith. The hunch was confirmed by his parting words: He would *continue* to pray for my conversion and salvation. I guess that may depend, in his mind, on whether or not I get every one of these words right. It was a point of view that conflicted with that of his more progressive colleagues, like Father Eugene, who advocated flexibility in response to faith in a changing world.

"I know little about heaven, because I know only from my own senses what is real and what is not," Father Eugene had declared from the podium as the conference's closing speaker. "We never have final answers, yet we each tend to cling to our reality and narrow band of private observances as if they are absolute truth. We must remain open to what is real," he beseeched his colleagues, "because we never really *know* what it is. . . . Meaning in life today is not simply going back and imitating how it used to be when we remember it in a different way. It's a process of maturity." In the silence that followed Father Eugene's closing words, I glanced around the room, landing on the middle-aged face of the monk who had described faith as an "ongoing attempt." This was the same man who had explained to me that the word *salvation* is derived from the Greek root *sodzo,* which means "to be made whole, complete, to take that which is broken and fix it." To allow oneself to be led by God to this kind of salvation is, according to Catholicism, the meaning of grace.

Brother John waved to me as I pulled out of the monastery parking lot, pointed toward the intersection at the foot of Saint John's campus where two roads meet to form a perfect cross. One direction leads to the chapel, the other to the world and its secular attempts at *sodzo*. As I made my way toward strip malls and drive-thrus, I felt I now better understood why someone—even a peer—would choose to join a monastery as a way of pursuing inner completion and selfless service. But I also remained convinced that the brave attempt at spiritual wholeness—or holiness—was equally attainable, given concerted effort, under less vaulted ceilings, or no ceiling at all.

Chapter Five

Joseph Smith came of age during the spiritual fervor that swept parts of early nineteenth-century America, when Protestant faiths such as the Methodism, Presbyterianism, and the Baptist Church actively competed for converts. While most members of Joseph Smith's family were persuaded by the Presbyterian Church, the teenage boy remained unconvinced and turned to his Bible for guidance. "If any of you lack wisdom, let him ask of God, that giveth to all men liberally, and upbraideth not; and it shall be given," promised the first passage Smith happened upon.[1] So, falling to his knees, Smith prayed for wisdom as he contemplated which church of God he should join.

According to Smith, a dreamy figure of God with Jesus by his side appeared before him with a holy directive: join none, until further notice. Though shared with just a few, Smith's claim of a divine visitation quickly spread, making him the subject of a countywide persecution. Various religious establishments set out to discredit the teenager who threatened to steal their thunder with his tale of God's ambivalence toward their modes of piety.

A few years later, the still tender-aged Smith had another vision, a message mediated by an ethereal prophet on behalf of God. As recounted in The Book of Mormon, the prophet—Moroni—appeared in an ever-expanding bubble of white light until its brilliance filled Smith's bedroom. Among other things, Moroni revealed the whereabouts of a spiritual treasure buried in a hillside of upstate New York, which was said to include a book of gold plates with hiero-glyphic text, two stones in silver bows, and a breastplate. The stones, fastened to the breastplate, were reported to serve as a kind of ancient crystal ball used by old-world clairvoyants to predict the future and explain the past. Smith dug up the mysterious package and, using the stones, translated the encrypted plates. The translations are known today as The Book of Mormon—the seminal scripture distinguishing Mormonism from other Christian denominations. To Smith's mind, the information inscribed on the golden plates set the record straight, exposing existent Christian denominations as diluted, incomplete, and worse—heretical.

According to Smith's translation, Jesus, after his resurrection, paid an extended visit to "the promised land" of the Americas. Indeed, Smith claimed, North America was destined to cohost Christ's eventual return—a "New Zion," he called it—prophesied to take place in both Jerusalem and the sleepy town of Independence, Missouri. Modern-day Mormons call themselves "Latter-Day Saints," spreading their own version of the Christian gospel and living out the latter days before Christ's imminent trek from the Middle East to America's Middle West.

In 1844, during one of Smith's and his followers' many failed attempts to be peaceably accepted by the citizens of a new state—this time Illinois—Smith and his brother were attacked and killed by an intolerant mob. Without the unifying leadership of their founding prophet, the Mormons argued over who should be appointed as his successor. Just over a hundred and fifty years later, the founding church has split into more than twenty-five offshoots, each claim-ing a lineage of prophets traceable to Joseph Smith. The Salt Lake City–based Church of Jesus Christ of Latter-Day Saints has attracted the broadest sup-port, with over five million followers in the United States and eleven million worldwide. It is statistically the fastest-growing Christian church in America.

Testifying with Mormon Missionaries

As a latchkey preteen home alone after school, I was under strict orders never to answer a stranger's knock at the door. Dutifully complying, I remember the awkwardness of hearing an unexpected visitor and freezing in my tracks to silently wait out their retreat. Sometimes, overcome by curiosity, I would quietly tiptoe down the entryway and peer through the tiny glass hole to get a glimpse at the potentially menacing creature on the other side. Most of the time, it was an Amway or Avon salesperson, sporting the signature case and an exaggerated smile.

But on occasion, through that peephole, I'd see a pair of preppy girls not much older than I was. The wide-angle lens of my peephole made it impossible to read the cover of the black book they cradled, like a baby, in the fold of their arms, the message of which they seemed eager to share. Without fail, they always gave the door one last hearty rap before turning their attention to my neighbors.

The girls and their routine visits remained a curiosity to my adolescent psyche, right up there with the identity and whereabouts of the Bradys' first spouses. One summer, when their afternoon visits became more frequent, I asked my mother what the girls with the black books were after. "Your soul and allowance," she quipped with postworkday sarcasm.

Twenty years later, the indefatigable door-to-door practice of young Mormon missionaries continues. To experience this firsthand, I contacted the Latter-Day Saints' headquarters in Salt Lake City, which in turn put me in touch with six young female missionaries sharing an apartment in the Boston area, near where I was living at the time. Over the phone, Sister

Williams was immediately cheerful about the prospect of my accompanying her on her daily sidewalk ritual.

"So when does your day start?" I asked, wondering when we should meet.

"Six-thirty—sharp. Do you want to just come over then?" the gentle voice suggested.

Between Native American medicine people, the Amish, the Benedictines, and now the Mormons, I was beginning to long for religious loafers.

In the pale light of dawn, I located the four-story apartment building in one of the city's bustling immigrant suburbs. Rapping my knuckles on the door, I was amused by the role reversal and wondered if I wasn't the one now being sized up through the peephole. Finally the door handle turned, and a fresh-faced girl of about twenty welcomed me into modest quarters. Inside, there were a sitting room, a cramped kitchen, a single bathroom, and one sizable bedroom to accommodate six mattresses, where the young women slept like peas in an economical pod.

The smell of baking blueberry muffins wafted from the kitchen, where four of the six girls circled a small table and read aloud from their *Book of Mormon*. Sister Williams and Sister Riley, as they referred to themselves, had been assigned to the local Spanish-speaking community, and were sequestered in the adjacent room, practicing their newly acquired language with tandem readings from *The Book of Mormon*'s Spanish edition. In the greater Boston area, as in most cities, the Mormon Church proselytizes in communities of all ethnicities, dividing and conquering the mapped grid. It deploys missionaries who speak, however crudely, the predominant language of any given neighborhood, from Cambodian to Creole.

To train for this, volunteers submit to a two-month full-immersion course offered to male congregants at the age of nineteen and to females as soon as they turn twenty-one. Indoctrinated, the able-bodied saplings are then shipped to a faraway state for a span of eighteen months to two years.

Nudging my way into the kitchen table talk and a freshly buttered muffin, I was provided with a swift lesson on the life of a Mormon missionary. It is an unpaid position, I learned, adopted by sixty thousand individuals worldwide (compared with about six thousand missionaries affiliated with the Roman Catholic Church). Like a devotional boot camp, the commitment is a sacrifice of time with ongoing drills of obedience. Every moment of the twenty-four-hour cycle is designated: when to rise, eat, study Scripture, practice languages, proselytize (typically between 10:00 A.M. and 10:00 P.M.), volunteer for public service, sleep, grocery shop, launder, and write home. And like the military, the Mormon Church recruits its faithful foot soldiers at an age when their vitality and flexibility are high and their lives uncomplicated. Ripe with passion to be a part of something, indeed to have a mission, the girls I met were absorbed—mind, body, and spirit—in loyalty to their cause.

"Faith can't grow without practice," declared Sister Williams, who suspended her bachelor's degree in law and diplomacy for her stint as a missionary. Like the Benedictines, Mormon missionary youths believe that communal existence and all-consuming service provide the best possible incubator for faith. For Mormons, additionally, there is no better end to a long day's religious workout than being able to report the procurement of a new member for the church. As a nightly protocol, the missionaries speak by phone to their district supervisor, giving a full accounting of the hours worked, contacts made, and baptisms pledged. Looking around the cozy apartment, I half expected to see Converter of the Month plaques tacked to its walls.

"Do you ever get to sleep in or escape into a movie theater for an afternoon?" I asked Sister Williams, whose nose was buried in the small print of her black book.

"No, but I sometimes wish we could," she said, taking time for a smile, "especially the sleeping-in part. But you feel it and move through it, reminding yourself that it's not your time, it's God's."

Sister Williams linked her ambition to manifest "the Kingdom on earth" with her faith's reigning precept that every believer strive to achieve "godhood." Unlike those who feel they are saved when they are "born again," Mormons believe the holy water rite is but an initiation into a life-long process of earning salvation by achieving an exalted state of humanness. "Like any father," said Sister Williams, "God wants us to have what He has, but we have to work for it."

By mastering unwavering discipline, charity, and worship, Joseph Smith's followers are promised eternal paradise, a destination that, according to Mormon doctrine, has three distinct tiers. "We want to take as many people with us as we can," explained Sister Williams, pulling out the palm-size flip chart each missionary carries as a handy visual aid. Skipping over the criteria, she showed me the gradations of heaven as animated by lustrous cotton-candy-colored bubbles. The more good thoughts and deeds accomplished, the higher one ascends. While the lower dusty pink echelon is infinitely spacious, the hot pink penthouse promises only limited seating, reserved for those who've indeed succeeded in achieving "the status of God" while on earth. Missionary duty guarantees the young volunteers a space in at least one of the heavenly bubbles. It also offers them something rare in today's America: an archetypal, ritualized coming-of-age experience.

Preparing to set out, the sisters stood with coats, bags, books, and pamphlets in hand. Together they recited the mission statement taped to their door: "We build the Kingdom by ensuring conversion through the balanced effort, by fearlessly testifying of the truths revealed through *The Book of Mormon,* and by bringing others to Christ through the understanding of His Atonement and by establishing the central role of the Savior in our lives." I bowed my head with theirs while they prayed for protection as we prepared to charge Boston's busy streets.

Since most missionaries are not permitted to operate a car—even for proselytizing purposes—public transportation plays an essential role in their mission. I followed the two Spanish-speaking sisters to the bus station. Along the way, they spoke longingly of their founding prophet, Joseph Smith. His martyred memory seemed to inspire the very spring in their step. Smith was about their age, they pointed out, when he "fearlessly" persisted in his quest to know which of the many Christian churches of his time was "right." Hearing the sisters herald their founder's legacy as "*the* one" God has personally restored and legitimated, I was reminded of Gene Begay, who regarded the spectrum of spiritual practice as merely complementary ways of communing with the one Creator. "But it wasn't that simple in the minds of the missionaries," Gene had acknowledged, adding that his people were "forced to choose" between their ways and the ways of Christian missionaries. As the sisters and I boarded the bus, I thought, too, of their prophet and the religious chauvinism that killed him when the people of nineteenth-century Illinois decided their town was not big enough for his truth.

Steadying myself as the bus continued along its route, I asked my companions how many people they approach in the course of an average day. "About forty, give or take a few," Sister Williams calculated, as she approached a morning commuter.

"Hi, how are you today?" she asked an unassuming woman in Spanish.

The two talked for some time, not about God or Mormonism, but about where this woman resided, what she did for a living, how many children she had, and most important—her name. Whenever the sisters addressed a potential *investigator* (the Mormon term for an individual who expresses interest in knowing more about their faith), it was invariably by their first name, often repeated. Sister Williams masterfully worked the bus, stretching people's comfort zones without tearing them. If it was aloofness and sophistication her audience responded to, she sat a little farther away and offered words more sparingly; if it was a friend they sought, she scooted in, affirming them with her presence and genuine warmth, calling them again and again by name. If it was breezy conversation they liked, she was as lighthearted as a twenty-one-year-old should be. All of this left a surprising number of people wanting more.

"Maria, have you ever heard of *The Book of Mormon?*" Sister Williams asked, delivering her punch line as we neared our stop. Maria had not. "Maria, have you seen our commercials on TV?" She didn't think so, but couldn't say for certain. And within a hundred yards of our destination: "Maria, would you be interested in giving me your phone number so I can call you and find a time for us to come to your home and talk to you further?" After being declined access, Sister Williams politely thanked her listener—by name—suggesting that if she were ever to change her mind, she need only call the church's toll-free number.

As we made our way to the front of the bus, I took note of the people the sisters had targeted among the crowded seats, many of their faces slack with lonely sadness, others hardened by it. In these times, the missionaries offer a rare commodity, and many of their listeners are apparently grateful for the attention, especially that of a vibrant young woman ardent to share and willing to listen. The fact that it happened to be the gospel she was imparting seemed of little consequence to many who lent their ear. "The gospel isn't hard; life is," I overheard Sister Williams say. "The gospel makes it worth living." Others she confronted were clearly uninterested, deflecting her exuberance with apathetic stares. A few people looked visibly disturbed, even disgusted by the young women's advances. I witnessed one man deride the sisters' "stupidity" in relinquishing themselves to "a glorified tax-exempt exploit." But the two never lost their composure.

One of Sister Williams's roommates, Sister Savatdy—a Cambodian immigrant of tiny build and monumental energy—had defined her prose-lytizing practice metaphorically: "If you see a building on fire, you have the instinct to rush over and help people. That's what we're doing with this daily outreach." In that moment, I got the sense that her unspoken impression of me was that of one more person hanging precariously from a blazing window.

I asked the overachieving Sister Williams what gave her such unwavering certainty. "The Holy Spirit working through me, stirring in me," she said. I asked her what that very personal "stirring" felt like. "Sometimes it comes in a thought—a thought that you know is not yours—which can arrive just in time for someone who needs to hear it, even though you weren't consciously aware that they needed to hear it. The Holy Spirit works differently every time," she added. "If you're obedient, He will be your constant companion. The more you experience His presence, the easier it is to detect."

Two bus rides and a short walk later, we arrived at the sisters' first house call, with Anna, a thirty-something mother of three who operates a day care center out of her home. Anna, wearing industrial plastic gloves and a medical mask over her nose and mouth, was scrubbing away at the outside stairway when we poked our heads around the corner. Surprised to see the missionaries, she snapped off her gloves and pulled back her mask, realizing in that moment that she'd forgotten about the appointment. "Eeeh," she sighed guiltily at the familiar sight of the sisters, "I've been so busy, I haven't been able to do my homework." As a way of charting each investigator's progression toward baptism, it is customary for the missionaries to hand out study assignments from *The Book of Mormon*.

Having traveled nearly an hour to reach the appointment with Anna, the sisters managed to conceal their disappointment in her lack of progress, agreeing, with farewells in Spanish, to call her soon to reschedule. "People need a *lot* of encouragement," Sister Riley said, as we retraced our steps and boarded another bus to carry us to our next appointments. Both were also busts: one young woman had a splitting migraine, the other a father who didn't allow missionaries in his home.

The women shuffled appointments via a pay phone to accommodate the schedule gap, and we climbed aboard another bus. Sister Williams's eyes feasted on the lunchtime crowd, while Sister Riley slipped into a nearby seat, presumably to rest her feet. Of the two, Sister Riley was clearly more introverted, and had a much harder time peddling her faith to

strangers. Her gregarious partner, on the other hand, in a matter of minutes, unloaded three pamphlets, jotted down two phone numbers, and tra-
versed one heated rejection. Caught up in watching Sister Williams the
way one does a talented street performer, I suddenly realized Sister Riley
had disappeared. I scanned the bus—our roving chapel—my eyes landing
in its back pew. Sister Riley sat alone, her arms loosely folded, her body
moving with the rhythm of the bus's sway, her eyes grazing the floor. I
knew in that instant she believed she was failing.

Taking the empty seat next to hers, I said something about how challenging it would be for me to talk to countless, often caustic strangers day
after day in a city and language not my own. At first she was silent, but
then, softly, she responded, "It's something I'm working through. I don't
always like to talk. Sometimes I want to be alone, be quiet, process things.
But I can't. We have to keep moving, keep talking."

Though out of her element, Sister Riley would not give up. Her mission
had become an outpost she refused to abandon, a height from which she
observed the changing topography of herself. "The highs and lows of being
a missionary are very pronounced," she acknowledged. "But this is the best
school for life. I've learned what kind of person I want to be, I've learned to
care for something besides myself." I found myself admiring her gutsy act of
simply staying, when it would be so easy to slip away, back to Utah and
quiet suburban bedrooms where doors can be shut and things can be
processed. And yet, it seemed almost unfair that this girl should be pushed
by her church and family to perform in a manner so obviously inorganic to
her nature, to measure her service to God by standards she could not meet.

The mouth of the bus hissed as it opened and spit us out onto concrete,
pointed in the direction of our next appointment. Yaremi, a woman of
about twenty from the Dominican Republic, answered the door to her
parents' tiny duplex, inviting us in. Bracing her arching back with one
hand, she lowered herself onto the couch, more attentive to the soap opera
blaring from the television than to the sisters. Visibly unsettled, the sisters
politely asked if "it" could be turned off, avoiding not only the images
coming from the box but the very word used to describe it. For missionaries, television, newspapers, magazines, non-Mormon books, music (except
for hymns), personal phone calls, alcohol, and even caffeine are banned by
the church.

Peace was gained with the push of a button, and the sisters asked
Yaremi about her pregnancy and health, her job and family, then eased

into the status of her homework. Yaremi was in the process of receiving
the six foundational Mormon teachings that must be committed to memory before baptism can be performed, instruction covering doctrinal
beliefs, daily practices, ethics, financial responsibility to the church, the history of Mormonism, and the life story of Joseph Smith. Under our
scrutiny, Yaremi blushed at the sisters' request for a full progress report. "I
kind of forgot to do the reading," she said in Spanish. The sisters looked
concerned.

Yaremi did want to be baptized into the Mormon Church, she assured
them, just as her mother had been. To jump-start her new week, the sisters
suggested "a particularly inspiring passage" from *The Book of Mormon* and
reminded her of the importance of church attendance—another prerequi-
site of baptism. "I don't have a skirt that fits," Yaremi said sheepishly.
Promising to do what they could to find her some maternity wear, the sisters then asked Yaremi to lead us in a closing prayer.

On each of the days I spent with the missionaries, I counted an average
of eighteen group prayers. They were like conference calls to God, halting
the process of living in order to check in with the Creator. We prayed during morning Scripture study, upon leaving the apartment, upon arriving at
another's home, before any morsel of food or drink passed our lips, before
we moved from one place to the next, and sometimes—quickies—while
standing on subway platforms or at bus stops. We even prayed before I put
the car in gear, when chauffeuring the missionaries a time or two to particularly remote appointments, since, like the Amish, they are permitted, with
good reason, to ride as a *passenger* in a volunteer's car.

Yaremi hung her head, saying she was too shy to pray out loud. Sister
Williams encouraged her with the "easy way to pray" formula they had
taught her during one of their previous visits: "In God's name state what
you are thankful for and then what you need, in the name of Jesus. Amen."
Yaremi met her with more lip-locked head shaking, so Sister Williams
picked up the slack.

I tried to close my eyes as I listened to Sister Williams's spoken prayer,
but they sneaked open to watch. Barely versed in Spanish, I was only able
to understand a little of what was said, and my eyes roamed from the three
bowed heads to the adjoining dining room. There, they rested on a pair of
porcelain Buddhas displayed on a mirrored shelf. Miniature people clung to
each of the protruding Buddha bellies, like puppies clamoring for mother's
milk. I wondered if Yaremi's mother had purchased them simply as deco-

ration for her dining room, or if they held spiritual significance for her. Glancing back to the missionaries and Yaremi, whose eyes were still shut tight in prayer, I again thought about the fundamental difference between "exclusive" religions like Mormonism that claim sole authority over divine revelation, and those—like Buddhism and Native American traditions—that tend to approach ultimate truth more inclusively. Staring at the porcelain figures, I recalled the Buddhist parable about blind people touching different parts of an elephant. The moral of the short story is that the more perspectives one is capable of assimilating, the more accurate—and complete—one's vision of reality becomes.

"Amen," said Sister Williams, snapping my attention back to the mission at hand—one last pep talk to make certain Yaremi knew they "loved and supported" her. Back on the pavement, Sister Williams unfolded her trusty map. "Leading someone to baptism is pure joy," she said, satisfied. Pulling an apple from her bag—a substitute for lunch—she walked, talked, navigated, and chewed.

At the end of the first heavily scheduled day, we boarded a bus heading in the direction of the missionaries' apartment, bringing that day's transportation totals to nine bus rides, six subway stops, and innumerable invigorating walks. The engine droned, the city's fumes of productivity wafted through the open windows, and the street lamps marked our mileage, further tranquilizing my tired mind and body. I registered only snippets of the sisters' dialogues as they attempted to connect with other passengers, their spiel seeping deeper into my subconscious. Sitting across from me was a Hispanic woman of about fifty. I detected a heaviness hanging over her, and impulsively I reached for one of the sisters' pamphlets to hand to her, wondering, in that second, if it might ease her aches and pains the way it seemed to for some people. This impulse surprised me, as my second thought was how presumptuous it suddenly felt to assume that what speaks to one soul will speak equally to another. When I verbalized this perspective to Sister Williams, she disagreed that her tactics imposed anything on others. "We just share the gospel of salvation," she said, "and whoever's ready to hear it, hears it."

However, the people most willing to listen to the missionaries didn't seem as swayed by the theological details of their gospel as they did by the old-fashioned neighborly kindness. Many of the converts I met spoke of a previous lack—or loss—of a sense of community, an absence they felt the members of the Mormon Church had filled.

Later in the week, en route to one of the Spanish-speaking missionaries' afternoon appointments, we stopped by the home of Lourdes, a Puerto Rican woman in her mid-forties who'd been converted through the random knock upon her door. Now an active member, Lourdes sometimes volunteered her time to assist the missionaries when they visited people who were incapacitated and needed help with cooking and cleaning. Standing in her kitchen as she fried pork chops for her own family of four, I asked Lourdes why she had turned from Catholicism to the Mormon faith. "The Catholic Church was so cold," she said. "Nobody talked to each other, everybody kept to themselves. The Mormon Church is like a family," she added before pausing to stir her crock pot of beans. "Even though at first my husband was suspicious of Mormons, he went to the services and, like me, felt like he found his home."

The notion of finding a home in one's faith was something I'd heard—and would continue to hear—from people of every religious tradition. Having visited various local Mormon churches—called *wards*—to observe their three-hour, interactive services, I found it remarkable that, like an extended family, everyone indeed seemed to know everyone else's name and intimate goings-on. While this sort of intimacy is to be expected among smaller congregations like the Amish, the Mormons seem to be achieving this sense of connection despite their vaster numbers. "When I had knee surgery," Lourdes offered as an example of Mormon kinship, "sisters and members from the LDS Church came over to cook, clean, and help me with the kids—for *eight weeks* they came! That's why when I have the chance, I volunteer to go with the missionaries to help other people."

As a binding vow of baptism, in addition to community service each new member promises to tithe 10 percent of their monthly income to the Mormon Church. As a result, the organization is able to operate an array of programs that support an internal welfare system, build new temples, provide scholarships to Mormon students, and—to ensure it all continues and grows—proselytize around the globe.

Eventually parting ways with the Spanish-speaking sisters, I tracked down their roommates so I could join them for one final house call. A woman named Marion, who had been successfully proselytized some four years earlier by the sisters' male missionary counterparts, had called to request a dinnertime visit. I was told these kinds of requests are not uncommon among active members in the church who miss the one-on-one attention they received during their conversion process. The sisters were happy to oblige, combining their two-person teams for the occasion.

Marion was waiting for us at the bus stop when we stepped off; she explained she'd been too excited about our visit to wait for us in her apartment. Escorting us through her neighborhood, Marion gravitated toward me, assuming that I, too, was a missionary. (Without so much as a nanosecond pause in her elated chatter, I was unable to correct her impression.) Although this wouldn't be my only incident of mistaken identity, it was the first time I *felt* what it was like to be a missionary in someone's eyes. Though these young women and men tend to be half the age of those they counsel, they are often revered as oracles of the Mormon faith, perhaps because they indeed seem to have an answer—or at least a scriptural reference—for everything.

Marion's dialogue propelled our walk, which ended in her postage-stamp kitchen where we sat elbow to elbow around her table, passing among us piping-hot mashed potatoes and gravy, fried chicken, green beans, and pineapple upside-down cake—a feast she'd "spent all day preparing in our honor." I interrupted Marion's stream of consciousness to ask her how she had come to join the Mormon Church. Without hesitation, she launched into the memory of her fortieth birthday, a day, she said, she had planned to be her last. With an overdose of depressants waiting on her nightstand, Marion traveled across town to visit her brother for—unbeknownst to him—a final farewell. On her fateful bus ride back, she was confronted by a pair of "elders" (male Mormon missionaries)—all of nineteen and twenty years old. Hoping to "get rid of them," Marion agreed to accept their free copy of *The Book of Mormon*, but when she reached home, she promptly tossed the little black book into the trash can. As she tipped a handful of pills into her mouth, "a loud voice" spoke to her, instructing her to retrieve the book she had thrown away. She spit out the pills, fished out the book, and read without stopping until every word was absorbed.

Later the next day, the two elders appeared at her door uninvited, having tracked down her address through the phone book using the name she had given them. Keeping the smartly dressed boys at arm's length, Marion insisted they were wasting their time on a woman with a chronic case of multiple personality disorder—an affliction she had suffered from since childhood. Though admittedly her mood had been lifted momentarily by the book the elders had given her, she said she was incurably hopeless from a lifetime of struggle, depression, and blackouts. She was convinced that not even God—and especially not a few sweet boys from Utah—could save her. After listening to her story, one of the elders told her that he disagreed with her and her string of doctors' diagnoses. He was certain Marion was plagued with none other than an old-fashioned case of spirit possession, a condition he offered to exorcise.

Marion's refusal brought the elders back to her door day after day, until finally they came reinforced by a small cavalry of more young men in pressed white shirts and dark ties. As members of the all-male Mormon "restored" priesthood, the young men were each ordained with the authority to act "in the name of God."

Marion only remembers agreeing to allow the persistent priestly delegation inside, hoping to curb her neighbors' curious stares. She says she then blacked out for the hours that followed. The missionaries later relayed to Marion the details of their intervention with the spirit residing inside of her, a petulant masculine voice hurling violent threats at the young men. Marion said she woke up on her kitchen floor, in tears and exhausted, surrounded by the vaguely familiar, also exhausted faces of her six visitors.

That night Marion was baptized by a priest in the Mormon Church—a process he streamlined given her unusual circumstances. "Since then," Marion said, visibly relieved, "I've never had another episode and not one blackout. I'm not always happy," she qualified, "but I'm always at *peace*. Keeping Christ-centered brings me peace."

Marion lifted the bowl of mashed potatoes, offering us seconds even though our plates were still crowded with lukewarm firsts. The sisters' forks had been mostly suspended in midbite during Marion's story. But Marion hadn't put so much as a morsel of food on her own plate. I tried to offer her some of her own green bean casserole. "Having you all in my home is such a blessing," she said, refusing. "Your presence is my food."

I looked around the table at the sisters, who very apparently hadn't been briefed about the details surrounding Marion's conversion. Most of these girls had grown up in tranquil towns and protective families, buffered by white middle-class Americans whose language and life experience mirrored their own. I wasn't sure, in the long run, who was getting more out of this program, this graduate course in salvation: people like Marion, whose life had evidently been saved by a tag team of missionaries, or the young believers themselves. Before long, the young women would return to their routine lives, but not without the permanent imprint of having been with, and cared for, people vastly different from themselves.

Just before ten o'clock, we stepped into the darkness outside Marion's front door, thanked her for her hospitality, and walked back, mostly in silence, to the bus stop. Once on board, I slumped into a seat, taxed by the week and by Marion's finale, marveling at the ever-ready Energizer sisters as they tirelessly beat their drum for the last minutes left on the clock.

With their catchphrases ricocheting off all corners of the bus, I was surprised to look up and find Sister Savatdy sitting alone across from me, uncharacteristically sedate. I asked her if she was okay. She ambled around random thoughts until settling on what preoccupied her: she had just completed her last day as a missionary. Sister Savatdy had voluntarily served her church for five hundred and forty-seven days. Tonight, instead of preparing for the next day's appointments, she would return to the communal apartment and begin packing for the flight that would take her back to California, to her family, friends, and a paying office job.

Friendly but guarded, Sister Savatdy avoided showing any emotion about her imminent departure, even to her housemates, some of whom overheard our conversation and stopped to offer their attention and girlish affection. In a detached way, Sister Savatdy admitted uneasiness about having once again to contend with the impulses and distractions that had, for the last year and a half, been deflected by her schedule, her virtual sorority for God, and their mission. In a matter of hours, Sompong Savatdy would have a lot more in common with all the people, like me, whose doors are the ones that get knocked upon.

Chapter Six

n the mid-1800s, a man named Phineas P. Quimby experienced a chronic
case of tuberculosis that compelled him to investigate alternatives to the conventional medicine of his time. Abandoning his work as a clockmaker, he
began experimenting with a variety of mind-over-matter techniques, such as
hypnotism and magnetism. Quimby thus reportedly healed himself of his condition, attracting a roster of patients and pupils. A few of these disciples went on
to develop and propagate their own systems of healing, inspired—at least ini-
tially—by Quimby's mind-body research.

Mary Morse Baker, now known as Mrs. Mary Baker Eddy, was one such
protégée. Under Quimby's guidance, Mrs. Eddy attempted to arrest her own
array of illnesses. Attributing at least temporary abatement of her symptoms to
Quimby's techniques, she more fully committed herself to examining and
understanding his noninvasive, drug-free approach to health care.

Many years after her last visit with Quimby, Mrs. Eddy slipped on a patch
of ice, incurring a severe injury that would become the catalyst for a life-altering
change. Bedridden, Mrs. Eddy sought comfort in her Bible, a source upon
which Quimby's secular approach to healing did not rely. Opening to a passage
that detailed a miracle Jesus performed by calling upon the powers of his
omnipresent Father, Mrs. Eddy was suddenly struck by the conclusion that

such healing was also within her grasp as a child of God. She claims she was instantly—and permanently—healed by the certainty of her realization.

Mrs. *Eddy grew hopeful that others could be taught how to access God's will in order to restore health and harmony. Distancing herself from Quimby's irreligious legacy in developing her own methodology, Mrs. Eddy dedicated nearly every waking moment to compiling* Science and Health with Key to the Scriptures—*a seven-hundred-page Christianity-based metaphysical manual peppered with her reinterpretations of biblical references.*

Though Mrs. Eddy anticipated that the text would be embraced by Christians everywhere, she and her findings were instead marginalized by the Christian establishment. Consequently, Mrs. Eddy became one of the first American women to found her own church. She also founded a metaphysical college and a publishing society—a press that would turn out the Nobel Prize–winning newspaper the Christian Science Monitor. *With a growing grassroots following, Mrs. Eddy documented her healing successes and those of her students, striving to prove their viability as a measurable and repeatable science, and a practical way of life.*

Shortly after the 1879 genesis of Eddy's First Church of Christ, Scientist, one of her former students, Emma Curtis Hopkins, with the help of others committed to the science of prayer, gave birth to the movement popularly known as "New Thought." The most formidable New Thought institutions endure today as the Church of Religious Science, Divine Science, and the largest— Unity Church.

While Christian Science and the multiple schools of New Thought are independent of one another, they share the basic foundational belief that prayer—or "divinely realigned thought"—can positively alter the course of any condition, in an individual or in society. While New Thoughters tend to employ prayer as a complement to conventional or alternative medicine, Christian Science explicitly advocates prayer "treatment" as a substitute for both.

It is impossible to calculate how many people are affiliated with what has collectively been called "Practical Christianity." As the founder of the largest of these churches, Mrs. Eddy early on prohibited the tallying of membership. And beyond her fellowship are thousands of others, some of whom practice the principles of scientific prayer without formal affiliation to any church.

Praying with Practical Christians

It took me some time to follow Practical Christian reasoning, to understand this faith as something more than an eccentric optimists' club. Breezing by the Christian Science Reading Rooms prominently centered on main streets all across America, one can't help but look curiously at the people who call themselves "Scientists" but choose prayer over modern science whether treating a weak heart, a broken bone, a toothache, or acute depression. How many times have we all tried to wish away—or flatly deny—the ailments, hardships, and fears of everyday existence, only to have them catch up with us later? But those who live—and die—by this faith are convinced that it is the *disbeliever* who is imprudently delusional, having accepted pain and suffering as a fait accompli. These devout believers consider crises—a tornado watch, a failing marriage, a life-threatening illness, defeat, hunger—not as concrete reality, but as false and tattered *impressions* of reality. They prescribe repair work: a subtle and spiritual shift in thought from which will come tangible improvement.

Eager for an up-close look at their seminal practice of prayer, I attended a three-day "Pioneers of the Spiritual Millennium" conference, an annual gathering of Christian Science teenagers who travel from all ends of the earth to the world headquarters of their "Mother Church." Navigating the complex of high-rises and castlelike edifices covering an entire city block of prime real estate in downtown Boston, I finally found my way to the hulking doors of the domed and turreted sanctum of "science and health."

Taking a balcony seat in the chapel, with its three-thousand-person capacity, I was engulfed by youthful enthusiasm as the inaugural speaker, the consummate pollster of human behavior, George Gallup, Jr., took the podium. In his brief address, Mr. Gallup predicted that, while the central event of the twentieth century had been the exploration of outer space, we could expect the twenty-first century to be dedicated to the exploration of *inner space*. To Gallup's pioneering audience, *inner space* appeared to be a territory of unlimited potential—an interior moonscape that indeed promised to reveal much about life on this planet. Hoping to further their founder's leap into the depths of faith, these teens were studying to be the masters of their own destiny through prayerful conviction.

Belief in the power of prayer is not unique to Practical Christians: in a poll conducted by the Gallup Organization for *Life* magazine, 90 percent of Americans said they pray on a regular basis.[1] But Christian Scientists envision dramatic healing and change through a twist on the traditional notion of heavenly dialogue: not by *asking* God to heal illness, but by believing that illness does not exist. This bold denial of the validity and impact of the material world is the metaphysical crux of this revivalist faith. As the sixteen-year-old "pioneer" sitting next to me elaborated, "I don't ask God for help or mercy. I live my life knowing God has given us *all* free access to health, peace, and happiness, and He *wants* these things for us. It is our challenge to trust in this truth, a reality as invisible—and real—as the oxygen we breathe. 'When fear disappears,'" she quoted, well schooled in her founder's writings, "'the foundation of disease is gone.'"[2]

I continued my conversation with the girl and one of her friends over a pizza in a nearby shopping mall. The two summed up their spiritual practice as a way of "proactively directing" their lives in a time when most people their age "feel at the mercy of everything and everyone around them." Mary Baker Eddy had insisted that, contrary to conventional assumption, our thoughts are not simply innocuous meanderings contained within the privacy of our heads. Rather, our second-to-second opinions, expectations, and ideas—however unconscious—have their own kind of mass, like bits of sediment, that accumulates and clogs. A reminder over the school PA that it's once again flu season, or the publication of a statistic that girls are less adept than boys in science, are the kinds of toxic messages these budding believers attempt to filter from their ears and minds. "As a spiritual being, you have to be careful what kind of information you absorb," declared one of the girls.

In a cultural environment that defines us by what we wear and drive, by where we work, eat, live, and vacation, by the products we use, and by the color of our skin, these Practical Christians attempt to protect the boundaries of identity with the power of deliberate and devotional thought. At least this is how the Practical Christian philosophy was further explained to me by the chairman of the Christian Science Board of Directors, Virginia Harris.

As heir to Mrs. Eddy's throne, Mrs. Harris is the official spokesperson for the Christian Science faith, and currently the only female head of a major religious sect. I had ascended twenty-five floors to meet with Mrs. Harris in her office situated next to the Mother Church and overlooking South Boston's Dorchester Bay. Glancing out the window over her shoulder as she described her beliefs and practices—a kind of spiritualized revision of Nietzsche's *Übermensch*—I was taken back to the age of ten, when I was obsessed with a superheroine known as Wonder Woman.

For a number of years, Wonder Woman and I spent a portion of every afternoon together. I identified, as did many of my peers, with her feminist liberation camouflaged in a vibrantly patriotic strapless bathing suit. Along with the help of Charlie's Angels and the Bionic Woman, she captured the hearts and minds of a nation of girls who finally had their own larger-than-life ensemble to emulate and admire.

In the flush of my Wonder Woman phase, I spent the weekend at my grandparents' house nestled in the foothills of New Mexico's Sandia Mountains. It was an arid summer day. My grandmother granted permission for outdoor romping, so long as I stayed safely away from the street. Recruiting a neighbor girl, a natural stand-in for the bionic Lindsay Wagner, I of course cast myself as my favorite heroine. Sneaking tinfoil and my grandmother's fancy gold belt outside, I molded myself a pair of bullet-stopping bracelets and cinched up the leotard I had taken to wearing in the event that my special powers were unexpectedly called upon.

Transformed, my cohort and I reconvened behind my grandparents' two-and-a-half-story home. We briefed each other: a plot to end the world was being hatched by a group of villains atop my grandparents' roof. Mission one: scale the wall. This assignment wasn't all that challenging, considering that my grandfather had built a ladder for his own roof access. We stealthily made our way upward. The villains fired, but I deflected their bullets with swift wrist action. Bionic Woman decided that the scoundrels had suddenly parachuted over the edge, leaving us with the one option of jumping after them.

Without hesitation we soared off the rooftop, expecting the slow-motion landing the Wonder and Bionic Women always demonstrated on TV. Instead we hit the ground with a meaty thud. Miraculously, both of us bounced to our feet, unscathed.

Emboldened, we reenacted the scene three more times before my grandmother happened to glance out the window as our legs, torsos, and heads flew past, in that order. From my landing spot I could hear her screaming for my grandfather, who grabbed me by my golden belt and asked if he could speak to me—*"immediately."* He wondered whether my grandmother needed new spectacles, or if it had indeed been us she had seen falling from the sky. His hard intake of breath in response to my admission made me grasp just how dangerous and stupid he believed my superhuman maneuvers to be.

The truth was, though, it hadn't occurred to me that I could be hurt. I was *Wonder* Woman, for god's sake. And my partner was *bionic*. We were invincible and going into syndication. I knew my grandfather, as a mere mortal, could neither fully understand nor accept such things.

Of course, now that I'm older and "know better," I'm as surprised as anyone that I didn't spend the better half of my childhood in a body cast. But at the time I *wholeheartedly* trusted that my powers superseded the laws of the physical world.

I looked into the eyes of the leader of the Christian Science Church as she suggested that there was nothing fantastic about her belief in the supernatural. For her, its foundation rests on God's power as much as it does on her own. But what my adolescent free falls and Mrs. Harris's adult leaps have in common is an unquestioning, childlike faith in the perfect outcome of every moment. This is the Practical Christian tenet heralded by Jesus when he said to his fellow believers, "I tell you the truth, unless you change and become like little children, you will never enter the Kingdom of heaven."[3]

Christian Science asserts that as we become adults and are more reluctant to believe unhesitatingly in anything—in particular our intrinsic perfection and wholeness—we open the door to suffering. Indoctrinated with the mind-set of disasters, hazards, handicaps, statistics, war, and depravity, we each succumb to a spiritually contaminating acceptance of how inadequate, limited, and doomed we "are." Through a slow process of assimilation, this psychological fatalism becomes a self-fulfilling prophecy that reflects a sinful world in the midst of disintegration.

Hoping for more solid footing on this "higher" ground of Practical Christian thinking, I sought out a second opinion in Rev. Eric Butterworth, a leading proponent of New Thought—a close, or distant, relative to Christian Science, depending on whom you talk to. As a veteran Unity minister now in his seventies, Rev. Butterworth rejects what he calls "institutionalism and staid religious concepts." He considers himself "Emersonian," after Ralph Waldo Emerson, whose work as a nineteenth-century minister and philosopher has had a lasting influence on the New Thought movement.

"Emerson had a saying," relayed Rev. Butterworth from his spacious Greenwich, Connecticut, home, "'that when you break with the God of tradition and destroy the God of the intellect, God will fire you with His presence.' It sounds like an agnostic thought, but it isn't. When we get out of the institutional framework we can really get at the root of our spiritual nature."

Rev. Butterworth spoke of the religious mainstream from experience, having begun his career as an altar boy in the Episcopal Church. "I accepted this role without question," he recalled. "I dutifully went to altar-boy school, learned about the sacraments and so forth." One day after a service, young Butterworth pulled back the pleated curtain covering the altar and, much to his surprise, beheld an unkempt storage area of old furniture, chipped vases, dusty books, and odd pieces of lumber—"an accumulation of junk." The sight was so inconsistent with his youthful understanding of the altar's import that it caused him to examine more closely his entire religious setting. "As an altar boy you spend a lot of time just sitting quietly, and I would spend that time trying to figure out what this religion thing was all about," he said. "That altar experience became for me what [the apostle] Paul called 'the thorn in my side'—my remembrance of emptiness, which has helped me greatly in the long run."

In his lifelong search for God's fullness, Rev. Butterworth has come to the conclusion that "what it's really about" is divinity *in motion*. "God is a force that can't be pinned down no matter what you do," he exclaimed. "If you have to *find* God, you're lost before you start, because God isn't to be found. God is to be accepted, to be experienced, to be accessed. That's the purpose of deep prayer, to be still enough to attune ourselves to what already exists." Rev. Butterworth illustrated his idea of God as a force like gravity: "I drop a ball, it bounces—gravity did its work. You can't tax or strain an infinite process like gravity, just as you can't tax or strain God—infinite mind, love, and healing." I found Rev. Butterworth's choice of metaphor ironic, given that I was already equating my childhood experiments in gravity with his beliefs and practices.

To learn to attune oneself to the divine principles that Rev. Butterworth says are omnipresent, one must study Christianity's founding teacher. "Jesus was the Christ," he said, "because he was conscious of the divine depth in himself, and because he helped others discover the depths in themselves— 'He that believeth in me, the works that I do shall he do also, and even greater than these,' proclaimed Jesus. But nearly everyone missed it because they were too busy worshiping him. The teacher points to the truth, and the student worships the pointer—that's the way it's always been." To Rev. Butterworth, the recorded miracles of Jesus were examples that God hoped *each and every one* of his human offspring would awaken to, dispelling their own—and each other's—blindness, disease, sin, callousness, and even death. It's a profound recasting of traditional Christianity. *Evil is not intrinsic in us or in the world but exists only in our misaligned thought.*

Rev. Butterworth's radical statements did not end there. "Ultimately the focus of all religious institutions should be to put themselves out of business," he said. "I've been criticized by some of my peers in the Unity movement for saying that," he added. "But I think the dynamic should be like a college; college is devoted to one thing: training people to get along *without* the teacher and the institution, to thrive in an independent career.

"Our need is not to find *the* religion," he continued, "it is to find our self. And I can find myself in poetry, in the lyrical lines of Walt Whitman; I can find myself in Shakespeare; I can find myself in nature, studying the growing things around me; I can find myself in the knowledge of the physical body and its exciting possibilities of healing. Or I can go through all those experiences and learn more about myself by virtue of the fact that I've indulged in some intellectual pursuits. But no one religion has a monopoly on truth. The only kind of religion that offers hope for *all* persons is a religion of oneness—oneness with all life, all substance, all intelligence, all love, all people."

It is with the single focus of oneness—or unity—that Rev. Butterworth prays for change. "There are no such things as miracles," he was quick to clarify, "for when we truly understand the process of this kind of prayer, we know that the 'miraculous' result is as normal and natural as the growth of a flower."

What's considered "normal and natural" in the realm of scientific prayer can vary. Some results are said to be strictly internal, apparent only to the individual experiencing them. Others would qualify *by most standards* as bona fide miracles, like the sudden repair of a broken bone. Then there are the accounts that verge on the comic. One Christian Scientist shared with me an instance of healing performed by her Christian Science mentor, who came home one day to find that her dog had died. Upon discovering her beloved pet's lifeless body, the woman took down his leash and insisted, as Jesus had to Lazarus, that the dog rise and walk. When the dog didn't comply, the woman stayed true to her faith: She denied the "illusion of death" and took her dog for a walk. Or more accurately, a drag. On the second loop around the block, I was told, the pooch began to cough, his lungs suddenly filling with air, his tail resuming its contented churn, and he subsequently continued to walk—of his own accord—for another few years, giving everyone time for proper good-byes.

Virginia Harris had detailed a less bizarre, but no less startling, example of resurrection in recounting her own near-death experience. Broadsided at high speed, she was severely injured and trapped in her mangled car for nearly an hour, struggling to stay conscious while paramedics worked to wrest her from the wreckage. "I was very afraid, but I knew I couldn't let that fear take over," she remembered. "Going in and out of consciousness, I knew that my survival was between me and God. I knew that if I could stay conscious, I could pray, and if I was praying, I knew I was alive. So I tried to keep my mind focused on God's power being everywhere and being supreme, and knowing there were other cars involved, I expanded my knowingness of this truth to include them."

Mrs. Harris was rushed by ambulance to the emergency room, where the doctors' unpromising prognoses were delivered to her husband. Set to be wheeled in for emergency surgery, Mrs. Harris, half delirious, flashed to times in her life when she had felt the protection of God's love and presence all around her. Much to the shock of the medical staff, Mrs. Harris— with her husband's support—declined surgery, opting instead for the incision-free, drug-free treatment of prayer. Reluctantly, they released and delivered her to her home by ambulance, where she lay in bed, fighting to stay alive, at times, she admits, questioning her decision, one that I agreed didn't sound particularly *practical*. "There was a time during those few days when I did think I was dying," she acknowledged. "There were moments of pain, of fear and doubt, when the mental and physical pull to give in to death was strong. I wondered if I had enough spiritual muscle to pull it off. I wondered if I was being stupid. My three sons would come in and stroke my face and crawl into bed with me, and the tears would just roll down because I didn't want to die; I wanted to be making the best decision to ensure that. But through it all, I felt I was being cared for and I *expected* healing." After three days, Mrs. Harris experienced dramatic improvement, and after two weeks, she says, it was as if the accident had never happened.

I stared at Mrs. Harris's delicate hands balancing a bone china cup and saucer, her pinky slightly raised. I glanced around at her neoclassical furniture, fine artwork, coordinated fabric walls, and back to her tailored skirt suit and crossed legs shimmering in silky hose—all in the same soothing color scheme. Something about Mrs. Harris—who looked more likely to be lunching at a country club than defying the pull of death—felt incongruous. I was perplexed.

Although I had come across a number of studies conducted over the last decade by medical institutions, like Duke University, validating prayer as an effective complement to some of their patients' conventional medical treatments, no double-blind tests have conclusively proved the effectiveness of prayer as an all-out *substitute* for medicine. With archives of corroborated healing testimonies documented by Christian Scientists, Virginia Harris believes it's only a matter of time before their personal experiences will be scientifically verified.

Until then, Practical Christians must rely on themselves—and others—for validation. In anticipation of her students' need for support and assistance, particularly in traumatic situations, Mrs. Eddy established a protocol to accredit for-hire pray-ers. Mrs. Harris had spoken of one such person who she believed was instrumental to her own recovery.

I of course was eager to make an appointment with one of these "prayer practitioners," hoping for more insight into the practice, and perhaps to benefit from its professed powers. Prayer practitioners will tackle just about anything a person might bring to them—from the absurd to the dire. Since at the time I didn't have any physical ailments, I decided to hand my practitioner the challenge of expunging my one long-held nasty habit: nail biting. I was told such things could be cured using Mrs. Eddy's power of prayer, even in one appointment.

Now, there are garden-variety run-of-the-mill nail-biters, and then there are the Olympic hopefuls; during the more stressful times in my life, I have trained with the gusto of a gold medal contender. Born to a long maternal line of high-strung women, with no shortage of hair twirlers, smokers, and drinkers in the bunch, I chose biting as my trade. Over time, I came to feel almost duty bound to carry forward generations of tradition. To overcome my handicap would be to sever my ties to the idiosyncrasies of my clan, like a refusal to participate in a secret society's handshake.

Stuffing all this self-analysis into a nutshell, I handed it to my practitioner, who sat across from me in a regal gold-leaf chair. "It's rather easy to see the underlying thought below a broken arm, or an illness, or a behavioral addiction," she finally said in response to my stated desire to stop gnawing at myself. "The hard part," she added as the underpinning of her prayer technique, "is the clarity of *unseeing* it." Asking me no further questions, she explained that she prefers "*not* to know the ins and outs of a patient's perceptions or condition." A Practical Christian refuses to indulge or personify a disease, no matter how visibly apparent. They will never, for example, describe a tumor as "your" cancer. Nor will they entertain details of an ailment or accident. It's considered insurance against turning the "illusion" of affliction into an actuality. Never so much as glancing at my hands, my practitioner asked me if I wanted her to do "a treatment."

One of the most remarkable claims of those who practice scientific prayer is that the method can be effective even on people who do not believe in it. Mary Baker Eddy documented volumes of accounts of having healed individuals stricken with various disabilities, although she claimed they did not know the first thing about Christian Science or its unique approach to prayer. "As long as the *practitioner's* thought stays on perfection," confirmed my practitioner, "the error can be corrected, even if the person is in disbelief." Having nothing to lose by accepting this mental medicine, I went ahead with her offer for treatment. I was hopeful of nothing short of the miraculous need for a weekly manicure.

My practitioner chose to perform the treatment *after* I'd left her office, which I'm told is not uncommon. As I made my way home, I imagined her focusing on my innate wholeness and harmony as a child of God, changing with her own thought my attachment to my habit. Or maybe her thoughts were riveted on my being *in* my family while not *of* it. This was all speculation, of course, as the details of my "self-tailored" treatment were never divulged.

———

Curious about the rigidity of her practice, I had asked Mrs. Harris how her fellow church members would have reacted had she chosen to let the doctors wheel her into surgery that day of her car accident. She assured me that while Christian Science does not integrate conventional medicine or "alternative therapies" into its prayer, it also does not wholly disregard their potential effectiveness. "We've just found that it's more conducive to have your faith going one direction or the other," she explained. "Modern medicine can be highly effective," she conceded, "when supplemented with both the doctor and the patient's conviction that it *will* be." Mrs. Harris went on to say that if at any time in the process of prayer treatment a Christian Scientist feels there is something else they should be doing, as in seeking medical assistance—either for themselves or their child—they are encouraged to do so. "Just as I have personally been handed cases from the medical realm that they were unable to help, which I have had success with, everyone must do what makes them most comfortable and seems most effective."

Addressing the obvious flaw in her declaration of free will, I pointed out that children whose parents make choices *for* them don't exactly have the ability to assess and assert what's most comfortable and effective when it comes to the complexities of health care. I could tell Mrs. Harris had been challenged on this point many times before, but instead of getting defensive, she got personal.

"When I was six," she recalled, "my brother was put under hospital care for a bronchial condition, and he died there in that sterile hospital room. I remember it vividly." The loss was especially intense for Mrs. Harris's mother, a dedicated Christian Scientist who had married a nonpracticing Lutheran. Mrs. Harris said her mother was haunted by thoughts that if she'd only had stronger faith and insisted on treating her son with prayer, he might still be living. And Mrs. Harris's father endured the guilt of having insisted on the medical route that failed them. Mrs. Harris attested that Christian Science parents have experienced, firsthand, the effectiveness of prayer—a curative method she successfully employed with her own now-adult sons. "No one has a hundred percent success rate," she argued, citing the statistic that fifty-two thousand children die every year under professional medical care. "Every Christian Science practitioner and every pediatrician does their very best to, within their discipline and care system, cure and save lives."

A few days after my appointment with my own practitioner, I received a bill for fifty dollars, intimating that the intangible antidote had been administered. Now, some months later, I am still attached to my habit. On certain days when I'm feeling particularly unmiraculous, I think to myself: I should just accept my shortcomings and move on; who wants to be *perfect* anyway? Hearing the word *perfection* routinely batted around Christian Science and New Thought circles had started to get to me. I called Rev. Butterworth to ask him to elaborate on exactly how this concept informs his practice, sharing with him my distaste for what struck me as an unhealthy obsession with flawlessness.

"What's wrong with a little heartache and disappointment, some throbbing melancholy, even a bout of illness, imperfection, or injury?" I asked.

As Rev. Butterworth addressed my question, he explained that I had wrongly taken his faith's repetitive talk of perfection at face value. While there are those who literally translate biblical passages like "Be ye therefore perfect, even as your Father which is in heaven is perfect,"[4] Rev. Butterworth interprets it thus: "There's an absolute sense and a relative sense of perfection. Absolute means achieving a fulfillment of the seed—a seed grows, unfolds, and becomes a perfect blossom. There's no room for anything less than perfection in nature; the plant has no other alternative but to be perfect. But man has the role of consciousness to contend with." Unlike the seed, man must be mindful not to let his own thoughts stop his natural progression. "It's not easy to alter, to transform, but it can be done," declared Rev. Butterworth. "That's what our study of truth is all about: as one changes the general attitudes and expectations one's grown accustomed to, a force of healing and metamorphosis is released."

However, he cautioned, the outcome of change might not resemble what we hope it will, for while he considered his practice a science, he did not expect it to be predictable. "We cannot control or force outcome," he said, "but rather identify completely with wholeness, awareness, and transcendence," letting the higher wisdom of God take care of the rest. In other words, even if a treatment is not a success in the medical sense, Practical Christians do not necessarily consider it a failure. Lack of outward evidence does not preclude an inward healing: a form of enlightenment or transcendence to a higher level of morality, self-awareness, love, forgiveness, or peace.

During the time I spent with Virginia Harris, I found myself intrigued by the unique blend of faith and volition that seemed to equip her with unflappable focus, cheeriness, and optimism. In fact, nearly every one of the prayer-centered believers I met exuded alert good-naturedness, seemingly determined not to let the antagonisms of an average day sneak up and apprehend them. While some Christians prepare for the "end days" like squirrels for the first snow, Practical Christians project a more sanguine view. Though they too hope to help usher in the second coming of Christ, they do not envision it as an end to life as we know it. What is coming, they say, is already here. "Now," cried the apostle, "is the accepted time; behold, now is the day of salvation."[5]

It is the "nowness" of this way of life that I found particularly resonant, the conviction that there is no paradise to *wait* on and prepare for. Paradise—defined by these Practical Christians as inner and outer harmony—is attainable in every moment. As Mary Baker Eddy lamented: "If half the attention given to hygiene were given to the study of Christian Science and to the spiritualization of thought, this alone would usher in [Christ's] millennium."[6]

Crossing through the Christian Science courtyard after attending a Sunday service, I strolled alongside an expansive marble reflecting pond. It was a serene, meditative pool with a glassy surface, water silently spilling over its rounded edges in constant regeneration. I assumed it was intended to symbolize the divine flow I had heard invoked again and again in the presence of these believers. As I walked, my reflection followed me, as did the reflections of people walking beside me. We all appeared to be effortlessly gliding over the surface of the water, animating this faith's ideal that inside every man and woman rests a miracle waiting to unfold. "[B]ehold," said Jesus, "the kingdom of God is within you."[7]

Chapter Seven

n the cusp of the era now commonly referred to as "B.C.," Jesus of Nazareth lived and taught. He spread his spiritual message to his largely illiterate fellow townspeople the same way itinerant teachers, religious leaders, and philosophers before him had: through the spoken word. Addressing people one at a time or in throngs, the original preacher of Christianity delivered a message of God's unconditional love for humankind, God's omnipotence, and God's direct accessibility to all classes of people who are pure in heart, with an emphasis on the poor and disenfranchised. Eventually, in an effort to broaden his discourse, Jesus traveled to surrounding Mediterranean townships accompanied by disciples whom he would often dispatch to preach and heal as he himself did.

An avid convert and the church's first theologian, Saint Paul never laid eyes on Jesus before his crucifixion. Nevertheless, he took up the arduous and sometimes dangerous task of evangelizing the masses, one city center at a time, with the messages of Christ and the example of his life. "House churches" became the central meeting places for first-century converts, willing hosts providing a designated space for group worship and study, for the celebration of the sacraments, such as baptism and the Eucharist, and for the preaching of the gospel, occasionally orated by Saint Paul himself. Many of these home-owning patrons—both men and women—acted as local leaders of their grassroots congregations, nurturing a faith that as yet had no scripture.

As the early Christian flock expanded, some felt "called" to join Saint Paul's mission, becoming wandering "charismatics," or propagators of the new and evolving gospel. By the end of the first century, parts of what would become the Christian Bible were being recorded in written form, though the authors' identities have long been disputed. With a written liturgy, the teaching of Christianity became more formalized, lessening the margin of inaccuracy accounted to oral tradition.

Two millennia later, the written text of Christianity is now widely available, though the role of the preacher is no less exercised, as modern Christian leaders continue to convey a now-ancient philosophy the same way Christ did: by word of mouth. Perhaps the central ritual of Protestant Christianity, preaching is not exclusive to any one of its many branches, but instead has become a common link between billions of believers who now distinguish themselves with names such as Baptist, Lutheran, Episcopalian, or Pentecostal. Given their legacy of reformation, preachers from all Protestant denominations must every week confront the momentous challenge of continually interpreting, articulating, and rejuvenating a two-thousand-year-old message.

Spreading the Word with Preachers

Throughout my adolescence, my Grandpa Pete was my constant companion. Every Sunday morning at exactly eight o'clock, he would swing by in his banana-yellow MG, his knees hugging his ears as he drove, and whisk me away to our own secret sanctum. At the same corner table by the window, over chocolate milk and glazed twists, my grandpa would enchant me with improvised sermons on life and people, morality, priorities, honor, love, honesty, prudence, and character—all for his congregation of one. He was my own doughnut-loving Confucius, and his philosophical musings were the closest thing I ever had to religion. As Huston Smith once described the great Chinese philosopher: "[Confucius] presented himself to his students as their fellow traveler, committed to the task of becoming fully human but modest in how far he had gotten with that task."[1] Pete's humbling and ennobling testaments of his efforts to become—and help me become—more fully human have only appreciated with time.

We've all had teachers who, in their best moments, have provided a model that serves to inspire us, and Christians who feel called to preach their "good news" offer themselves to their brethren for this purpose. They not only oversee common rites of passage such as baptism, marriage, death, and burial, but also help fellow believers reckon their faith, thoughts, and actions within a complex, ever-shifting world. In turning to some of America's Protestant ministers—both well known and not—I hoped to observe the transmission of God's will and Jesus' example from pulpit to pew.

Rev. Peter Gomes was reared in a Southern Baptist church in Plymouth, Massachusetts, and is now the minister for the Anglican Memorial Church at Harvard University. The Memorial Church congregation consists largely of mild-mannered students, professors, and sundry Cambridge intellectuals who arrive punctually for the one-hour Sunday services presided over by their highly regarded preacher, who is also a bestselling author. Each week a gifted choir obscured behind an antique lattice begins the service with a selected collection of hymns. On the choir's final, elongated note, Rev. Gomes strides across the stage to take his place behind a cylindrical pulpit perched high above his flock.

The first time I saw him preach, Rev. Gomes tackled what he deemed "a common anxiety among Christians": the relationship between religion and money. "The moral of the text is inescapable," he declared from up high. "Jesus approves of those who give more than they think they can afford." Rev. Gomes reminded us of "the poor widow" of biblical times who tithed from what little she held in her possession—a gesture of far greater substance, he suggested, than more abundant sums given out of surplus. Personalizing his homily, he spoke of his own childhood memories of his parents—both working-class African-Americans, whose first debt addressed each month was their promissory note to God: 10 percent of their income, no matter what the personal hardships of the time. Rev. Gomes quoted Winston Churchill, who once said: "We make a living by what we save; but we make a life by what we give." Rev. Gomes declared that in examining how we give, we come to see life as increasingly worth living. "And that," he affirmed to his mostly privileged, mostly Caucasian listeners, "is what Jesus had in mind."

Agreeing to talk in private about his practice of preaching, Rev. Gomes escorted me to one of his church's many chambers, a room of rich, dark mahogany brightened only by large oil paintings of distinguished-looking men. Rev. Gomes is surrounded by the gaze of those who've come before him, and I asked him if he feels challenged by the task of delivering ancient messages to his college campus congregation.

"There is a general conceit," he began, "that suggests that somehow we are different people in different places in the world than when these religious truths were first articulated. My life's experience tells me that this is not so. People are still needy, they're still frightened, they're still venal and mean, and they still have moments of great joy and exaltation. I see no change at all in the human condition from some nomadic pre-Hebrew tribes in the wilderness to the most sophisticated of Western civilizations as we engage the twenty-first century."

Rev. Gomes went on to say that there has never been a point in history when the masses willingly embraced biblical concepts. It's always been left up to the "priestly consciousness" to continue trying, in every generation, to awaken a response. "The reason we keep doing it is not that we're successful at it," he said. "It is because we're *not* successful at it, and somebody has to keep waving that banner. And therefore it is even more important to do it now, in a time when we are even less susceptible to these appeals than were our grandparents, who lived, in many ways, in a less complicated world." But the particular character of his largely unaffiliated and transient audience makes Rev. Gomes's mission that much more appealing to him. "Religion is a foreign language to a lot of them, and therefore that makes it both demanding and fascinating to teach."

Gomes's teaching style appeals to the intellect, fitting in a church situated in what Bob Dylan once referred to as the "green pastures" of Harvard University. But I was curious to explore other congregational profiles, and decided to dedicate some weeks to service-hopping in the Bible Belt. As I was driving the perimeters of New Orleans one evening, the balmy air pulled me farther and farther west toward the setting sun until I soared into a nearby town. WELCOME TO HAHNVILLE read the sign posted on the highway.

Having stumbled upon a township with my name, I decided to explore its modest streets. Driving past two invitingly open doors next to which was stenciled "The Philadelphia Baptist Church," I stopped someone just about to enter and asked if I could join their about-to-begin service. I was immediately enveloped in southern hospitality as embodied by a few elderly African-American women. These women, wearing bold-colored skirt suits, lacy blouses, and white doilies draped over the crowns of their heads, led me into their chapel for the seven o'clock "revival."

The Reverend Dr. Joseph Johnson, Jr., officiated, a responsibility he managed not from a raised lectern, but from the floor, at eye level with his congregants. His podium served only as a side table for a glass of water and an extra handkerchief. To the left sat a three-piece band—guitar, drums, and bass—waiting for its cue; to the right sat a quorum of male elders in thronelike chairs, a kind of apostleship that coached from the sidelines, like warm-up batters encouraging their man at the plate.

Abruptly, Rev. Johnson began. "People are looking for answers in a pill, a pipe, a bottle, and one-eight-hundred psychic networks," he declared, not wasting any time in building his injunction against "mis-guided seeking."

"Help us, Jesus," one of the apostles implored.

"M-hmm," seconded another.

"God will take care of you," Rev. Johnson affirmed. "He doesn't want you to trust your bank account, your lawyer, your doctor—he wants you to trust in *Him!* So He challenges us. Challenge makes us stronger! No need to call one-eight-hundred-Sagittarius-and-Gemini. You need to call Jesus, like Israel did!" Rev. Johnson's momentum sent him across the floor, as if sideswiped by a sudden gust of holy wind, shuffling and stomping his feet. His three-piece backup band kicked in, and a rain of *amen*s and *hal-lelujah*s were showered from the pews. Staying an octave above the flurry he had stirred, Rev. Johnson's words were met one for one, his congrega-tion never deserting him in the divine commotion. "PRAYER IS POWER!" Rev. Johnson roared.

"Speak up!" the genteel lady next to me hollered, as if her soul was hard of hearing.

"No prayer is NO power!" he plowed forward, the strain on his throat eliciting empathetic pains in mine. "God is bringing us through a *process.* And he is never in a hurry, but he is never late. He'll let you go into the lion's mouth so he is able to deliver you OUT." Nearly every pair of eyes in the tiny chapel was closed, every hand raised, palms tilted like satellite dishes locking onto their signal, a roomful of worshipers attuned to their preacher. With arms waving in the air, some congregants moved to the front of the chapel to pair up with one of the deacons now standing, who laid their hands on whoever approached the bench, threading personalized prayers into the sermon that never slowed.

Watching everything unfold, I thought about what few opportunities we are given in our daily lives to close our eyes in public, to feel secure enough to truly let go of monitoring everything around us, trusting some-one else to stand watch over our worries so that we can briefly step away from them. For the next two hours, safe in the haven of their chapel, everyone's guard dropped—an infectious exercise that both unburdened and energized men and women alike.

At the end of the service, everyone indeed seemed revived, including me. Bear-hugged by all the strangers around me, I took my leave just as the band was catching its second wind.

On my way out of town, weather reports confirmed a hovering hurricane's intention to pummel New Orleans, giving me reason to head inland. I set my sights on Plains, Georgia, a small town preparing for its annual peanut festival, a weekend-long celebration of its most important regional crop. As our country's most famed peanut farmer to date, Plains's own Jimmy Carter was to preside over the festival, as well as the Sunday School class at his local Maranatha Baptist Church, a duty he upholds whenever he's in town. I purchased a map and some fuel and settled in for the late-night drive.

I located the Maranatha Church just before ten on Sunday morning, assuming I'd be first in line for the eleven o'clock service. Instead I found myself stuck in a bottleneck at the base of the church parking lot. Buses blockaded the entrances, dumping out loads of tourists who seemed happy to be taking a break from their southern plantation and swamp tours for a little religion, Jimmy Carter–style. Joining the snaking line on the sidewalk, I finally reached the front door, only to be halted by the chest of a church bouncer. Physically blocking me from entering, he informed me that the last seat had just been taken. "You'll have to go to the TV room," he said, referring to the overflow area where closed-circuit monitors broadcast live from the sanctuary. Exasperated, I begrudgingly followed his instructions, taking a detour to the bathroom, which inadvertently led me through a side door and into the church.

"Do you already have a seat?" another, less hulking guard asked.

"Yes, I do," I heard myself lie, unable to accept that after traveling all this way I'd be stuck in front of a TV. Stopping at a row of smiling grandmothers, they kindly moved their pocketbooks to make room for me.

For the next hour, everyone quietly fanned themselves with church programs while they waited, the room warm with anticipation. Secret Service agents secured the corners of the building, nonchalantly exchanging information with one another—and others we couldn't see—through the cuffs of their sleeves. Everyone, in turn, fanned themselves a little faster.

At long last, there was movement. A woman breezed up the aisle, looking more familiar as she approached. Stepping through the roped-off row in front of mine, Rosalynn Carter took her usual seat in the section reserved for actual members of the church, a group that, reflecting the size of the town, totaled about forty. I wondered how the locals felt about being besieged by tourists whenever Jimmy—as he's casually referred to by

Plains residents—was in town and at their pulpit. But then I thought of how many congregations prayerfully strategize to attract this many warm bodies, and the clear benefits of celebrity seemed evident.

As soon as Mrs. Carter settled in, Maranatha's resident minister, the Reverend Dr. John G. Ariail, appeared, and cued the choir into a sedate version of "This Joy That I Have." Holding both sides of the podium, he began the sermon that would precede Carter's. Rev. Ariail spoke of the world's hunger crisis ("eleven million people starving while we have a country of excessive obesity") and of America's obsession with money ("we think we're poor because we don't have the wealth of Bill Gates"). His homily emerged as a cautionary tale of the insatiable desires of a country that constitutes 5 percent of the world's population while consuming close to 50 percent of its natural resources. He urged us not to compart-. mentalize our Christian values, but to be *thoroughly* and mindfully Christian, for above all, Jesus detested hypocrisy. Though his message was relevant and compelling, nearly everyone—with the exception of the church regulars—seemed to view Dr. Ariail as a warm-up act, the opening band that receives only halfhearted attention no matter how hard it plays.

The room's posture shifted as Jimmy Carter made his entrance, all eyes straining. Looking nearly the same as when he'd occupied the White House more than twenty years before, Carter exuded the confidence of someone who's as accustomed to microphones as the rest of us are to telephones.

"It is the twenty-year anniversary of the Camp David Accord," he announced by way of self-introduction, referring to his brokerage of the lasting peace agreement between Egypt and Israel. After a round of applause, the versatile Sunday school teacher moved on to that week's Scripture lesson.

Mr. Carter humbly admitted that he felt tested by it. "The Song of Solomon has always been hard to teach," he said in his relaxed drawl, citing the section's conspicuous absence of theology, morality, or even the mention of God's name. "Instead it's about erotic, physical love between men and women," he declared. "It expresses the way God feels about us as His creation; He's *passionately* in love with us, intense love for us and for the church, the kind of love illustrated by Mary anointing Jesus' feet with precious oil and wiping them with her hair. No matter what happens to us, nothing can separate us from the love of God."

Carter urged us to reciprocate God's adoration with "benevolent acts," such as helping the Salvation Army, or building houses for the poor, something he has taught by example through his association with the nonprofit organization Habitat for Humanity. In concluding, former president Carter said that at the end of life, there are only two important things to measure: those we have loved—particularly the seemingly *unlovable*—and those who have loved us.

While Carter's humanitarian record is unquestionably built upon passion, his technique for *teaching* about such emotions was decidedly dispassionate. Or perhaps it was only in comparison to the energetic revival I'd attended a few days earlier. As at Rev. Gomes's Harvard service, everyone in the Plains chapel remained reserved; not a single arm shot upward, no one erupted in an *amen* or a *Thank you, Jesus,* despite the former president's routine mention of his spiritual founder's name. And no one felt compelled to encourage Mr. Carter to "speak up," wanting their bones to rattle with his spoken word. Both churches were Southern Baptist, but these bused-in listeners seemed paralyzed in comparison to the elderly ladies in doilies from Hahnville. I realized then that if I were ever to become a routine churchgoer, my house of worship would have to be the kind that moved the mind, the spirit, and the body.

Thanking us all for coming, Mr. Carter joined his wife outside on the chapel lawn (the one I was told he sometimes mows while Mrs. Carter vacuums the carpets inside) to pose with individuals and tour groups desirous of souvenir photographs. The line moved efficiently, some church volunteers snapping the pictures while others systematically guided people by their elbows in and out of the frame, saving the Carters from anyone's attempts at chitchat. The former first couple seemed plenty aware that most of the people who'd occupied their pews that morning had come to relish this Kodak moment as much as, if not more than, the biblical lesson imparted. I wondered if, especially in these celebrity-driven times, it was inevitable that the luminance of the messenger will sometimes outshine the illumination of the message.

Having sent numerous requests through Mr. Carter's office in the weeks preceding this service, I waited around, hoping for an opportunity to briefly discuss his conviction to spread the gospel. I got as far as a handshake and an introduction, which was suddenly interrupted by a blue-suited arm that reached in to lead the former president by *his* elbow to an idling chauffeured town car. A bit stunned by his abrupt departure, I watched the unmarked car whisk Jimmy and Rosalynn away, back into the protection and normalcy of their private enclave.

Intrigued by the idea of talking to a preacher who, unlike our former president, actively seeks out the limelight as a platform for his spiritual message, I approached the Reverend Robert Schuller. Each week, Rev. Schuller shares his "positive theology" with live and TV audiences on *The Hour of Power,* one of the most popular religious programs in the world.

Raised on a small Iowa farm with the doctrine of our inherent unworthiness and habit of sin, Rev. Schuller offers his worldwide cast of communicants something drastically different. He delivers accessible, feel-good theology sweetened with themes of self-improvement, self-esteem, forgiveness, and God's universal love. Rev. Schuller has himself called his program "religious kindergarten," suggesting that if people want something less elementary, they'll look elsewhere. Until then, he's happy to cater to those who find his straightforward doctrine therapeutic and appetizing as they lounge in the privacy of their own home, or even their car.

In 1955 Rev. Schuller became the visionary behind the first drive-in church, his Southern California congregants encouraged to "come as you are" and enjoy, from the comfort and anonymity of an automobile, his Sunday services delivered from atop the rented theater's snack bar. Though Rev. Schuller has since traded in his rooftop pulpit for the multimillion-dollar high-tech "Crystal Cathedral," he continues to uphold his legacy, reserving a section of his enormous parking lot for his congregational overflow, or for those who simply prefer the drive-in venue for their weekly dose of God.

On the day of my interview with Rev. Schuller, two days before Easter, I arrived early for a grand tour of the grounds. The place is a virtual eternityland ornamented with sculpted hedges, impressive fountains, imposing palatial structures, a well-stocked souvenir shop, and life-size biblical scenes cast in bronze. Some religious leaders might choose to direct the tens of millions in cash toward something that someone in need could actually bite into or take shelter in. Criticized for his architectural extravagance, Rev. Schuller asserts that he only builds structures that "qualify as *art*—something that when seen and experienced through the senses inspires and uplifts the human person to a better, more ennobling life." I can't say that beholding the 1980s-dated space-age Crystal Cathedral uplifted me personally, but nearly everyone I encountered in and around the cathedral beamed with awe and pride at their own Emerald City.

Ushered into Rev. Schuller's expansive high-rise office suite, I was greeted warmly by his smile, handshake, and a self-deprecating playfulness I hadn't expected. Knowing he was pressed for time—one of the year's two biggest Christian holidays was nipping at his heels—I jumped right to the purpose of my visit.

I began by asking him to please "write" his own job description. After a few seconds of reflection he said, "To communicate to human beings who they are and what their potential for living can be on every level—physical, spiritual, and professional. And I fulfill that mission," he added, sticking with his architectural fixation, "by building into their thought processes a system of thinking that accepts faith as the basic engineering principle in the design and structure of a thing called 'personality.'"

The Bible, like many other religious texts, can be read as both lenient and severe, and its messages are often veiled, illusory, and even contradictory. Thus what is presented as truth—the gospel—is largely determined by the personality of its interpreter. While Rev. Schuller is schooled in dogma, he chooses instead to focus his weekly message on "the spirit." He says that the "indoctrinating and cognitive approach" popular among his ministerial colleagues appeals to the brain, defining "our beliefs about God, and how our beliefs about God differ from others'." In contrast, he appeals to "the heart," suggesting that the accumulation of information *about* Christianity does not make someone authentically Christian.

As a disseminator of the gospel of the heart, Rev. Schuller aims not only to inspire but to console his local congregation and broader TV audience. His motto is *Find a need and fill it, find a hurt and heal it.* "I think we're entering a new age," Rev. Schuller declared, "where . . . spirit is finally more important even than substance. That's a provocative statement that many of us probably wish weren't so. But if you have all the right substance, and yet at the bottom of it is an arrogant know-it-all spirit . . . it's not going to work."

Asked about his influences, Rev. Schuller pointed to Norman Vincent Peale's philosophy of positive thinking, and holocaust survivor and psychiatrist Victor Frankel's studies of our search for meaning and purpose. Inspired by these men, Rev. Schuller has configured his own brand of spiritualized pop psychology, intermingling the vernacular of the self-help genre with the dialect of the Bible.

To experience Rev. Schuller's sermons live, I attended three out of his *five* back-to-back Easter services, held to accommodate the swarm of visitors who flooded his two-thousand-eight-hundred–seat cathedral. (It also doesn't hurt, Rev. Schuller had said to me with a wink, to have five recorded shows from which to select the best "takes" for a delayed broadcast.) While escorting me to an open seat, an usher commented on the team of volunteers who had worked through the night to transform the cathedral's stage into the bountiful floral glory we now beheld. It was indeed a fragrant spectacle, one that could easily be mistaken for the setting of a royal funeral, or an ambitious float in the Rose Bowl parade.

I took my seat just as the full orchestra, world-class choir, and sixteen-thousand–pipe organ began to wow the massive congregation. Rev. Schuller took his place behind the pulpit, beaming proudly. Allowing a long applause intended both for the entertainment and for him, Rev. Schuller began his address with a plea for donations to help build another addition to the crystal kingdom. "We've raised about five million dollars for the new visitors' center building designed by architect Richard Meier," Rev. Schuller said. "But it will cost eighteen million more to actually build the building, so if anyone wants to give a million, let's talk," he joked. He used a variation of the one-liner in each of his services, and the congregants, who'd just deposited checks and bills into plates circulated by ushers, duly laughed every time. Never short on positive thinking, Rev. Schuller assured his listeners—an active donor base of about 650,000 people—that the construction would be completed within two years.

"But it's *Easter,*" he continued, as if to interrupt himself for the real public service announcement, shifting into the rhapsodic enunciation of the consummate storyteller. "The message of Easter is that life is e-ter-nal," he began. "And the promise is that if we choose to, we can live in the center of divine love forevermore, because that's where Jesus is, and that's where *I'm* going. Or," he said, "you can live sep-ar-ated from divine love for-ever-more." Looking around his congregation, he spoke as if he were sitting alone with each one of us. "Somebody once asked me," he reminisced, leaning an elbow on his podium, " 'Do you think there's a hell?' " Taking a beat to shine his signature half-grin, Rev. Schuller continued, "I said to them, 'I certainly hope so. Otherwise heaven would be a *hell* of a place.' "

Curious about how this self-licensed Realtor of heaven perceived his audience, I had earlier pressed Rev. Schuller to describe whom he envisions when he writes and delivers his sermons. "I think, whether we like to admit it or not, we as preachers are talking not so much to our listeners, but to *ourselves*. They say you can tell a minister's sins by what he's always preaching against. Basically, a sermon—a message—if it has passion and sincerity, is a witness. And a witness means I'm telling the story of what I've seen, what I experience. For me, the self who I'm preaching to"—he paused, concocting his own composite—"is someone who wants to be a good person, who wants to be a respected person, an intelligent, helpful, and humble person."

It was a perspective I later found mirrored in the words of another preacher, Fred Craddock, in his book *Overhearing the Gospel*. Craddock wrote: "The teacher or preacher does not thrill and move the hearers with a message on the uncertainties of life while proceeding on his own way *certainly*. The communicator is striving to become while urging others to become."[2] Or, to quote one of my grandfather's more colloquial phrases, "You teach best what you most need to learn."

Regally adorned in his floor-length embroidered robe, presiding over his pulpit of blooming grandeur, and inflated on the Godzilla-size TV screens, Rev. Schuller looked as certain as they come. And yet I also saw how his position might feel like a vulnerable one, millions of viewers presuming him to be all that was projected onto the screen. During our conversation, I had asked Rev. Schuller if he ever got nervous or self-conscious behind the pulpit. "Oh, yes I do," he said without hesitation. "I'm probably the most insecure preacher you will ever meet."

"You mean you get butterflies?" I asked.

"No, not butterflies," he qualified, "I just never, ever feel that I am adequately prepared. And I'm called to deliver a solo performance without anybody monitoring what I should say, or reminding me to make my points. I've chosen spontaneity when I preach, which means the subconscious is ahead of the conscious. And what it really means is that I am very dependent upon what I call the Holy Spirit, the God who inspires words and ideas to tumble out in an effective way. But I *personally* never know if they've been effective. When I finish Sunday morning on that pulpit, I walk down the steps into my private mezzanine office, and no one is allowed in there until my wife [also *The Hour of Power* executive producer] comes from the machine room where she watches the show. When she says, 'That was great, very good, Bob,' I can breathe again knowing I got through another one." Rev. Schuller exhaled deeply through his nose with closed eyes, releasing the very private anxieties of a public speaker. "If I was told suddenly that I had but thirty seconds to live," he added, opening his eyes, "my last words would be *'Thank God* I don't have to preach another sermon next Sunday.'"

Schuller wrapped up his third tidy twenty-five-minute Easter sermon—each remarkably similar to the others, for a man of spontaneity. In doing so, he reiterated his recurrent theme: "You deal with facts by becoming knowledgeable. You deal with mysteries by becoming wise enough to be a positive-thinking believer."

His departure from the pulpit was as unceremonious as his entrance had been grand. Against the background of the live orchestra, I imagined the robed minister fleeing through the empty hallways toward his private mezzanine office, where he would wait with held breath until his wife arrived. There, away from the spotlight, his effectiveness would be affirmed by the one who knew him best, urging him with her words to be his own positive-thinking believer.

Like my grandfather's impassioned sermons, which eventually matured inside of me, Rev. Schuller's messages—the ones millions of people overhear him deliver to *himself*—transform and expand at the rate he does. While this TV-savvy preacher may or may not be leading people into the deepest form of self-inquiry or a disciplined daily practice, he is sowing plenty of seeds of potentiality into the personalities of his captive audience.

Whether the preachers I observed were addressing the skeptical intellectual, the earnestly devout, the tourist, the channel flipper, or simply themselves, their styles were appropriately tailored to match their audiences. But while their presentations were diverse, their message was mostly unified, each pair of hands waving the "banner," as Rev. Gomes had called it, of unconditional love, sacrifice, charity, gratitude, morality, and, of course, salvation.

Chapter Eight

riginating as two distinct sects born of the Protestant Reformation, Universalism and Unitarianism were each named, by their detractors, after heresies. The early Unitarians earned their name by renouncing the holy trinity and the tenet of Original Sin in preference for a unified God and a belief in the inherent goodness and potential of humankind. Founding Universalists rejected the notion of a God who would save only some of his children, advocating instead the doctrine of universal salvation. As one nineteenth-century minister who served in both Unitarian and Universalist churches prior to their merger observed, "the [Universalist] thinks God is too good to damn them, and the [Unitarian] thinks they are too good to be damned forever."[1]

Origen, an ascetic hermit whom Roman Catholics claim as one of their third-century "desert fathers," was credited by early Unitarians and Universalists for having laid the foundation that became their "heretical" faiths. Origen stressed the unconditional humanity of Jesus, argued against the existence of hell, and taught of a benevolent God who offered salvation to all people. In 1961, having traveled parallel tracks nurtured by countless theologians, philosophers, reformers, and martyrs, the two Origen-inspired denominations wedded and expanded their symbiotic philosophies. Under the umbrella of Unitarian Universalism, they together embraced individual liberty, free will, reason, inquiry, independent communication with God, religious tolerance, humanitarianism, and the gospel of universal salvation.

An active Universalist of the nineteenth century—the founder of the American Red Cross, Clara Barton—once declared, "I have an almost complete disregard of precedent, and a faith in the possibility of something better. It irritates me to be told how things always have been done. . . . I defy the tyranny of precedent. I cannot afford the luxury of a closed mind. I go for anything new that might improve the past."[2]

Clara Barton was one of many to illuminate in letter and action her church's radical refusal to be bound to the status quo, or usurped by any creed other than the libertarian precept "We agree to disagree." Reflecting the fledgling faith's doctrine that no one religion, sect, individual, or scripture is the sole custodian of truth, another Unitarian, Thomas Jefferson, once said, "Were I to be the founder of a new [religious] sect, I would call them Apiarians, and, after the example of the bee, advise them to extract the honey of every sect."[3]

Today, Unitarian Universalists are a living embodiment of America's religious pluralism, identified as everything from Jewish to pagan, Buddhist to humanist, Christian to agnostic, and even atheist—an ever-widening diversity that might have surprised even the likes of Jefferson. With just over two hundred thousand registered members in the United States, the Unitarian Universalists' influential presence continues to belie its modest census.

Spreading the Wealth
with Unitarian Universalists

When I was seven, my mother, who began her professional life as a social worker, took on an extracurricular activity as the volunteer director of a Vietnamese resettlement program. She was appointed by the governor's office to help Southeast Asian refugee families acclimate to our hometown of Omaha, Nebraska. Believing that my exposure to her work would be an invaluable education, my mother hauled me around from one tiny, overcrowded apartment to the next as she advised traumatized, largely non-English-speaking people on how to survive in their new, sometimes hostile environment. With a meager budget and inadequate training, she mostly accomplished this with the aid of a pocket dictionary, fumbling her translations one word at a time, while I sat in the corner acting bored.

At the end of every visit, those being counseled would—with body language and a few words of broken English—thank my mother profusely. One family, the Phams, would approach me after each session and present me—as the unofficial ambassador of my mother—with a box of chocolate-covered maraschino cherries. The first time this token of appreciation was bequeathed, I ripped open the box on the drive home and gleefully popped the delicious-sounding delicacy into my mouth. And then I gagged. In all my seven years, I had never disliked any edible thing more than that pickled fruit disguised as candy.

Yet when we returned the next week, I unhesitatingly accepted a new box of toxic cherries, following my mother's silent direction to do so graciously—an unmistakable signal she delivered with a firm squeeze of my hand. Several times during the car ride home I suggested dedicating a few minutes of the Phams' next tutorial to the subject of good American candy. *"They have nothing,"* my mother finally said in exasperation, her focus pulling dangerously from the road to my bewildered face. "Their gift to you is a *sacrifice* to them," she said in that particular tone that denotes parental finality.

I stopped complaining *out loud*. Given my obliviousness to Southeast Asian politics and the realities of poverty, I did not understand until much later the dimensions of my mother's words.

Over time, the tower of cellophane boxes of petrifying cherries on my dresser grew. They became a child's lesson in helping others not for the fruits of reward, but as the natural course of one's daily life.

Oddly, it was that first (and last) bite into a chocolate-covered maraschino cherry that returned to me when I attended a Unitarian Universalist Sunday service in Gloucester, Massachusetts, at the first Universalist Church founded on American soil, in 1779. From well-worn benches, we sang hymns inspired by an assortment of world religions and then gave our attention to a sermon that explored morality without ever mentioning the word *God*. I was astonished at how different this approach to faith seemed from that of its Christian counterparts.

While some people are drawn to religion for its supernatural premise, Unitarian Universalists tend to extol a more pragmatic view, regarding their church as a shelter for both individual expression and collective obligation. Recounting examples of heroic character from the chronicles of modern history rather than the pages of biblical record, the Gloucester minister hoped to make the power to improve the world tangible to each of us. It is, after all, the practice of public service in the interest of social justice that most unites Unitarian Universalists from Massachusetts with those in other states and around the world.

Concluding her sermon, the minister reminded us of the many church-sponsored programs in which we could participate, from volunteering opportunities and demonstrations, to organizational committee meetings and a donation campaign to furnish emergency kits to distant peoples in crisis. "And don't forget to visit the table on your way out if you're interested in knowing more about upcoming legislative bills," the minister added.

For Unitarian Universalists, "dying to the self" means putting the community before—or at least on par with—one's own interests. They elevate the "Do unto others as you would have them do unto you" maxim not as a way of accumulating heavenly favor—for they believe we are all already "saved"—but as a worldview steeped in common sense and human decency. While nearly every religion teaches some form of mastering oneself in order to be of service to others, the resonance of the Unitarian Universalist message lies in its distinctly nondogmatic tenor. What emerges from these fellowships is social action influenced by a long tradition of intellectuals, transcendentalists, and social reformers such as Susan B. Anthony, Dorothea Dix, Ralph Waldo Emerson, and Henry David Thoreau, to name but a few. Occasionally a democratic consensus surfaces and organizational positions are adopted, but diversity reigns, even in activism. In one sample congregation, one might encounter a committee of people dedicated to women's rights, another to public education, a handful rallying around environmental issues, and the rest focusing their time, energy, and donation dollars on a local homeless shelter.

But while the Unitarian Universalist libertarian spirit is regarded as a model of tolerance, some—even inside the church—argue that their once-revolutionary religious movement now runs the risk of drowning in the pool of ineffectual all-inclusiveness. When I asked one Unitarian Universalist minister about her members' more traditional ritualistic practices, she hesitated, then said with a sigh, "They're kind of hard to get hold of, since they can be just about anything." While her congregation is "Christian-leaning," she joked, the last time Jesus Christ's name was spoken inside her church was when their janitor bumped his head on the basement rafter.

However eclectic, the expression of the Unitarian Universalist movement is reflected in the biblical injunction "Be ye doers of the word, and not hearers only," and in Thomas Jefferson's personal declaration "It is in our lives, and not our words that our religion must be read."[4]

While people of other religions might consider their greatest spiritual "doing" to be prayer, meditation, worship, or proselytizing, Unitarian Universalists are more inclined to invest their faith in an action they believe will measurably better the earthly quality of another person's life. "Religion to us must have an impact on the world," writes Dr. William F. Schulz, a recent president of the national Unitarian Universalist Association and now president of the human rights advocacy group Amnesty International. "It cannot be all chanting and incense or even coffee and conversation," he adds. "We have every day just one more chance to retrieve history from the edge of perfidy."[5]

Entering his sparsely furnished midtown Manhattan office for just a little coffee and conversation, I was struck by Dr. Schulz's collection of Amnesty posters, each showing a fixed stare of strife and fortitude representing hundreds of thousands more undocumented. A third-generation Unitarian Universalist and longtime minister, Dr. Schulz is a dyed-in-the-wool religious liberal shaped by the zeitgeist of the 1960s, a time he remembers as demonstrating "a heightened sense of our possibilities as a nation, as well as the moral obligations that were being unmet." A serious man with gentle eyes, Dr. Schulz wore a suit and a trim beard that I imagined grew more wildly in his earlier days of nonviolent protest.

Considering his faith's differing—or nonexistent—definitions of the Creator, I asked Dr. Schulz to share his own. "I personally understand God as the source of grace and of blessings that come to us unheralded or undeserved," he began. "I don't perceive God in any anthropomorphic way, or as an actor in the world, but I would not be uncomfortable with the use of the word *God* as the source of life's plenitude and graciousness," he added, reflecting the natural mysticism spawned by Unitarianism in the 1830s. "I feel [obligated] to work for social justice, because not everyone has equal access to that plenitude." In the final analysis, Dr. Schulz suggested, the important question is not whether God exists, but rather whether our attitude toward creation is one of "trust, generosity, and enchantment; or suspicion, indifference, and cynicism."

Dr. Schulz's perspective reminded me of something Rev. Peter Gomes had said when I asked him if he observed an "American way" of practicing religion and religious values. "Yes, I think there is an American way of reading the Bible and an American view of how to practice," Gomes said. "It's an attempt to reconcile our uniquely American individualism with our historic and strong sense of communitarianism." Rev. Gomes went on to say that, as a culture, we oscillate between belief in a purely personal relationship to God and a belief influenced by our Puritan forebears, who were communally minded. "They believed in holy societies," Rev. Gomes said of the Puritans, "and even though they had deeply horizontal relationships—conviction of sin, conviction of grace, election, and so on—they nevertheless believed in building as ideal replicas of a holy society as they could. We've lived ever since between 'me, myself, and I' as the sole definition of how the religious life is to be practiced, and a notion that our job is to reform our neighbors and society and the world, and set up an exemplary public and communal life."

Dr. Schulz is a contemporary proponent of these communal values on a global scale. He doesn't believe in an intervening Creator, but feels that God is leaving the unfolding of creation entirely up to us. I asked Dr. Schulz how he remains hopeful and energized in his cause when Amnesty International makes him a witness to the worst of human nature. "Any religious person needs to be committed to living a balanced life," he said, "and that is particularly true if you're dealing with horrific events and occurrences. If I myself am not healthy, I'm not in a position to help anyone else. So I work very hard to achieve that balance so I can remain useful." To do this, Dr. Schulz makes time for his family, for fun, for spiritual reflection, and for pursuits that have "absolutely nothing to do with Amnesty and human rights."

He is also motivated by the people he meets who have endured very literal pain and injury and yet have emerged, as he said, "whole, or if not whole, have enough spirit in them to become whole again. There is that saying—I think it's in Ecclesiastes: 'He who increaseth knowledge, increaseth sorrow.' And it is certainly true that I experience sorrow frequently at what I hear and learn. But knowing that Amnesty has freed forty thousand prisoners of conscience since it was founded in 1961, I'm also given great, great satisfaction, and that contributes profoundly to the personal balance that keeps me going."

Balance between action and introspection was an idea cited again and again during my interactions with Unitarian Universalists. Among them there seemed to be a movement—gaining momentum over the last few decades—to integrate personal development with social betterment. Having long done their part to shore up society's outer banks, Unitarian Universalists were beginning to explore the "inner space" that George Gallup, Jr., had invoked at the Christian Science conference. One congregant I met sitting in the pews of the Gloucester "UU" church said that she had noticed more members beginning "to investigate their spiritual nature through some form of consistent practice outside of activism."

When I asked Dr. Schulz if he had noticed this trend among fellow congregants, he said he had. "There's an old Zen saying: 'After ecstasy, the laundry,'" he said pointing out that most Unitarian Universalists have been plenty good at the latter, and now it seemed more were learning to soften their loads of responsibility with a measure of ecstasy.

Though I had through my twenties—weaned from my mother's prodding hand squeezes—given time and energy to help those "less fortunate" than I, exposure to Unitarian Universalism caused me to take a closer look at that part of my life. In examining my less conscious motives, I came to see that the volunteer work I had done had been equally about assisting myself, trying to soothe for strangers the underlying afflictions and fears that I, too, confronted. It seemed that even my most apparently selfless act satisfied some need of my own. And yet my effort to reach out to people in need has always been the gesture that has kept me aboveground, engaged in a world from which it is, more and more, too easy to retreat.

Striving to live out our national schoolhouse pledge of allegiance to liberty and justice for all, Unitarian Universalists experience an ongoing conversion of self in their commitment to scatter more evenly the abundance that exists in pockets of creation.

> *Swiftly arose and spread around me the peace and knowledge that pass all the*
>   *argument of the earth,*
> *And I know that the hand of God is the promise of my own,*
> *And I know that the spirit of God is the brother of my own,*
> *And that all the men ever born are also my brothers, and the women my*
>   *sisters and lovers,*
> *And that a kelson of the creation is love*
> *And limitless are leaves stiff or drooping in the fields. . . .*
>
> —WALT WHITMAN, *Leaves of Grass*[6]

Spiritualism

Chapter Nine

The fundamental beliefs and practices of Spiritualism reach back to the beginning of recorded history—and possibly further, to the first human attempt to make contact with ancestors and gods from the spirit realm. A Swedish scientist, Emanuel Swedenborg, is credited with being the first notable "modern" practitioner of Spiritualism. Living in the eighteenth century, Swedenborg claimed to communicate with angels and spirits—entities that had previously inhabited bodies on the physical plane. From these communications Swedenborg is said to have developed clairvoyance and psychic sensitivity, allowing him to elucidate the past and foretell the future. He was also believed by some to be able to mediate contact between a living person and a deceased loved one. Integrating these beliefs with his Christian faith, Swedenborg helped Spiritualism evolve from a marginalized novelty to a legitimate religious movement of nineteenth-century America.

While modest enclaves of Swedenborg's followers can still be found, most modern American Spiritualists recognize Dr. Andrew Jackson Davis as their founding father. Davis is remembered most for his clairvoyant diagnoses of disease and illness. "Spirits have aided me many times," Dr. Davis once wrote, "but they do not control either my person or my reason. They can and do perform kindly offices for those on earth, but benefits can only be secured on the *condition that we allow them to become our teachers and not our Masters—that we accept them as companions, not as Gods to be worshipped."[1]*

Meanwhile, a broader fascination with the phenomena was taking hold of Americans in the mid-1800s, inspired by one family's haunting experience. Having moved into a tiny cottage in Hydesville, New York, the devoutly Methodist Fox family complained of a loud—and invisible—roommate who they said caused the sounds of heavy footsteps, sliding furniture, rattling windows, shaking floorboards, and sharp raps as if doors and tables were being struck. Desperate for sleep and frightened by the inexplicable disturbances, Katie and Margaretta Fox, twelve and fifteen years old respectively, mustered the courage to confront their bodiless bedfellow, devising a form of Morse code by which sequences of tapping sounds corresponded to letters of the alphabet. Character by character, the unsettled ghost spelled out its identity: C-h-a-r-l-e-s-B-R-o-s-n-a, followed by an account of the tragic end he claimed to have met at the hands of a previous occupant of the cottage. Characterizing himself as an itinerant peddler, Charles B. Rosna is said to have explained to the Fox family—letter by letter—that his body was buried in their cellar.

News of the conversations between the girls and their talkative ghost spread through the small town, and beyond. The Fox family began accepting visitors into their home to observe and confirm for themselves the existence of Mr. Rosna and other spirits who occasionally nudged their way into the discussions. For years thereafter, the girls toured the United States as "the famous Fox sisters," demonstrating and promoting spirit communication as both verifiable and meaningful. The Fox sisters were regarded as living proof for others who began meeting regularly to develop their own mediumship—a term commonly used to describe the ability to communicate with those "in spirit."

While these experiences blossomed into a multitude of denominations, a majority of Spiritualists joined forces to establish their practice as a unified faith. Ratified in 1948 by the Federation of Spiritual Churches, some of the guiding principles include the directives to abhor war and uphold peace, to condemn all prejudice and unfair discrimination, to work to abolish the death penalty, to demand reform of penal and mental institutions, to advocate planned parenthood, and to generally commit to improving the quality of life for all peoples, everywhere.[2] Reflecting the fundamental concepts of its monotheistic predecessors, Spiritualism asserts a belief in one God infinite and omnipresent, the oneness ("brotherhood") of humankind, and a celestial law of positive or negative retribution for all earthly actions.

With the twentieth century's Spiritualist movement in full swing, the public's focus shifted away from the Fox family. It was at about that time that a wall of the abandoned Fox family cottage collapsed, unearthing a male skeleton and his tin trunk, stuffed with rusty housewares and decayed laces.

Since then, the movement has continued to grow and diversify, making an accurate estimate of membership impossible. But Spiritualists far and wide uphold their shared founders' principles, practicing direct communication with the deceased.

Listening with Spiritualists

I was twenty-one years old and living alone in a narrow shoebox of a house perched defiantly over a Hollywood canyon. Nothing seemed out of the ordinary the night I parked in my usual spot, climbed down the darkened stairway that led to my front door, and fumbled to find the right key, as I had hundreds of times before. Turning the handle and stepping into the darkness of my kitchen, I suddenly sensed an intruder. I couldn't now say for certain what it was that tipped me off—a faint shuffle, scratch, or flicker? I only remember arriving at my point of panic, not the split seconds that carried me there.

But as my eyes adjusted to the shadows, I saw no one and heard nothing, other than the rattling of my own rib cage. I sent my arm out to flip on a light, and looked around, craning my neck to peer down the hallway leading to my bedroom. There, I was confronted not by the ski-masked man I had imagined, but by a diaphanous image of my grandmother gliding effortlessly through the corridor.

The heavy object I had grabbed for self-defense slipped out of my hand and onto the floor.

Was I hallucinating? Had someone spiked my dinner? My mind groped as if for its fallen spectacles, desperate to make rational sense of this unfathomable sighting. My skin tingled with the sensation of a thousand tiny needles.

I had just spoken to my grandmother a few days earlier, and the conversation rushed back to me.

My grandparents' Sunday-morning phone calls were one of the few predictable things in my life. I always answered the 8 A.M. ring half-asleep, and they always apologized for waking me up. I could picture them, both on the phone at once: my grandpa manning the powder blue push-button upstairs, my grandma, the yellow rotary attached to her kitchen wall. Always allowing me a few minutes to adjust to daylight, my grandfather's delectable doughnut sermons would be transported to my faraway ears as I listened with closed eyes. We would then exchange familiar updates: I would confirm with minor detail that I was still eating, dating, and working; they would confirm that they were still talking, keeping busy, and taking their medication—my grandfather for his blood pressure, my grandmother for her diabetes and "nerves." When our weekly script ended, we'd say good-bye. It was my habit to listen for their twin clicks before hanging up and rolling over, back to sleep.

But on this particular Sunday, a few days earlier, my grandparents and I had strayed from our tradition. Having slept undisturbed till late morning, I woke with a start and dialed their number. They assured me from their respective phones that they had only been unusually preoccupied, and the rest of our conversation went as usual, until the good-bye. "Be good, chicken legs," my grandpa always liked to say. "Don't forget to eat," my grandma would helpfully remind. "If you need a few bucks, you *don't* know where to find us," the patriarch would joke. "Talk to you guys next week," I'd throw in to get us around the corner. My grandpa was responsible for the collective "We love ya," and I, the final "Love you too," bringing us to the crescendo of a three-way "B-bye."

This week, though, at the end of the line I'd heard only one click. I waited. No second click. I waited. "Hello?" I called through the still line. Silence. Still no click.

"I love you," my grandmother's measured voice had finally said, closing the space between us with uncanny certainty.

Taken aback, I realized how long it had been since my grandmother had uttered those words for herself.

"I . . . I love you too," I echoed, but it spun out of me more like a question. Almost simultaneously came my grandmother's belated click.

Standing in my now-empty hallway, I felt weak.

Though there was no longer even a trace of her translucent image, I could still feel her presence, that same eerie, palpable density taking up space in the room. Inhaling a few deep breaths to collect my tears and my fear, I distinctly heard her voice. Not a memory of her voice, but her actual oral tone spoken through my entire body, like an intercom reverberating from my cells, gliding along my bones, and reaching into my brain. Along with sound waves came the sensation of her emotions, vicarious swells of euphoria crashing over my shock and sadness, her elation airy and intoxicating. I experienced the serenity of a woman who, in the span of her seventy-odd years, had possessed many things, but never the luxury of sustainable joy or real tranquillity. Though she spoke with the sensibility of her earthly personality and with a complete awareness of the past, it was as if my grandmother no longer felt entrapped by who she had been, or thought she was. I reveled in meeting for what felt like the first time someone I'd long known, briefly holding, like a firefly cupped in two hands, a light that glowed with the promise of something gentler and more eternal than this place.

In this way, my grandmother and I talked for a while. For how long, I don't know, as the space we shared seemed a timeless bubble. Much of what she said would only be of interest to someone who knew our family well, disclosing decades of muted hopes and disrobed denial. But one wish she expressed does seem broadly relevant: that those she loved might rest easier knowing that her death was but a transition into another, and quite possibly better, expression of life.

"What's it like where you are now?" I asked her.

"Edgeless," said the woman who'd spent her life dangling from emotionally dangerous heights.

"What are you *doing*?" I wondered.

"Waiting," she said calmly.

"For what?" I asked.

"I don't know," she marveled. "Someone is coming to explain, and I need to wait here for them."

And then, as miraculously as she had appeared, my grandmother was gone, as if pulled like taffy in another direction. The signal of her voice thinned, the particles of her presence recoiled, and the space around me once again became just my own. I wondered if the "someone" she was expecting had finally come. Or if she'd suddenly been drawn to another family member or friend. Or perhaps she could no longer overcome what I couldn't hide from her, that small reserve of disbelief in me that was unable—or unwilling—to accept her visit as reality.

Scanning everything around me, I didn't—couldn't—move for fear of erasing what might have just happened. I had the urge to gather, like evidence, each word I had heard, to dust for her silvery fingerprints, to trace her flowing image—still fresh in my mind's eye—and permanently print it in my memory.

The telephone's muffled, then desperately shrill, ring scattered my altered state. I became chilled, wondering who might be on the other end. I wasn't prepared to speak, nor was I eager for confirmation of what most of me had begun to accept. I let the first rings pass me by, half believing that the implications of seeing and hearing my grandmother's wispy image could somehow be undone if I simply didn't answer.

The machine dutifully intercepted the call, my cheerful recorded greeting played. Only then did I gingerly lift the receiver to my ear. The sound of tears familiar to me trickled through the line and poured out of the tiny speaker of my phone. "Mom," I said, trying to think of something to comfort her. She gulped air. "Grandma . . . my mom," she managed to get out before struggling for more breath, "passed away. Come home." Out of words, she just sobbed.

There is nothing more startling than coming, without warning, face-to-face with the defenseless child inside of one's own parent. I, too, was wordless, feeling sheer despair for my mother—for the finality of all that her mother had been, and all that she had not. But I also felt strangely relieved and light—a kind of contained exhilaration—as I reconciled all the moments between the turn of my front doorknob to now. I held the certainty in me, like a map to a once rumored treasure, that "losing" my grandmother was ultimately a redistribution of mass, not an annihilation of it.

Spiritualists' core belief is that death is but a continuation of life, a realm we on earth can readily access. To them, my experience would be nothing out of the ordinary, nothing overtly phenomenal. In fact, these believers make it their most focused practice to conjure such communication *at will.*

Looking into this practice of ethereal dialogue, I came across the spirit medium and bestselling author James Van Praagh. A self-proclaimed conduit between earth and the afterlife, Van Praagh has enabled hundreds of people to contact their deceased loved ones. He's even demonstrated his ability for millions of viewers on popular TV shows like *Larry King Live.*

Responding to my request to meet, Van Praagh invited me to his home in Laguna, California, to discuss his perspective on the basic beliefs and practices of Spiritualism.

As I breezed down the 5 freeway toward Laguna, traffic suddenly became lethargic. I reclined my seat a notch, turned up the radio, and settled in for delay. Jarred out of daydream, I caught the glare of flashing red lights surging up behind me in my side mirror, then screaming past. As I inched forward, I saw two stalled semis, unscathed as far as I could tell. Then, drawing closer, I beheld what had come between their massive cargoes: a sporty yellow car crumpled like a paper bag. A procession of accidental mourners, three lanes of cars rolled past the aftermath of an irrevocable change in a stranger's life. My thoughts immediately went to the family, those for whom the sound of the phone ringing would never be the same. The cars in front of me slowed to a near halt, exercising their voyeuristic rights before speeding off to make up for lost time. I pictured drivers turning up their radios to drown out the thoughts that inevitably arise when you know it could just as easily have been you.

As I came upon the lapping body of the Pacific Ocean, death crossed my mind again, this time through thoughts of my great-aunt Mary, who lived—and died—on this rim of California coast. Memories of her came to me the rest of the way to Laguna, in particular of our trip to Disneyland and her insistence that we pose for souvenir pictures inside a replica of the *Starship Enterprise,* our arms wrapped chummily around wax figures of Captain Kirk and his crew. The grin of an older woman eternally ready for life and for a laugh was preserved in my own mental snapshot of my grandpa's big sister, Mary.

Greeted by Van Praagh at his door, I apologized for being more than a little late and recounted the freeway accident. We talked as he led me through his yard and up a path to an overhang of canyon with ocean views. "People don't want to look at real mortality," he said in response, signaling me to take a seat at a tiny weathered table. "We may gawk at a scene, but in actuality we divert our glances. Otherwise we'd be living very differently."

Van Praagh had an inviting demeanor that was compatible with his boyish grin and clear azure eyes, which crinkle around the edges when he talks. His lightheartedness prompted me to wonder aloud about his spiritual practice: what helps keep a man who spends a lot of time talking to dead people so uncommonly buoyant?

"Meditation helps a lot," he said. "It gets me grounded to the earth. I don't get to meditate in a formal way every day, but I do make a concerted effort to 'connect' daily, whether it's saying good morning to the flowers, or looking at the ocean, or connecting to the trees—some way of saying thank you and acknowledging life and one's existence on this earth. If we can stay clear and connected to the simple but remarkable fact of being alive, our essence, which is very childlike—not childish—is free."

Having mentioned that he'd just recently moved into his home, Van Praagh gestured with his hands to the landscape he planned to embellish with even more flowers and trees. "It's when I don't connect," he explained, bringing his hands back, "that the illusions, and fears, and the 'outside' start to cave in on me. And that's when I know I need to get back, once again, to my true self, my real self."

Like all Spiritualists, Van Praagh believes that underneath our fears, anxieties, and sense of alienation is a "real self" made of pure spirit with perfect perception. Uncovering this higher self is, however, a process of mystical evolution. Indeed, the whole system of spiritualistic thinking stems from the idea that we each take on successive lives for the single purpose of realizing our shared luminance and higher consciousness. This notion of recovering a real self—of supernatural stuff packed inside the mortal coil of personality and ego—has similarly been cited by many others from various traditions as their motive for daily practice. Through rituals like baptism, prayer, meditation, song—and, for Spiritualists, communion with spirits—believers of nearly every faith find ways to conjure a more ideal self. Reconnecting to this divine nature allows a glimpse of what Spiritualists believe will one day be their permanent state of grace in the afterlife.

Having once imagined himself in a priestly collar, Van Praagh came to his own awareness of this more "spirit-centered real self" while attending Catholic seminary. "The seminary is where my sense of Catholicism ended and my sense of spirituality began," he declared. "The turning point for me occurred over one Easter weekend when each student was instructed to enter a small altar room and pray alone for an hour. In that hour I got the sense—I don't know if someone 'spoke' to me or I just felt it—that what I was praying to was much, much larger than what I'd been taught by the Catholic Church. And suddenly the hypocrisy of it all hit me, and I couldn't handle it—whether the many starving people who could eat based on the gold in the Vatican, or how one man called a 'priest' has the authority to say you are or you are not forgiven, or how the Church insists that

God can only be found in its building, and true holiness can only come in its form. I started asking myself, Why can't God and holiness be found everywhere? And then I started seeing the destructiveness of fear being imparted by religion—not just the Catholic Church, of course—and so eventually I decided my connection to God, my spirituality, would have to exist outside the self-sanctified walls of institutions."

Going it alone, Van Praagh subscribed to the liberal belief system of Spiritualism without formally affiliating himself with any one of its churches, though he often attends their services as a guest medium. Like most serious "channelers," he hopes his autonomously honed skills will not only offer peace of mind to those who seek confirmation of life after death, but potentially help unlock the most perplexing mysteries of life on earth. Like sleuths of the ethers, Spiritualists piece together clues that might explain the deeper meanings behind human existence.

And then there are the less lofty insights many Spiritualists seek out on a daily basis—polling their personal spirit guides on everything from where to live, to what line of work to pursue, to choosing the "right" doctor. This ongoing counsel can occur in simple mental dialogue, or through automatic writing using a pen and paper, or via a device such as a Ouija board, runes, or tarot cards. Some Spiritualists use a pendulum to expedite answers—a weighted string or chain that rotates clockwise or counter-clockwise in a yes or a no response to questions. I once came across a Spiritualist in a grocery store who was holding her rose quartz pendulum up as she walked down the aisles, soliciting advice from her spirit guides—or perhaps her higher self—for which items to add to her basket.

Not all self-proclaimed Spiritualists are fully developed mediums, and so they are left to rely on devices, and sometimes fellow believers, to translate their ethereal messages for them. But Van Praagh insists that every single person is a natural-born channel to *Spirit*—a gender-inclusive term he uses in place of *God*. We engage Spirit every day without even necessarily realizing it, Van Praagh said. "I mean *everybody*," he emphasized, "whether you're an accountant, a medical professional, or a truck driver—you're interacting with Spirit all the time, through images, words, or feelings. All inspiration, and much of what we call 'intuition,' is the working of Spirit. But to develop reception takes practice," he cautioned. "Not many people are willing to dedicate the time it takes to tune in, because we're in a society that is moving quickly, interested in instant results. Spirit vibrates at its *own* frequency, going on forever, for eternity."

In preparation for my meeting with Van Praagh, I had attended a few services at a beachside Spiritualist church founded in 1877, near Cape Cod. IN HONOR OF THE REDMEN read the sign nailed above the entrance of the octagonal dwelling. Built to resemble a traditional wigwam, the site was established by a Boston medium who hoped to honor Native American spirit guides with a kind of home away from home. More than a hundred years later—squeezed between summer homes, nautical gear shops, and pizza parlors—the wigwam looked more like an awkward memorial to the nineteenth-century notion of the Native American as noble savage.

Entering the wigwam with a group of about twenty people, I sat in one of the late-twentieth-century plastic folding chairs configured in a large circle. With carefree attention to time, the service began fifteen minutes late. Its first order of business was hands-on healing. Unlike certain services I'd attended in Evangelical churches, this Spiritualist version of healing was not the least bit theatrical. It was as solemn and straightforward as a silent group prayer, with those seeking relief invited to sit around the "healing pole": a thick tree trunk rooted at the center of the room, said to have been "sensitized" by the Micmac Indians after the wigwam was built. Other congregants stood to volunteer their hands, which they laid on the backs, shoulders, and heads of those who'd come forward for help. We all closed our eyes, and were asked to visualize the healing energy of Spirit infiltrating the source of each malady.

Like Practical Christians, Spiritualists believe that wholeness and health exist in infinite, ever-present abundance. For Spiritualists, it is a cast of unseen guides that assists in the accessing of that potential. The collaboration to heal is made possible by the medium's focused concentration, raising one's own inner vibration to match the higher, healing frequency of Spirit.

Almost all of the volunteer healers indicated completion of their task by shaking out their hands as if they'd just washed them and couldn't find a towel. Then those wrapped around the tree trunk opened their eyes and quietly thanked the person standing behind them. Our single circle restored with the readjustment of a few chairs, we then sang distinctly Christian hymns praising God, building to a warbling finale of "Amazing Grace": ". . . Wa-as bli-ind, bu-ut . . . no-ow . . . I-I . . . see." As we delivered our last off-key note, a woman ambled up to the empty podium

with the help of her cane, letting the room stew in a dramatic pause before beginning her "talk"—the more casual Spiritualist rendition of a
sermon.

Following her eyes around the room as she acknowledged her listeners,
I took note of the group's profile: about 70 percent Caucasian women in
their forties and fifties, the rest middle-aged men. To warm up her fellow
mediums, the visiting speaker from Pittsburgh first shared the story of her
most recent escapade with her "unseen friends," who during her drive east
had telepathically navigated her safely around a widespread forest fire
burning out of control. "Once again, they pulled me through," she said of
her invisible travel companions, lots of heads in the room bobbing in
agreement.

Closing her eyes, the woman seemed to go away from us for a moment,
as if she were tuning her insides the way one does a staticky radio. Van
Praagh would later elaborate on the idea of "vibrational tuning" for me:
"The hardest part of hearing is discerning the difference between your
inner voice and that of Spirit," he explained. "It requires a kind of stepping
aside from yourself. Perfecting this ability determines the clarity of a good
medium, because when you're going through a channel, the spirit's own
biases will color things; their earthly personalities come through—their dis-
likes, sense of humor, the whole character of their earth life. The quicker
you can translate whatever words, feelings, and images come in—avoiding
your own editing or second-guessing—the more clear and accurate the
message will be."

After the medium had worked her way clockwise around the room,
spontaneously relaying words, feelings, and images from the spirit realm to
about half of us, she started losing steam. She reminded her understanding
comrades of how exhausting ethereal communication can be. An enthusiastic younger woman—the spitting image of Sally Field—popped out of
her seat to volunteer relief. Visibly nervous, the young woman suggested
that it might be "good" for her to publicly test her receptor skills. Standing
to the side of the podium rather than behind it, as if she hadn't yet earned
that right, the pinch-hitting medium closed her eyes. Her first few messages
seemed to resonate with those receiving them, for tears welled in their
eyes. Through this woman, a deceased husband identified himself by his
beloved car and favorite blue coffee mug, hoping to assure his wife of their
unceasing companionship. The mediating woman tapped into the spirit of
a grandmother who wanted to remind her forty-something grandson of the

ruby ring she wore, the treats she always baked for him, and the long walks they'd taken together, also promising intimate guardianship.

I was next. As she gazed in my direction, a big smile came over her face.

"There's a girl standing behind you," she said. "She's wearing a kind of prim seventeenth-century dress. She's not a relative, and maybe not even one of your personal guides, but she has a message for you. She's saying that emotionally you are very heavy right now, very burdened, and that this will continue through the winter, until spring, when you will begin to feel light again. She's showing me an image of a young colt leaping freely through a field."

A leaping colt? Burdened through winter? The others before me had been given concrete descriptions of sentimental objects, physical likenesses, familiar places, even particular smells linked to loved ones who had died. Why, I wondered, did I get the random Pilgrim girl? It was true, I did feel a bit overwhelmed at the time, but we're all burdened by one thing or another, and most of us are bound to feel a little heavier in winter. Maybe, despite her vagueness, a girl from the seventeenth century really had gone out of her way, and time frame, to try and unburden me, or at least, with her choice of costume, reflect back to me the pilgrimage I had indeed embarked upon. But frankly, mine felt like the sort of generic "reading" that gives skeptics fodder to criticize a Spiritualist's practice.

Among the congregation of ghost receivers—some of whom seemed tuned in, others tuned out—I decided it would be fine with me if I was never again contacted by a disembodied Pilgrim or Indian chief. Though I remain intrigued by the idea of spirits communicating from beyond the grave, if that indelible night with my grandmother proves to be my life's only true spirit communion, my appetite for the other side has been plenty gratified.

In spending time with Spiritualists who psychically comb the airwaves for advice, support, and companionship, I observed some hazards. Inherent to the practice is the impulse to sneak quick-fix answers to the tests in life we seem meant to study for. Not to mention that the source of these answers can be as dubious as the drunk guy at a party. And a few Spiritualists I met seemed much closer to their circle of invisible friends than to embodied ones, a unique case of cloistering oneself in one's own secret spirit world.

I'd arrived at Van Praagh's house with some of these preconceptions. He, in turn, attempted to illustrate how better understanding the afterlife can usefully inform our earthly life. "There are many levels to our being-ness," he began. "What we see here on earth is a physical body, but we actually have *seven* main bodies—all vibrating at different rates of speed, all living at different levels, accumulating understanding, or consciousness, that will eventually be integrated. When we pass out of the physical realm and into the astral, and then into the etheric body, we're at varying levels of awareness. When you first pass over, there's an immediate expansiveness, a deep realization of who you are—your true self."

This had seemed to be the case with my grandmother, who appeared to embody the self she'd wanted to be, speaking to me unencumbered by misery. Van Praagh explained that when a spirit contacts someone on earth, it's as if they slip back into their most comfortable pair of shoes. I thought about how my grandmother's fleeting image in my hallway had not resembled the aged body she had left behind, but instead the glowing beauty of her roaring twenties. It was as if she was reclaiming that version of herself, slipping it back on as the chosen garment of her life.

In elaborating the mechanics of the out-of-body experience, Van Praagh hoped to clarify what it is we're supposed to be doing while we *have* bodies. It is, he reiterated, our shared task to transcend the self-absorption and burdensome emotions, circumstances, and logistics of everyday life so that we can restore—if only momentarily—our original interior.

During our conversation, to give his concepts a personal context, Van Praagh occasionally referred to facts about my life that I had not yet disclosed to him, like the death of my grandmother. Unlike those of the Sally Field look-alike from the wigwam church, Van Praagh's antennae seemed fine-tuned and far-reaching. Eventually he asked for my permission to more formally "read" me—an ethical courtesy usually expressed by mediums before peering into another's life. Curious about what he might find, I gave my permission. Van Praagh's gaze drifted over my right shoulder, as if someone had just walked up behind me.

"Who's Mary—an aunt?" he asked. He began to describe an older woman "who is witty and adventuresome," a comment I noticed he made in the present tense. I told him I indeed had, or have—depending on how you want to look at it—an unconventional great-aunt who fit that name and description. "She feels a strong kinship with you," he said, pausing for more translation. "She says you were thinking of her, so she's just returning the thought," he added, as if I'd inadvertently paged her.

His focus subtly shifted to another direction, as if someone else were calling to him from his yard.

"There's a large Irish family standing with you, your grandmother's side," he ventured.

"They would be Irish," I confirmed, sneaking a peek over my shoulder half expecting a reunion, but finding only tall trees, sun-dappled and still. Van Praagh paused, seeming to be carrying on a silent discussion with the invisible ancestral delegation. He was like an old-time telephone operator who connected person-to-person calls, and then listened in on the conversation.

"Many people who pass over struggle with the aftermath of their alcoholism and feelings of weakness and guilt, just like your grandmother," he stated matter-of-factly. My grandmother had indeed struggled with alcoholism while she was alive. "Alcoholics typically experience a lot of regret once they leave the body," he went on. "They suddenly see the cause and effect, and feel like they've ruined other people's lives. A majority of my readings turn out to be about regret and forgiveness. The spirit cannot move forward until those they were close to on earth forgive them. A living person's thoughts of blame and guilt can actually hold back a spirit's progression like invisible chains." He assured me that my grandmother was not bound this way, that my family members had very successfully released her. "But for those who can't or don't," he continued, "the progress of both—the one here and the one in spirit—digresses, so I try and assist in the forgiveness process, so both parties can move forward.

"I've done readings where I've had to acknowledge to someone, 'You're right, your mother did not love you.' And they'll break down and talk about how their life was ruined because she didn't love them. There are so many opportunities of growth here on earth, but not enough people see it like that. They see themselves as being slaves to a system, burdened, survival-oriented, and then they allow the martyr complex of 'Look at what this earth and all of its people are doing to me' to set in, instead of taking responsibility and gaining a peaceful understanding of, and control over, one's life." In his unique brand of spirit therapy, Van Praagh points out that we tend to overpersonalize our disappointments. "I try and help people realize that the individuals they're still angry with were simply stuck and ill-equipped. When they come to terms with this, ideally they can then begin the process of letting go of the past and put that energy back into *living*."

Having taken up the better part of his afternoon, I thanked Van Praagh for his time. "I wonder," he said, as we headed back down his bluff, "as you talk to this variety of religious leaders and spiritual teachers, if you won't find that a lot of it isn't the same stuff, just said differently." His words echoed the ecumenical spirit of Gene Begay, William Schulz, and others. "No matter how much ceremony or language is involved," Van Praagh added, "what we all do boils down to love. I don't care if it's on top of the Himalayas or at sea level on the Bowery, it comes down to *love yourself and love others as you love yourself*. I guess my daily practice in keeping attuned to that universal truth is to stay a part of this world—to stay *in* it."

After my grandmother's death—the first personal loss I was old enough to grieve—I realized that mourning is something we must ultimately undergo alone. For this reason I did not share my visitation with my family until long after the fact. The personal nature of the encounter helped me understand why skeptics may never get proof of the existence of the supernatural, since firsthand experience of it seems dependent upon an innocent willingness to see and hear—a state of being that was apparently ripe in me at the age of twenty-one.

At one point in our conversation, Van Praagh had said, "I'm not concerned with whether or not people believe in the fourth dimension. I think what matters most is that we simply question, search, and feel *more*." I found myself in agreement, having never felt a need to convince anyone—related or otherwise—of my grandmother's unexpected house call. Yet every time I come across someone with an encounter similar to mine, I can't help but wonder how many more faint flickers, flashes, and sideways glances pass by us, each day, undetected.

Judaism

Chapter Ten

Some four thousand years ago a man called Abraham, whose forebears had prayed to multiple gods, professed his belief in one universal God. Despite strife, adversity, and dispersion, Abraham's descendants became a new nation of "Israelites," a remarkably cohesive people bound together by the Ten Commandments given to them by God through Moses. Around these divine injunctions, laws and traditions emerged—a way of life governed by reason, justice, worship, celebration, and eventually rabbinic prudence and teaching.

It wasn't until the nineteenth century that Judaism went the way of other world religions, formally fracturing into a multiplicity of interpretation and observance. Over the last two hundred years, three primary divisions have represented the changing identity of modern Judaism.

The first to challenge tradition and conventional worship, early-nineteenth-century German Jews established a liberal branch of their faith now commonly known as "Reform." Favoring a less restricted interpretation of Jewish law, the early Reformers emphasized the ethical over the ritual, the scientific and rational over the emotional, and supported the rights and equality of women. In some ways they have become defined more by what they do not do and believe than by what they do. Today the Reform movement, which varies widely in its worship practices, claims a 50 percent plurality of America's affiliated Jewish population.

In reaction to the Reform movement, the rigorously observant stepped forward to formally identify themselves as "Orthodox," a 10 percent contingent loyal to the literal interpretation of Jewish law and tradition as set forth in the Torah (the first five books of the Hebrew Bible) and elaborated on by the rabbis of the first century. And in an effort to both preserve tradition and respond to modernity and changing needs, the Conservative movement planted itself between the polarities of Orthodox and Reform.

Adding to the expression of contemporary Judaism is a movement that can be traced back to medieval Europe. An alternative style of worship, it found an audience in illiterate peasant Jews disenfranchised from study and erudition. Calling themselves "Hasidim"—or pious ones—they eventually migrated to the United States and brought with them the underground dissemination of mysticism: the secretive and ancient teachings of the Kabbalah, an esoteric text concerned with "angels, demons, charms, dream interpretation, Messiah predictions, and numerology."[1] Today, Kabbalah teachers—affiliated with any one of the three "branches" of Judaism—are more abundant than ever as Jewish mysticism attracts the interest of Jews and gentiles alike.

Across the spectrum—from fundamentalism to reconstructionism—Jewish practice is a triune of worship, learning, and deed, as expressed through some degree of prayer, scripture study, and prescribed moral and ritual action. The Torah, along with the Talmud (rabbinic elaboration), provides the world's fifteen million Jews—an estimated six million of whom reside in the United States—with a guide to religious observance, as well as ethical standards for daily life.

Sanctifying with Jews

I wove through the suburban back streets of Memphis, in search of the Baron Hirsch Congregation, having been invited to observe its evening prayers by the temple's rabbi, Rafael Grossman. Yes, one of America's largest Orthodox Jewish temples flourishes right in the heart of Elvis country. Upon arriving, I was cordially greeted by the rabbi, though Orthodox custom prevented him from shaking my hand, as physical contact with any woman other than one's wife is forbidden.

Shown to the back of the prayer hall, I was asked to take a seat in the last few rows, partitioned by clear plastic bars. I felt quarantined, without even the company of other women, as *daily* temple prayers (as opposed to Sabbath and holiday services) are historically a male-only ritual. This custom is commonly justified by the belief that women are intrinsically closer to God and thus not obligated to perform the same time-intensive observances as their male counterparts. Looking at it more cynically, however, the arrangement seemed to help guarantee that dinner would be on the table upon their return home.

Through my translucent bars, I had a clear view of the back of the male worshipers' heads, each topped by a *yarmulke*—or skull cap—as a physical reminder of their obligations to God. In apparent contrast, they were tethered to earth and its obligations by the cell phones and beepers clipped to their belts. Yet the intermingling of modern gadgetry with religious iconography spoke to the strength of Judaism in its firm *and* flexible design. It is a faith that has repeatedly been forced to adapt to new cultures and circumstances. Cell phones and the Internet are just the latest challenges for rabbis who must define for their congregants the appropriate balance between the material world and the religious life. In this specialized world-view, even the latest technology can be a part of one's religious observance if used to honor God by, for example, upholding justice and freedom, or as a way of forging an honest living to support one's family and communal responsibilities.

But for this hour, all electronic devices were turned off. Each man faced east toward Jerusalem, before beginning the rhythmic bob indicative of *davening*—a Yiddish word that emphasizes the One to whom prayer is directed. The rabbi was indiscernible in their midst as the requisite quorum of men rocked back and forth, reciting in whispers the prescribed liturgy from the holy books they held open in their hands. Some draped their tasseled prayer shawls over their heads like blinders, to block out all that might distract from their course. Each man, moving through the liturgy at his own pace, spouted verse, song, and exclamations at various moments—a hypnotic, symphonic murmur periodically punctuated by *"Adonai!,"* one of the Hebraic names for God. When the room fell silent again and all limbs had been stilled, the men closed their books, adding to the day's religious observance a few private and unscripted prayers.

Taking his leave of the congregants, Rabbi Grossman led me down a long hallway and into his sprawling office. An entire wall was covered with framed photographs of the rabbi flanked by other formidable clergymen and former U.S. presidents. As the *fifty-second* consecutive rabbi born to his family, he was clearly doing them proud. Propping open his back door, Rabbi Grossman inhaled the evening's sticky summer breeze before filling his lungs with smoke from a newly lit cigarette. "I need to quit," he said as he exhaled, eyeing the stick of tobacco between his fingers as if he had no idea how it had found its way there. Taking a seat nearby, I asked the rabbi about his more intentional choices as leader of his local community of Orthodox Jews.

"I had two experiences in my life that were metamorphic to my work," he began. "I went stone deaf when I was five years old. A successful surgery at the age of ten restored my hearing, but my speech remained profoundly impeded." Rabbi Grossman went on to explain that since his arduous rehabilitation he has never taken the gift of communication for granted, embracing "verbalizing and teaching" not because he was the heir to a religious legacy, but because it was his heartfelt, hard-earned passion.

But he didn't fully understand his role as a religious leader, he further explained, until the death of his teenage eldest daughter, which occurred many years into his career. In bottomless despair, Rabbi Grossman felt no alternative but to reconcile the past with the future. Consciously, he sought ways to direct his love for his daughter into a redemptive channel, affirming and sanctifying the lives of those around him. "I don't sleep very much," he admitted. "My work keeps me busy about fifteen hours a day, except on the Sabbath, of course," he added with a smile of fatigued fulfillment.

With the hindsight of his sixty-plus years, Rabbi Grossman has concluded that while earthly outcomes are far from arbitrary, they cannot always be neatly explained, or understood. "There is that which we leave to God and God alone," he declared, as with the death of his daughter. But there is also that which God leaves to us, he emphasized, pointing to the Jewish obligation of *Tikkun Olam,* translated as "repairing the world."

I asked Rabbi Grossman if he thought it possible to have a relationship with, and faith in, God without daily practice. "In my view, no," he said bluntly. "Faith without practice is an abuse of faith. Faith that is completely limited to what is commonly known as 'spirituality'—self-indulgences, meditative singular experiences, and the like—lacks a dimension required of the religious person." To Rabbi Grossman, the concept of *Tikkun Olam* defines the heart of Judaism—an ancient handshake commitment between a Creator and His people who promised to leave the place of creation in better condition than they'd found it.

"If we're unable to do this—to give, love, and obey unconditionally in faith," Rabbi Grossman said, "then we are no different than the primitive man who is concerned only with survival. Who needs creative self-searching to the depths of one's being when death rages outside one's door? Judaism is committed to, and obsessed with, *life,*" he insisted, the cigarette butt that dangled from his hand suddenly more conspicuous than before. And yet the rabbi was not the first person I'd met who overlooked—or perhaps was motivated by—his own vices in his campaign to help save the world.

As with his acquired appreciation for speech, Rabbi Grossman had experienced an incident in his childhood that had given him a unique perspective on life and beating the odds. He recounted a time from his early teens when, over the course of one summer, his entire circle of close friends contracted polio. Grossman had swum with the same nine boys every day in a contaminated lake, but was somehow spared the disease that would eventually take four of his friends' lives and leave the rest permanently disabled.

Much later in his life, Rabbi Grossman had met Dr. Jonas Salk, the scientist responsible for the polio vaccine, and asked the doctor what had motivated him to find a cure. "The belief that there is a solution," Dr. Salk answered. In their ensuing conversation, Dr. Salk acknowledged that his optimism had not been contagious during his eleven-year struggle for funding; he'd been ridiculed by the media and many of his colleagues who didn't believe a vaccine was possible. Rabbi Grossman asked Dr. Salk what had given him such fortitude during those isolating years. "Faith," replied the man of science to the man of religion. "Faith that this *can* be done."

"Obviously in those years of insult and denigration," reflected Rabbi Grossman, "this wasn't done for the sake of self-glorification or edification. Dr. Salk's commitment was a *true* act of faith, a belief in the impossible that can change—even save—a life. And similarly, in all religious experience, it is the commitment and trust that there is something higher, greater, and better that can bring us to a point of love and being that indeed makes this whole existence a more meaningful and happier one."

I polled a number of rabbis to ask them which particular religious "experiences," as Rabbi Grossman had called them, they found most meaningful and essential to the sustenance of their faith. One Conservative rabbi and author, Harold Kushner, answered, "All of them." Elaborating, he said, "Not only do I pray as a Jew, but I eat as a Jew, I read as a Jew, I handle money as a Jew, and I respond as a Jew." While every religion has its own stock of rituals, Judaism embeds them into mundane daily acts to produce sacred purpose, sublime moments, and communal cohesion. And this, says Rabbi Kushner, is the "genius of Judaism."

But when pressed for which ritual *most* embodies their faith, Rabbi Kushner, along with the rest of the rabbis I spoke to, agreed that it was observance of the Sabbath—the only ritual singled out in the Ten Commandments. As proclaimed in the Hebrew Bible: "The children of Israel shall keep the Sabbath and observe it throughout their generations as an everlasting covenant."[2]

From sundown on Friday until nightfall on Saturday, the Jewish believer sets aside everyday routine to reorient his or her attention toward God. For this one day of every week, God's act of creation is commemorated. "For in six days the Lord made heaven and earth . . . and rested on the seventh day, wherefore the Lord blessed the Sabbath day and made it holy," declares Exodus.[3]

Reenacting the culmination of God's divine handiwork, Jews look to the Sabbath as a time to pause in their own earthly "creating," stand back, and marvel at the very miracle of creation. Through the twenty-four-hour Sabbath cycle, observant Jews are meant to revel in the interplay between physical liberation and spiritual surrender, shedding grudges, competition, anxieties, and all "manner of work" so that they may be drawn into the more sacred realm of unscheduled time, uninterrupted reflection, and unalloyed love. After six days marred by aggravation and overexertion, the seventh is given over to a deep sigh of satisfaction and gratitude stretching from dusk to dusk. In doing so, Jews find their way back to that less encumbered, more humble, and joyful self, described by some as the "true self."

I'd been invited to be a guest at a traditional Sabbath meal—the table ritual that marks the holy day of rest for Jews around the world. Because the Sabbath begins at sundown, my host, Rebecca, and I raced against the last moments of natural light ricocheting off high-rises on the Upper West Side of Manhattan. Once the sun set, all Sabbath rules would technically be in effect, including no handling of money, no using of motors and machines (which includes everything from cars to ovens), and generally no exertion that could be considered work.

Rebecca and I had hoped to make it to her temple in time for Kabbalat Shabbat prayer service, to formally inaugurate what we would later celebrate more intimately around a table with her friends. Checking her watch, Rebecca reached out to flag down a passing taxi, a habit of expedience that I imagined her Conservative rabbi father might frown upon. But the Sabbath had not officially begun, Rebecca defended, mindful of the exact hour and minute of a setting sun that had been prematurely obscured by her city's skyscrapers. Handpicking the borderline compromises she was, and was not, willing to make, Rebecca held open her wallet and asked me to fetch from it a few dollars to pay our driver, leaving her hands uncontaminated following the Sabbath injunction against the handling of currency.

Inside the progressive Conservative temple, we sang the Hebrew prayer songs alongside the male congregants, greeting the holy day. At the end of the short service, we wished the women *and* men around us—with kisses on cheeks—"Good Shabbos," before walking back to Rebecca's apartment.

Joined by six other guests, we assembled around the Sabbath candles, traditionally lit just before sundown by the woman of the house. Covering her head with the customary cloth, Rebecca whispered her prayer in Hebrew and then in English, waving her hands over the candle flame three times:

> Blessed art Thou, O Lord, Our God,
> King of the Universe,
> Who has sanctified us by the Ten Commandments,
> And commanded us to kindle the lights of the Sabbath.

Rebecca shielded her eyes with the warmed palms of her hands, as if to absorb the light they now held. "We welcome the Sabbath as if it were a bride," she said.

Taking our seats at the table, we all joined in the traditional songs of *"Shalom Aleichem"*—to welcome the Sabbath angels—and *"Eyshet Chayil"* (Woman of Valor), in honor of our host. Normally any child present is then blessed by the adults, but with our assemblage of single New Yorkers, we skipped right into chanting the kiddush, the blessing over the wine. Like Christians, Jews ceremonialize the sharing of bread and the fermented juice of the vine. Taking turns at the sink, we ritually washed our hands in silence, preparing ourselves both physically and mentally for the benediction of *motzi*—Hebrew for "Bring forth"—sung over the challah bread and the Sabbath day itself.

Endowed with the special meaning we had given it, our loaf was broken into pieces, which were dipped in salt before being passed around the table. Taking a chunk, I asked about the significance of the salt. No one had an answer. As with other practices steeped in family tradition, fully comprehending the underlying meaning of timeworn rituals was sometimes secondary to simply observing them. "I dip the bread in salt because that's what my grandmother always did," said the woman sitting across from me. The comment made me think of my own Jewish grandmother, into whose family I was adopted at the age of six, after she had already passed away. She had been raised in a Conservative home, which meant it was likely that she, too, dipped her challah bread in salt, and might have been able, were she still alive, to tell me and my tablemates why.

While we ate our Eastern European meal family-style, my host and her friends spoke of the challenges they face in attempting to integrate their workaday, fully Americanized lives with the traditions of their forebears.

"Ever since our emancipation in Europe—when Jews were first made citizens in the late 1700s—we've had this internal conflict," Rebecca said. Under new, less oppressive legislation, European Jews became more integrated with the rest of society. For some households, this mixing of cultures meant a watering down of religious tradition, posing a threat to the continuity and stability of Jewish identity.

Particularly in the last century, the Jewish-American population has worked for the causes of equality and freedom in their adopted homeland. For example, many Jews have been active on behalf of civil rights. But for some, these secular successes have taken the place of religious ones. "Our ongoing challenge as modern Jews," Rebecca added, "is to engage fully in American life without succumbing to the homogeneity of it."

One young man at the table suggested that in the attempt to live observantly, "Orthodox Jews have it easier than other Jews." Among the Orthodox, Jewish law is obeyed as a clearly defined, unquestioned obligation to God. The young man said that to practice Judaism the way he does—an approach set squarely between tradition and change—one must endlessly weigh every choice and its implications in the choreography of improvisational faith. But observing the Sabbath, with its built-in fellowship, seemed to be one easy and obvious choice for Rebecca and her friends to make.

Our bellies were soon full from the number of courses Rebecca had prepared, staying true to the Sabbath imperative that food be abundant and shared. At the end of the meal, my companions and I sang more songs praising God, pounding on the table in raucous celebration, as is the joy-filled custom on the day of rest. My six-hour Sabbath observance was capped by a guilt-free cab ride to a friend's house for some uninterrupted sleep. But for everyone else, scattering on foot toward their respective homes, the twenty-four-hour cycle of holy observance had just begun. Arriving at their buildings, some might choose to indulge in the luxury of an elevator ride. But their Orthodox neighbors would be relegated to the stairs—the act of pushing a button that completes an electrical circuit is deemed "work" by certain interpretations of Jewish law. A few lucky Orthodox Jews live in high-rise buildings equipped with "Shabbos elevators," programmed to stop automatically at every floor, so the Jewish passengers do not have to work at pushing the buttons—or exhaust themselves climbing twenty flights of stairs.

Waking on Saturday morning, at least some of my dinner companions would again return to synagogue, where a portion of the Torah would be read and discussed. On their way home, they would not run a quick errand, catch a movie, work out at the gym, or sneak into the office to lessen the week's workload. Most of them would not drive, use their home computers, pick up the phone, turn on the TV, or fix anything that had broken. Turning the notion of rest away from its everyday connotation of merely vegging out, observant Jews imbue their religious day off with activities that are emotionally and spiritually deepening. With a Saturday of city action buzzing around them, my new acquaintances would spend most of their time at home—theirs or someone else's—partaking of more family-style meals embellished with ancient song and old-fashioned conversation. It would be a day filled only with things simple, pleasurable, and intimate—all with God's blessing. As one father said to me, "Probably more Jewish babies are conceived on the Sabbath than any other day of the week."

Toward the end of the Sabbath day, the most religiously attentive would return to synagogue for one final worship service. Then, just after sundown on Saturday, when at least three stars can be found in the sky, the invisible bride of Sabbath retreats with the ceremony of *habdalah*—Hebrew for "division." In shadow, a braided candle with three wicks is lit and a hymn sung to God in appreciation for distinguishing the holy from the profane, darkness from light, the people of Israel from the rest of the nations, and the seventh day from the six days of creation. Everyone present holds their hands up to the flame, turning them over and over in acknowledgment of the polarity between light and shadow, good and evil, and the choices each person makes to ignite his or her life with one or the other. The intertwining candle is then doused in wine that has been blessed, and the aroma of sweet spices is inhaled as a reminder of the sweetness of the Sabbath as it departs—an ethereal sanctuary of time and the senses that, unlike a physical temple, can never be destroyed.

"It still amazes me," Rebecca later remarked in an e-mail to me, "that after habdalah, you're suddenly back in your regular, everyday life after having briefly transcended it. It's not an intense, heightened thing, but more like a slow-burn realization that the previous twenty-four hours were the most meaningful ones of the week. For that time, priorities like family and friends, self-examination, gratitude, and peacefulness were naturally in order."

Rodger Kamenetz is a poet, author, and proponent of the "Jewish Renewal movement." He described his more informal variation of the Sabbath to me over lunch in a Mediterranean café in the garden district of New Orleans. "My family's main accomplishment," he said, dragging a triangle of pita bread through a mound of hummus, "is to prepare a meal, sit down together, light the candles, say the blessings, experience that the Sabbath has come, and eat. But I'm hesitant to advertise the experience as any more than that," he hedged, "because sometimes it feels sacred, and sometimes it doesn't. Sometimes you just light these candles, say these prayers, and eat. That's it, no big deal. But other times, because you've done this week after week, it's accumulated a lot of meaning and you *experience* that. That's what discipline is: the benefit of accumulation."

For a few fleeting years of my childhood, I accumulated Sabbaths that were even more streamlined than Rodger Kamenetz's. When my parents were still married, we sometimes had Friday-night dinners at their friends' houses, though table conversation tended to revolve around the tenderness of the roast more than any spiritual meaning attached to the act of devouring it.

Sometime during his college years, my adopted father came to look upon his family's faith as one might an inheritance of vintage silver spoons—fragile, impractical things unfit for daily handling or use. When I was young, I overheard a conversation about "atheism," the meaning of which I did not fully grasp. Nonetheless, I understood enough to ask my dad if he was "one," to which he unflinchingly replied yes without further discussion.

My father is one of those people who, in addition to altogether sidestepping religion, refuses to talk about the past. To this day, that patrilineal side of my family's religious orientation—and what led to my father's rejection of it—remains an enigma to me. Over the years, however, two aspects of his feelings about Judaism have become starkly clear. First, my father's trials and tribulations, and his intellectual pursuits, led him to conclude that nothing can be entrusted entirely, as Rabbi Grossman had insisted, "to God and God alone." Second, my father's religious indifference is something he shares with a surprising number of American Jews.

This widening repudiation of religious convention and tradition is an obvious cause for alarm in the minds of many rabbis. Occasionally, I became the object—if only indirectly—of this rabbinical concern, as the girl with a vaguely Jewish last name, distinctly Irish face, and nonobservant

Jewish father. Out of most of the rabbis' mouths fell the same curious questions: Where do your Jewish relatives come from? How much Judaism
were you raised with? Have you thought of formally converting? Do you
plan to marry a Jewish man? I had only short, incomplete answers. With a
gentile mother, and thus an unqualified bloodline for Jewry, and no plans
for formal conversion, I am—in some rabbis' eyes—a reminder of their
modern crisis of cultural assimilation.

Hoping to glimpse the perspective responsible for the most dramatic revamp
of the ever-expanding Jewish-American tradition, I followed Rodger
Kamenetz's directions to a house of Reform Judaism he called "the cruise
ship synagogue." The largest Reform temple in New Orleans, the building
rivaled European duomos in measurement and ornament. Planting myself in
the lookout of the back row, I observed a preservice scene not unlike that of
other religious settings I'd visited recently. Most of the women made unig-
norable entrances, strutting proudly if not self-consciously down the aisle,
clad in designer clothes and bejeweled in reminders of earthly success. Ironically, today was Yom Kippur, the high holy day of atonement and inward
scrutiny. As the Scripture to which we were asked to turn rhetorically wondered: "When will redemption come? When we look upon others as we
would have them look upon us."[4]

Recalling the Memphis prayer service I had witnessed from behind
bars, I reflected upon how absorbed those men had been, not in themselves
or one another, but in prayer and God, how utterly unconcerned with the
distractions of earthliness they had seemed to be for that one appointed
hour. In contrast, the enormity of the New Orleans temple did nothing to
increase the intimacy between those inside and their God. The congregation's interest seemed fragile, barely surviving through prayers, Torah reading, sermon, and song, all delivered in English rather than Hebrew. I
thought of the late rabbi and advocate for Jewish reinvigoration Abraham
Heschel, who once wrote, "The modern temple suffers from a *severe
cold.* . . . What can come out of such an atmosphere? . . . People expect the
rabbi to conduct a service: efficient, expert service. But efficiency and
rapidity are no remedy against devotional sterility."[5]

As a result of their uneven attention to *personally* preserving the rituals
of their great-grandparents, many offspring of fully assimilated Jews are
coming of age religiously illiterate. Like Christians who attend church

only on Easter and Christmas, a large contingent of commitment-shy temple-goers pour into their houses of worship only a few times a year for the high holy days, presumably discarding most other aspects of daily observance. Gallup pollsters isolated this trend in the majority of Americans who say they can be "a good Christian or Jew without going to church or synagogue."[6]

Lamenting this trend in her own Los Angeles temple, another Reform rabbi, Lisa Edwards, told me, "These infrequent members come to the holy day services without any preparation. Whatever else they care about, they *learn* and practice often. But for some reason a lot of people in the Reform movement abandon that approach when it comes to religion and prayer. It's as if they make this annual pilgrimage to temple just to make *sure* they're still alienated from Judaism."

A self-proclaimed anarchist, Rodger Kamenetz agreed. "It's true," he said, when I shared Rabbi Edwards's comment with him. "A lot of people who go to temple—regardless of their denomination—see it as 'nothing happened to me, the rabbi and the synagogue failed because they didn't *move* me.'" Kamenetz said he had felt this way for years, until he realized there was another way to look at it. "So the rabbi is imperfect, the synagogue doesn't function all that well, the service is old and familiar and full of platitudes, and maybe the translation isn't gender-proper," he said, listing common complaints. "But we have to continually ask ourself: What am I bringing to it? You have to put yourself *into* the experience to make it happen."

Kamenetz says he repeatedly turns this question on himself, as well as on the adult students who come to him hoping to renew their interest in Judaism. "It's about working on ourselves to the point where we're better receivers," Kamenetz said. "You can tune in to a symphony on a five-dollar transistor radio, or a really nice sound system, or be there live in person. It's the same music, but not the same experience. That's where practice comes in for me. I don't see practice as duty and responsibility. I see it as a way to repeat an experience of connectedness."

In Kamenetz's view, no one is incapable of connecting to—even excelling at—Judaism. "*Everyone* has a devotion, everybody has a top authority," he said. As a teacher of Renewal—a free-form, experimental approach to Jewish practice—Kamenetz ascertains what it is each of his students is passionate about, and then teaches them to feel and express that passion through their religion. "Even if it's shopping at the mall, I think a person who's been devoted to materialism and success has learned discipline and commitment and care." Kamenetz is convinced that, "with minor adjustments," people can draw from the skills they've developed in other areas of their lives in order to succeed at being "proactively" Jewish.

"People are no longer satisfied with secondhand experience," Kamenetz theorized when I asked him why he thought so many people were seeking him out for his brand of spiritual guidance. "I think the broader interest in direct, more accessible experience has happened for a number of reasons—most primarily being a breakdown of authority, a breakdown of consensual reality. Our science is now saying that, in fact, the table is not solid, that we actually don't know anything concrete about time, space, where we come from, where we're going, who we are. Of course, we go through life as though we *do* know all these things, but underneath there's a haunting suspicion that our assumptions are all wrong." That, Kamenetz speculates, has fostered a return to the inner, less intellectualized realms of religious experience.

Kamenetz sees the pluralism of American religion as a catalyst for this shift. When different faiths line up side by side, it brings out the ancient syndrome of "God loves *us* more," he says. That in turn causes people to gravitate to one of two places: "Either fundamentalism, which encourages people to stick to 'mine' with a kind of tenacity that is, I think, tight-assed and doomed. Or, the other choice, which is a willingness to see one's particular tradition as *one* viable means to understand and access meaning and experience.

"No matter how we define our beliefs, we've all had these peak experiences—these *moments,*" Kamenetz declared. "It could be topping the summit of a mountain, listening to a piece of music, or simply looking into the face of another person—an experience, sometimes unexpected, of deep resonance, pain, or great joy that allows us to see the world in a different way." It is the clarity and connectedness provided in moments like these that Kamenetz believes can be replicated—even elongated—through an accumulation of spiritual practice.

Shortly after my meeting with Kamenetz, I crossed paths with a mentor and friend of his, a "Kabbalistic" rabbi named Jonathan Omer-Man. Like mystics of every creed, Rabbi Omer-Man has dedicated his life to the kind of visceral nearness to God of which Kamenetz had spoken.

A number of years ago, members of the Los Angeles Jewish community (the second largest in the country) had beseeched the much-younger Rabbi Omer-Man to move to their city and help solve their "apostasy crisis"—the conversion of their children to other faiths such as Buddhism and Hinduism. "What they then called 'cults,'" remembered Rabbi Omer-Man with a hint of a smirk, as I sat with him in his west Los Angeles Kabbalistic Center. Successful in his bid to win back at least some of those youthful Jewish defectors, twenty years later Rabbi Omer-man is now sought by Jews hoping for a spiritual renaissance *before* they fall away.

An unlikely spiritual deputy for Los Angeles County, Rabbi Omer-Man grew up in England in a "nonobservant Orthodox home." Orthodoxy was "the only game in town," he recalled, before the Reform movement had fully claimed its place at the table of Jewish faith. "Our neighborhood's Orthodoxy was not spiritually demanding," he explained, "though it was an important social identity." It was a declaration I'd heard from a number of Jews, whose faith and loyalty is seated more in their Jewish community and culture than in overt religious feelings. At the age of twenty-one, Omer-Man moved from London to Israel to live as a "secular Israeli." Soon after he arrived, however, he felt "a beckoning, a summoning," as he recalled. "And, of course, there are many doors to answer that. It was almost by chance that I chose the Jewish one, though Jerusalem is a pretty good place to choose a Jewish path."

Rabbi Omer-Man cringed when I asked him what "kind" of Judaism he had chosen to practice and teach as his center's resident mystic. "Some Jewish mystics are so 'open' their brains fall out," he said, stone-faced. I asked if he would then be comfortable with describing, in his own words, what it was he did as a rabbi. "I attempt to find and share answers within the Jewish mystical tradition to certain universal needs that people have, in a way that's appropriate for our time," he offered. "That might pertain to the quest for home, the quest for wholeness, or the quest for understanding what it means to have a 'path,' and the many ways in which the obstacles one encounters through life *are* the path."

I wondered why the ancient mystical traditions of Judaism had, until recently, been largely absent from America's Jewish landscape. Rabbi Omer-Man touched upon the effects of assimilation and the devastating loss of mystical teachers in the Holocaust, and then suggested that the larger variable was not limited to Judaism. "I think it [repression of mysticism] is a problem for all the Western religions, probably dating back to the fifteenth century—at least in European culture—with the discovery of humanism," he said. When intellectual society embraced and exploited rationality, he added, it did so largely at the expense of mystical traditions that taught and challenged people to access and enhance their intuitive senses. "So we're now living in a time when modernism and its dependence upon the intellect and the ego is crumbling. These sources just don't have the answers everyone thought they would."

As we talked, it became clear how Rabbi Omer-Man deals with Angelenos, people infamous for their vanity: he attempts to lead them away from *themselves*. We mastered our world, he said, "but the ability to overcome the self—to surrender—is something we almost lost. My hope is to wean people from the conquering mind, the acquisitive mind. The curious mind created Western civilization, and I'm not suggesting we dump it, but there is a point at which acquisitive curiousness becomes oppressive. Here we try to cultivate a balance of inner silence and outer involvement, with the understanding that spiritual wisdom is extremely subtle. People who go in search of big powerful experiences are often going the wrong direction. The intent should not be so much reaching out to conquer the world, but to breathe it in, to allow it to flow through you."

Rabbi Omer-Man's words evoked a Talmudic passage someone once paraphrased for me: Every Jew ought to keep two pieces of paper in his pocket. On one should be written "I am but dust and ashes," and on the other, "For me the world was created."

When I asked Rabbi Omer-Man what he considered his most valuable daily practice, he said, "That of blessing." Elaborating, he said, "To focus the mind on the blessing of creation is to find the divine spark in everything that exists in the world, and connect it with the source of all being. One of the first things I do in the morning is express gratitude for being alive," he explained, quoting, nearly verbatim, many others I had met from a variety of faiths. "Sometimes I can wake up feeling crusty and mean, irascible and misanthropic, and the spiritual work becomes finding ways to break through that."

I acknowledged my fair share of irascible and misanthropic mornings, explaining to Rabbi Omer-Man that I, too, had been looking for ways to break through that. "We each exist in a state of separation—in exile—though we yearn always for oneness," he said. "The best of us spend ninety percent of our time in this state of separation, and it is from this place that the majority of our spiritual work is done."

With devotion to both spiritual work and divine rest, religiously attentive Jews carry the blessing and the burden of *choosing* to be one of "the
chosen." Under any heading of Jewish observance, to embrace this calling
means to alter how one lives, indeed, to set one's life apart from the less
deliberate choices of others. Those who do make it to their temple for
service, or to their table for Sabbath, may come to discover that their
minipilgrimages produce much more than a confirmation of religious
estrangement. Indeed, in the faithful accumulation of experience, one may
find, as many I met have found, that even for 10 percent of nonseparation
it is worth *doing* Judaism.

Chapter Eleven

A ccording to a Princeton Religion Research Center report, only 3 to 4 percent of Americans are agnostic (those who doubt the existence of God) or atheist (those who firmly believe that God does not exist). The remaining 97 percent of individuals polled acknowledge "a belief in God, or a universal spirit."[1]

The same report stated that 69 percent of adult Americans say they have formal membership in a church, synagogue, or other religious body.[2] Presumably, a portion of the 28 percent who have spiritual/religious beliefs but no formal affiliation forge their own private practice, observing a faith outside the bounds of the collective and the institutional. For these uncategorized individuals, a daily practice may be every bit as devotional and disciplined as those ordained and taught by mainstream religions.

Improvising with the Self-Taught

Spending a few days sightseeing around Tennessee after my meeting with Rabbi Grossman, I recalled a newspaper article I once came across about a Memphis man who taught himself how to paint, fashioning canvases out of found objects and inscribing them with religiously provocative words, themes, and images. While I was waiting at a traffic signal, the man's name suddenly came to me: Light; Joe Light.

On a lark, I stopped in a Memphis gas station and looked through a phone book, dialing the first nondescript Light listed. A mellifluous southern voice answered, and when I asked if a *Joe* lived there, I got a promising "Hold on, darlin'" in return. The man who eventually came to the phone indeed seemed to be the one I was looking for. At the end of our conversation, we made a plan to meet the next afternoon at his home/art studio on the north side of town.

As I made my way through central Memphis toward its outskirts, the topography shifted from rolling green lawns to flat dirt and chain-link fencing. The grocery stores disappeared, the convenience stores and modestly steepled churches multiplied. I turned onto Joe Light's street where the rows of homes looked like giant wooden teeth in dire need of braces.

I stopped at the slumping structure that matched the number on my scrap of paper. A towering black man greeted me at the front door, ducking under its lintel and reaching across what seemed like miles to shake my hand. I immediately recognized his unmistakable grin from the article that I had originally read about artists in the area. As I stepped into the hallway, the home's interior appeared to be folding in on itself, the peeling walls and bowing floors attesting to the many years Joe, his wife, Rosie Lee, and their ten children have lived there.

Light and I sat down in his family room on a long brown couch that shared quarters with a lawn mower and other sundry objects. An antique refrigerator, a weathered door, a white vinyl purse, and odd pieces of lumber and scraps of cardboard had all become canvases for this artist's work. I explained my reason for spontaneously tracking him down, embarrassed to admit how little I knew about him. He didn't seem to mind, and was willing to fill me in on the events that had led him to pick up a brush as a way of talking about God. Or rather, as he came to explain—talking *for* God.

Light mostly stares straight ahead when he speaks, especially when he's remembering. So, sitting at his side, I watched his profile while he stared through the door at Rosie Lee sweeping the hallway floor. He took us back to the mid-1960s. "When I was a young fella," he said, "I had a lot of foolish things on my mind. I was what you might call a sinful person, a bad person. I broke probably every law in the Bible, but I didn't know better." Light had gone to church as a child with his parents and was twice baptized, but says he "just wasn't much interested in God."

That all changed one night with a whisper. Lying on a cot in a jail cell where he was doing time for some of those "foolish things," he heard an airy voice swirl around him like a draft through a cracked-open door.

"The whisper said it was *God,*" Light recalled. "I knew someone was pulling a prank on me," he added with a chuckle. But the voice did not relent, whispering, as if never needing a breath, throughout the night and into the next day, until Light could no longer shrug it off as a hoax. Feeling stalked by this inexhaustible voice, Light challenged it to prove its professed identity. In response, the voice directed Light's attention to a small window. "It said that it was going to send a bird to come to the windowsill. I was to 'take control of the bird' by speaking to it 'with my mind,' and it would obey my thoughts," explained Light.

"I felt like this was kind of stupid," he admitted. "But right away a bird came—a sparrow. Then the bird walked to and fro on the windowsill, following my mental directions. When I would 'tell' it to stop, it would stop dead still, like it was frozen. Then I'd tell it to walk again and it would walk, then I'd tell it to stop and it would stop. This went on for some time, and I thought maybe I was losing my mind or something." Eventually Light told the bird it was free to go, and it promptly took flight.

The ominous voice then asked Light to take a seat and simply listen.

What followed was a highly unusual lecture series that began with a description of "the levels of creation," and how all of existence—man, beast, and element—are related. For a number of days, Light sat as still as the bird on the sill while the voice talked of the genesis of earth and humankind, the history of Abraham and the Tower of Babel, teachings about morality, relationships, how to parent, and what it means to have an earthly mission. "He told me about so much I could spend another lifetime telling you," Light declared.

Light spent the remainder of his prison sentence absorbed in studying and comparing the Jewish and Christian Testaments against all that the whispering voice had conveyed. "Everything the voice told me, I later found confirmed in the *Hebrew* Bible," Light specified, still visibly astonished by this fact thirty years later. "I felt bad for having to double-check Him, but I was learning and I'm *still* learning." As he acknowledged this with a self-deprecating laugh, his upper denture came loose and seemed to chuckle on its own.

At first Light was careful not to tell people about what he interchangeably calls "the voice" and "God." "Some people hear what has happened to me and think, This man is *insane,* poor thing," Light acknowledged. Especially women, he added, recalling his first few dates as a free man, dinners that abruptly ended once he put his secret on the table.

But then Light met Rosie, a woman he eventually entrusted with the details of his unusual experiences. They've been together ever since. According to Light, Rosie even once heard the voice with her own ears. And she isn't the only one; a few of their children eavesdropped as well by placing their ear next to Light's, which, like an antique gramophone, projected the sound of the voice. When I had the opportunity to ask Rosie and her twenty-something daughter about it, their eyes simultaneously widened. While Rosie busied herself, as if to sweep away my question, her daughter confirmed that she, a few of her siblings, and her mother had indeed heard the voice emanating through her father's skull. But that's all she would say, as if to divulge any more would somehow summon the mysterious voice to dwell inside *her* head.

Light's family seemed content to experience God and all things that go bump in the night the way most people do: in the abstract. Still, they seemed accepting and respectful of their patriarch's intimacy with the voice that was now more inclined to speak "silently" to Light "between his thoughts." Light says he always copies down these telepathic messages verbatim. "Most of them come to me at night when it's quiet, sometimes in the *middle* of the night," he said, which is why he keeps paper and pen close at hand, forever prepared to take down the words and phrases he hears.

I asked Light why he thought God had singled him out as a trustee of his message. "I'm figuring it was to get my attention," he speculated, his gaze trained on his grandchildren playing in the hallway. "And for good reason, too. I learned a lot through that time in prison by just listening— about how to treat a wife and kids, about love, about things I never was taught before. My dad used to beat me, just tear me up. I thought that's the way you were supposed to raise kids. Now I know better. . . . I remember hearing my dad say he hated folks, he hated his cousin, and so forth. And my mother said it, too. Personally, I've found hate and pain destroys the mind. Love makes you healthy.

"That might be one of the reasons why God came to me and chose me to take this mission, to speak His mind so I could write it down. He might have thought He needed a type of person who's been through a lot of hard times in his life, but never hated—someone who could handle the backlash."

Many of Light's painted pieces revolve around folksy commentary like "Your brain is dead if you don't have a dream to live up to," or "When you take a chance on anything, you are gambling; *God* thought he had created only a good world and he lost." And then there are the instructive placards, like "God has spoken to me and I quote, 'tell the people to not eat the scavengers in the water, they are to help keep the waters clean, they eats all the filth in the water, they are unclean to you.'"

There have been times, Light says, when his messages have elicited angry responses from people who feel "threatened" by particular words and images Light has in the past displayed along the fence around his home. Offering examples of the people who've been provoked, Light spoke of the numerous pieces he'd crafted that proclaimed the authority of the Old Testament over that of the New Testament. Though he's riled more than a few of his predominantly Christian neighbors, Light says their reaction has been mild compared with that of certain Black Muslim groups, whose "hatred" is condemned by the voice Light hears; and these condemnations are routinely incorporated into his paintings. Light has even stirred some attention among members of the Ku Klux Klan, who have on occasion found themselves the subject of Light's artistic criticism. More cautious in the early years about publicly displaying his work, Light has come to the conclusion that "God wants the message out regardless of how it sounds, or who it upsets." So now Light freely exhibits his art wherever and whenever he has the opportunity, whether in his own front yard, in the homes of collectors, or in local and national museums, such as the Smithsonian.

In memorizing Light's profile, I began to understand why I had been drawn to his art and now his home. As he filled in the picture of his one-man ministry, I saw how it provided him with a vehicle for personal communion. Listening to him speak passionately about the divine origin and discipline of his craft reminded me of something the painter William Segal once said: "Almost every activity done with attention and presence can be a form of prayer. No matter what you are doing, if you do that with all your heart, and soul, and attention, it becomes a form of prayer which can lift you up."[3]

Light's life is a very literal illustration of this idea. His easel is his altar; or rather, a porch cluttered with sheets of metal, slats of wood and cardboard, found objects, a stash of disheveled brushes, and drippy pots of pigment. I had always thought of Judaism—or living according to the Hebrew Bible—as something that one could never do alone. It is a faith that by its very laws requires a quorum—a collective with which to pray, obey, repent, and rejoice in freedom. Listening to Light made me wonder: Can a person be Jewish if his house of worship is none but his own, and his authority of observance is a voice in his head? Is an expression of faith legitimate if it is not ordained? Is a religious identity recognizable only if it is ascribed?

As Light spoke more about his do-it-yourself Torah-derived rituals, he revealed some of the eccentric twists he puts on the tenets of conservative Judaism. He detailed for me which animals, and even which *parts* of an animal, are "acceptable" to eat, and how they should be cleaned, examined, and separately prepared. For Jews, to "keep kosher" is to uphold dietary restrictions cited in the Bible and elaborated by rabbinical law. But without a Jewish butcher or purveyor in his neighborhood, or an aisle of kosher food in his local grocery store, or a rabbi, or even a Jewish friend to consult, Light is left to improvise. "I clean my meat, fruit, and vegetables with washin' powder, like Cheer or Tide," he explained as one example of how he makes do. "The expensive kind is the best at getting all the chemicals and impurities off the food."

I asked Light if he'd ever been to a synagogue. "No," he declared, turn-

ing somber. "To be frank with ya, I'd feel out of place. I shouldn't feel like
that, but that's the way society has shaped up—it's not shaped up right. I
share their faith, and I serve the same God they serve, and live by the laws
of their Scripture, but there are certain things that have happened to the
Jews that they are remembering and acknowledging and celebrating; I
don't think it would be right for me to claim that."

Light's account of our awkwardly shaped society reminded me of
something Rabbi Grossman had said just a few days earlier: "Love is not
something we do when we love people such as ourselves. To love profoundly is to love that which is dissimilar, and to give oneself to something
beyond the self, like the artist who paints." Now his words seemed like a
premonition of the man I would soon meet on the other side of town.

Joe Light is what the art scene likes to call an "outsider" or "vernacular"
artist: a self-taught painter whose work doesn't conform to the orthodoxy
of fine art, but flows from the simple need for self-expression. Light's
approach to the spiritual dimension of his life is equally outsider and vernacular, listening for the whispers of God in his own way. In exchange for
his discipline and courage, Light feels God has blessed him with the greatest
gift of all: evidence of His existence. In return, Light says, God has asked
him to generously share with others the love and wisdom he is freely given.

Standing on his porch, Light pulled a piece of cardboard from the stack
of materials leaning against the side of his house. On it was his trademark
image: a sparrow resting like a crown atop a man's head. The sparrow
seems ready to take flight; it is Light's own emblem of faith, redemption,
and rebirth. His eyes locked on his self-portrait, Light said, "I did once ask
God why he came to me, but he didn't answer. He ain't answered yet."

Islam

Chapter Twelve

ifteen centuries ago, a boy named Muhammad was born in the million-square-mile tract of desert known as Arabia. Orphaned at birth and uneducated, Muhammad chose a simple life as a herdsman and trader that one might have expected would end as obscurely as it had begun. That all changed when the forty-year-old Muhammad began to hear the heavens, which rang like distant, hollow bells that shortened and sharpened into a distinct voice.

The voice revealed to Muhammad a destiny of prophecy that would renounce the paganism of his nomadic tribal people, and give birth to a new monotheistic religion. After twenty-three years of these divine visitations, Muhammad compiled his revelations of sacred verse into a scripture called the Qur'an, bearing the core message: Allah (God) is one, not many, and humankind, though many, is one. According to Islamic tradition, Muslims are descendants of Ishmael, while Jews (and their Christian offspring) descend from his brother Isaac; both are the sons of Abraham. "Oh people! You were created from a single male and female and made into nations and tribes that you may know each other," cries the Qur'an.[1] Distinguishing the highest purpose of human existence as the worship of its single and sovereign Creator, the Qur'an sets forth the obligatory expressions of piety, defines the propriety of interpersonal relationships, and expounds upon ethics, morality, and human rights, as well as the ultimate rewards and consequences of obeying or disregard-ing the scripture's guidelines. This system of beliefs and practices was named "Islam," and its faithful, "Muslims."

Acknowledging the existence of "one hundred and twenty-four thousand" other legitimate prophets—some cited in the Qur'an by name, such as David, Moses, and Jesus—Islamic tradition elevates Muhammad as the final prophet, whose message brings closure to God's progressive revelation. As the Qur'an states in its first-person plural voice: "For We assuredly sent amongst every people a messenger [with the command to] serve Allah and avoid evil."[2]

Because the Qur'an makes no distinctions of race, color, language, or coun-try, Muslims believe its revelations are explicitly intended for all people—each soul, in the end, confronted by the God it was born to recognize and serve. As one Islamic scholar writes: "Every man in every age does not, by himself, know what is good and what is evil, what is beneficial and what is harmful to him. . . . That is why God has spared man the risks of trial and error and revealed to him the Law which is the right and complete code of life for the entire human race."[3] In the Qur'an, it is not ethnicity, class, or geography that differentiates one person from another. Rather, it is the level of devotion to God. For the Qur'an commands every Muslim to look upon all others who believe in the oneness of God—regardless of their religious denomination—as their brother or sister in faith.

In addition to the impressive accomplishment of conveying the Qur'an and founding what would become the world's second-largest monotheistic faith, Muhammad is remembered and revered by Muslims as the noblest example of their beliefs and practices. Having spent the last twenty-two years of his life per-sonally guiding the first generation of Muslims, Muhammad's own words and deeds were closely observed, documented, and compiled into a living treatise on daily Islamic life called the Hadith. Along with the Qur'an, the Hadith is con-sidered the primary reference for living according to the tenets of Islam.

On the whole, daily Islamic worship has remained remarkably uniform from country to country and Muslim to Muslim. However, one group of Muslims called the Shiites (literally "partisans") is notable for its decisive split from the main house of Islam when, upon Muhammad's death, they chose to follow the leadership of Muhammad's cousin and son-in-law, Ali. In contrast, the Sunni majority (literally "traditionalists") remained loyal to the successor appointed by leading members of the Muslim community after Muhammad's death. In some cases, factions of the Shi'i have developed distinct forms of doctrine and worship. In both branches of Islam, small movements have emerged which have adopted a more militant stance on how to define Muslim identity and how to relate to non-Muslims. In the modern world, these more radical groups include the Middle-East-based Hamas, Al-Qaida, and Hizbollah.

Today, about 20 percent of the world's roughly one billion two hundred million Muslims are Shiites, primarily clustered around Iraq and Iran. The remaining 80 percent, who consider themselves Sunni, are spread as far and wide as India, Europe, Malaysia, Russia, China, Africa, and the Middle East. About six million Muslims reside in the United States. Because of population growth, immigration, and conversions, Islam is estimated to be the fastest-growing religion in America, with its faithful soon to be second only to Christians in numbers.

Fasting with Muslims

I had never worn the Muslim head covering before, so I stopped a well-concealed woman in front of a Boston mosque to ask for help with the swath of silky white fabric I held in my hand. The woman smiled and unhesitatingly draped the cloth over me as if I were a dinner table. Pulling one edge flat against my forehead and tucking the slack behind my ears, she expertly cinched and fastened the fabric under my chin with a safety pin she pulled from her pocket, leaving a window of space for my eyes, nose, and mouth. Satisfied, the woman unpinned and unfolded the cloth and handed it back to me, offering to supervise my reenactment of what she called *hijab*—the Arabic word for head covering, and the universal dress code for Islamic women.

As I felt my way through the steps, I asked her why Muslim women cover their heads, and sometimes faces. She cited the Qur'an's instruction to live modestly, a central tenet informing every Muslim man's and woman's speech, manner, rituals of worship, and dress. For a woman, the *hijab* and requisite full-body covering also deflect sexual innuendo and unwanted advances that could threaten her propriety. In other words, the woman implied, Muslim females are shrouded for their own sake.

While the Qur'an does not explicitly command women to obscure their *faces* under this protection plan, one of the four schools of Muslim authority—called *jurisprudence*—conservatively interprets complete head-to-toe concealment from the text. The woman went on to say that the Muslim majority conversely protects a woman's right to expose her face and hands, and that is why she and most other Muslim women in America "only" cover their heads and bodies. When I asked her what guidelines

Muslim men are bound to, she said the laws of religious authority compel them to cover the area from their navel to their knees.

Thanking her for her instruction and explanation, I headed back to my apartment, wondering as I walked how the standards for Muslim dress might be different if Muhammad had been an orphaned girl, and the ongoing Muslim authority a jury of women. Perhaps instead of draping people's faces to deter unwanted sexual advances, those whose overactive libido posed a threat to the peace would simply be fitted for pelvic lockboxes, the master keys kept safely in the possession of a mother or wife. But the woman in front of the mosque had insisted that for her, and the Muslim women she knows, wearing a *hijab* is not a case of coercion, nor is it even an imposition. Particularly for American Muslim women, endowed with civil rights and protections, the act of covering oneself is as much an elected practice as daily prayer, a bold public statement of faith, identity, and separation from the perceived vulgarity of the secularism that surrounds her. While most people spend—Muslims would say *waste*—an inordinate amount of time and energy trying to attract the attention of others, those devoted to Islam attempt to redirect those flirtatious and curious glances to God.

The morning after my *hijab* makeover, I awoke to my usual Pavlovian desire for coffee and a bagel. But as I climbed out of bed I remembered that it was, for every Muslim around the world, a holy day of fasting. I'd planned to adhere to this annual Islamic practice of self-sacrifice, which prohibits even a morsel of food or sip of water from passing one's lips from the time the sun rises to the moment it sets. So I went about my day, managing to stave off those pestering inner pokings of hunger, thirst, and caffeine withdrawal.

Ordaining a balance between spiritual practice and worldly responsibilities, the Qur'an says to neglect neither. It lays out a path of moderation that honors God, family, self, livelihood, and community—both immediate and extended—as one interconnected whole. In practice, during most of the year this precept of moderation requires intermittent pauses for prayer throughout the day, breaks from one's routine that others might squander on cigarettes or gossip. But during Ramadan—the ninth month on the Islamic calendar, commemorating Muhammad's first angelic visitation—Muslims fast as a concentrated gesture of attentiveness to the messages of their holy prophet, suppressing the appetite of the body as a way of arousing hunger in the soul. For this entire month, Muslims go about the tasks of their usual workday and home life while abstaining, during all daylight hours, from food, drink, and sexual relations. Meals are eaten only in the hours between dusk and dawn.

Around 5 P.M., just as the day's sun was beginning to relent—unlike the rumblings in my stomach—I dressed for the mosque. In a floor-length pleated skirt I once wore as part of a Halloween costume, a long-sleeved, high-necked blouse, and a *hijab* billowing from my head down to my waist, I was unrecognizable even to myself. Standing before a mirror, my face peeking back at me, I was amazed by how easily my sense of individual identity had been usurped by a few strategically placed pieces of cloth. I instantly became a part of a faith conglomerate. While I felt subjugated by what, for me, *was* a religious imposition, I had to admit my new look was a real time-saver. It relieved me of thirty minutes ordinarily given to primping—my hair dryer and accessories, makeup and a closetful of formfitting clothes suddenly unnecessary to the mission at hand.

My simplified grooming ritual reminded me of a time in my early twenties when, feeling overly self-conscious about my body's shape and my city's narrow vision of beauty, I took to wearing secondhand men's clothes. Frequenting Salvation Army stores, I'd rummage through their musty shelves and racks for oversized shirts, boxy pants, and earth-toned blazers in a mutinous assemblage of an asexual guise. I found security and an unexpected sense of empowerment in depriving others of the ability to see my body and objectify it or compare it to some ideal. For the first time I felt that my words and actions, alone, represented me—something I imagined many Muslim women could relate to.

But after about a year of living as the ghost of Charlie Chaplin, with a wardrobe my father complained belonged to "dead people," I donated my closet back to the Salvation Army. I decided that self-concealment was, for me, a cycle of life, not a way of life. From then on, I chose to dress not as a reaction to anything. I simply wore whatever happened to make me feel comfortable and alive, reintegrating my internal world with my external appearance.

Holding up the front of my cumbersome skirt so as not to trip, I began the ten-block trek from my apartment in Cambridge, down Prospect Avenue toward the Arabic-scripted building. I passed a pizza parlor along the way, where customers sat in window booths savagely wolfing down their slices. Salivating, I turned my thoughts back to Ramadan, to its reminder of how frequently we take for granted the essentials that God provides to sustain life, from the oxygen we breathe, to the water we drink, to the nourishment we ingest. As I watched the pizza eaters, I realized they were watching me. While my attire was intended to deflect attention, in this country it can have the opposite effect, piquing as much interest as a pair of hot pants.

Entering the mosque, thick with heat and heightened emotions, I blended in. No one questioned my presence amid this sea of uniformly dressed worshipers of every possible ethnicity. Joining the women downstairs in their segregated prayer quarters, I removed my shoes before stepping into the oversized room. Unlike other religions, in which segregation of the sexes tends to be observed only by the most conservative, separatism is standard fare in every mosque worldwide. It is another measure taken to prevent distraction from God and the Islamic law of proper conduct.

Though all the women looked so similar to me in their tents of anonymity, they easily recognized one another, kissing each familiar square of face as it entered the room. Though no one knew me, I was enthusiastically greeted just the same, women rising from their seated positions on the floor to kiss my cheeks and even my hand as a gesture of goodwill, particularly invigorated during Ramadan. I found a place on the floor among them and watched clusters of children romp freely around the bare room, unconfined by pews, ornate decorations, or mothers' scoldings. I felt unexpectedly relaxed among this group of strangers who wore no makeup and sported no new haircuts, fashions, or adornments. It was a room saturated with unqualified acceptance.

Arabic words, unintelligible to me, sprang from a loudspeaker mounted in the corner, an English translation trailing behind. In the temporary absence of their imam—a mosque's religious leader—a member of the congregation stepped forward in his place to make a statement, not an uncommon occurrence for a religion whose holy text encourages both spiritual unity and conscientious autonomy.

From a pulpit upstairs—invisible to those of us below—the male voice addressed the day's newspaper headlines. The U.S. Air Force had just bombed what they were calling a "terrorist university" in the hills of Afghanistan and a "terrorist-sponsored chemical plant" in Sudan, in retaliation for two embassy attacks believed to have been perpetrated by a Muslim group.[4] The feature article in the *Boston Globe* reported—prophetically, as it turned out—the turn of events as only the beginning of "new religious terrorism."[5] With palpable frustration and sadness, the voice criticized the media for its sometimes subtle, other times blatant equating of an isolated act of terrorism with the entire religion of Islam. In our era of sound-bite news, it seems stereotypes are more readily formed with these kinds of overused iconic phrases and borrowed images, and the associations, once assimilated, remain stubbornly present in us.

"Islam is all about the middle," the voice proclaimed through the mosque speaker. "Violence is not Islamic. Extremism of any kind is not *Islamic,*" he said, alluding to the etymology of his faith's very name: *salm,* meaning "to make peace." "We must continue to distinguish a Muslim and his opinions from the uncorrupted path of Islam," he beseeched his fellow congregants.

Within its text, the Qur'an commands its followers to behold humanity as God's perfect and precious creation, likening the taking of one innocent life to mass destruction. "The only true teacher is the Qur'an," the speaker intoned, stressing the relationship each Muslim has with God, independent of authority figures and their passions for power and revenge. "People will always humanize the teachings with their own perspectives, preferences, and agendas, so we have been given the Qur'an to refer to as our more complete, personal guide."

But how one *interprets* that personal guide is, in the end, personal. Tragically, violence justified as "holy war" with God's blessing—or even mandate—drives those on the fringe to unspeakable acts. On the day of his suicide bombing, by which he took the lives of five innocent civilians, a member of Hamas left a note to his mother stating: "Whoever believes that God's religion will be victorious without holy struggle, without blood, without body parts, is living under an illusion."[6] Unfortunately, the deep scars these relatively small but violent groups leave on our psyches require the mainstream Islamic majority to work that much harder to communicate its life-affirming message of peace and tolerance.

One aspect of Islam that all Muslims share is that of daily ritual observance. The Qur'an explicitly outlines five foundational requirements, called the "Pillars of Islam," for its followers: witness (a formal declaration that there is no deity except Allah, and that Muhammad is His messenger), prayer (scheduled five times daily), alms (charitable donations), fasting (at least through the month of Ramadan), and pilgrimage to Mecca (at least once in a lifetime).

Of their prescribed pillars, many Muslims consider fasting to be the most accurate reflection of devotion and character; the remaining practices, I was told, can be observed by rote, without true faith underlying them. By contrast, every sincere Muslim takes the journey of self-deprivation alone, proving their mettle to no one but God, as the emptiness of a belly and the purity of intention are not detectable by the naked eye. "You can't impress others with fasting, because only God is with you through every moment of the day," explained a woman sitting next to me. "Only He knows whether you are practicing with authenticity."

If fasting is a Muslim's private notice of deference to God, public prayer is the vehicle that delivers it. Every day of a devout Muslim's life is propelled by five precisely timed calls to prayer, each a humbling reminder—like the bell beckoning the monks to Saint John's Cathedral—of unceasing loyalty to God. During Ramadan, however, prayers increase in occurrence and length as a kind of spiritual spring cleaning.

In preparation for prayer, I followed the other women to the bathroom where we stood in line behind two sinks. I observed closely as the first pair of women paused at the faucet to verbally inaugurate their "ablutions"—the ceremonial washing required of every Muslim before formal prayer. *"Bismillah,"* they both uttered as they touched their hands to the water. A ubiquitous phrase in Muslim life, *Bismillah*—"In the name of God"—accompanies nearly every physical act throughout any given day, from cracking an egg, to starting a car, to picking up a child, to turning on a faucet. *Bismillah* is a kind of verbal nod to God, whose will is acknowledged as the constant generator of earthly existence.

The women then cupped their hands under the tap, rinsing out their mouths and then their nostrils, each three times, before sweeping their face, hairline, and neck with the same magic number of wet, graceful motions. To complete their ritual, the women also doused their forearms and then their ankles before stepping aside to make room for the next women in line. When it came my turn, I tried to be equally precise with my splashings, but purified the floor more than myself.

My nose still tingling from its first-ever minibaptism, I returned to the prayer room at least *symbolically* clean, joining the long row of women facing in the direction of Mecca—the birthplace of Muhammad and the heartfelt home of every one of his followers. My shoulders touched those of the women on either side of me, as did theirs the women next to them.

Although there was plenty of room to spread out, no one did. For a few moments we simply stood—still, silent, and connected, like a chain of paper dolls waiting to be unfolded.

The loudspeaker hummed with melodic Qur'anic verse, believed most potent when delivered in the original Arabic tongue of revelation. Unable to follow the literal meaning of the words, I simply imitated the other women as we dropped to our knees, folding over into a fetal position, touched our foreheads to the carpeted floor, and then rose back up onto our feet with an uninterrupted flow of movement.

I had prayed with strangers before, though usually without expectation of any kind of external communion. I always felt I had more to learn by observing others in their act of prayer than by momentarily escaping into my own, with the exception of my very personal involvement in the peyote circle. Not since that unforgettable night under the stars had I felt so intimately a part of another's divine discourse, though my sense of connection with these Muslim women was more abstract, as the language of their prayers was unintelligible to me. Yet our intermingled breath and closely linked bodies vivified the oneness of the Muslim creed, our support for one another's prayers spoken physically, rather than verbally.

"Allah Akbar"—"God is great"—the loudspeaker chirped as we again rose from the floor, our hands coming to rest over our ears, as if listening for the sea in a spiraled shell. The woman next to me whispered that the gesture isn't as much about listening as about surrendering: paying tribute to the One who has created the seas, the shells, and our place among them.

With that cycle of prayer complete, some women broke away from the group to tend to their children. Others remained stationary in deep concentration, touching the tips of their thumbs to each of their fingers, as if to remember, and then calculate, something owed. It seemed their reverence for God was matched only by their sense of grateful indebtedness to Him. Weighing the long-term consequences of their every word, thought, deed, and intention, devout Muslims live in a protracted effort to settle a celestial tab accrued for the blessings of existence and the reward of heaven.

Muslims believe that a cavalry of sleepless angels painstakingly records everything we do, say, and think for God's eventual review on the final Judgment Day. At the prophesied moment, privacy will no longer be safeguarded, each of life's ignoble plot points may no longer be revised. With the anticipation of this full-tilt investigation forever looming in the back of their minds, prudent Muslims are spurred to supplemental practice, whether through additional charity, random acts of kindness, memorization of the Qur'an, fasts apart from Ramadan, or optional prayers.

The women's finger-counting was one such extra-credit deposit, an investment made on their souls' behalf. Touching the thumb to the three joints of each finger, the women whispered *"Subhanallah"* ("Thanks be to God"), *"Alhamdulillah"* ("Praise be to God"), and *"Allah akbar"* ("God is great") until they reached ninety-nine, having swiftly traveled across both hands four times plus an extra finger. Rounding up their ongoing division of three, the women each offered a single *"Laillaha illa-Allah Muhammadun rasoolu-llah"* ("I bear witness that there is no deity but God and that Muhammad is His servant and messenger"), confirmed with a tap to the pinky.

And then, as if to humble themselves in the shadow of the greatness amassed in their one hundred praises, the women crowded their hands around their faces. As they did so, they pleaded with God to find their day of fasting acceptable, and to grant forgiveness for their personal transgressions.

The women dropped away from prayer formation one at a time, joining the others who'd already made the transition back to earthly time and physical necessity, savoring a fig and sipping water as the ceremonial end of the day's sacrificial fast. Nibbling the fruit, I struck up a conversation with a young woman whose childhood had been as nomadic and unconventional as my own.

"My parents met at Haight-Ashbury in the sixties, which sort of says it all," laughed Christina, an only child raised by her nonpracticing Jewish mother, who divorced, early on, her "disillusioned" Catholic father. While our family profiles were similar, the course of Christina's life held little else in common with my own. An academic overachiever, Christina graduated from high school at the age of fifteen, and from college at nineteen, with the single ambition of becoming a professional ballerina—a lifelong dream toppled by sudden injury. Wandering the streets of Paris reassessing her life's direction, Christina met a man. Originally from Morocco, the man was living the quintessential Parisian high life, unimpeded by the daily demands of the Muslim faith in which he'd been raised. After they'd lived together ("in sin") for two years, the man proposed to Christina, inspiring a prewedding trip to Morocco for the appropriate family introductions.

"I have to admit," Christina said, as we progressed from sweet fruits to a hearty meal of chicken, salad, and rice eaten with our fingers, "all my friends' warnings and the media hype about Muslim countries and Muslim men scared me. But I instantly fell in love with my fiancé's family and with Morocco, which was helpful, since I realized that if I married him, it would be a package deal." While her husband-to-be continued living an under-cover secular life, Christina found herself drawn to Islam, wanting to know more about the "ideals, values, principles, and the loving closeness between individual, family, and community" that she had witnessed among her future in-laws and their neighbors. "It was seeing how people *lived* Islam that made me want to live it," she explained.

I asked Christina if, given her childhood of nonconformity and discon-tinuity, she found Islam's structure and rooted consistency refreshing. "Yes," she acknowledged. "I was attracted to the stability of Islamic life. You know what's expected of you and what to expect from others," adding in afterthought, "and what to expect when you die, as much as that's possible." The theme of expectation was routinely invoked by the Muslims I would meet. It seemed their faith and its complex system of laws responded to the human desire to solve or eliminate unknown variables, to cement the criteria by which success and salvation are judged.

Pledging herself to both her God and her husband over the course of one week, Christina converted to Islam a few days before her Ramadan wedding, inaugurating her first religious fast and inspiring her husband to return to his Islamic roots. "I know so many women who met their hus-bands in disco clubs or bars, whose interest in Islam and eventual conver-sion brought the men back to observance," said Christina, now in her late twenties.

For those women, and for Christina, wearing the *hijab* outside of the mosque was the final—and most difficult—step in their faithful transforma-tion. "You have to be ready for that public declaration because people will say things to you about being Muslim, and your faith needs to be strong before you can respond to them." When I asked Christina what she's encountered wearing the *hijab,* she said with a sarcastic chuckle that she was often complimented on speaking "such good English for someone from another country." I imagined that was one of the least challenging com-ments she encountered.

Converts like Christina—people not from typically Muslim cultures— have come to compose 7 to 10 percent of America's Muslim population. Though there is a lack of conclusive data, many within the faith say American conversions have greatly increased since the late 1980s, when Islam was brought to the attention of mainstream America. One imam I met at a mosque in the suburbs of Boston commented that converts like Christina tend to be exceptional exemplars of Islamic practice. Motivated to "catch up," he said, newcomers are often more disciplined about the daily obligations than Muslims who've been born into the faith, who sometimes "get lazy."

A mere four years into her conversion, Christina indeed appeared to have been at it longer, from her ease in the company, and with the rituals, of her adopted Muslim sisterhood. "Oh, it's taken time," she assured me, recalling an early sense of inadequacy and insecurity on two fronts: child-bearing and fluency in Arabic—two "blessings" prized and praised by Islam. But though Christina is not yet a mother, nor is she fluent in Arabic, she has nonetheless found her place and peace in the mosque. "I can now say I am comfortable, not just with the identity change, but all the changes. That doesn't mean I don't miss certain things from my old life," she added, "like dancing and sports. Exposing your body for any purpose in front of a man who is not your husband is prohibited," she reminded me. "But there are alternatives and solutions to every boundary that might otherwise feel constricting; they just take a little creativity, like booking off-hours at the YMCA for a weekly [women-only] swim."

However, there are certain activities from her old life for which Christina will never find a Muslim-sanctioned alternative. "My husband and I don't go to the ballet, movies, or concerts," she acknowledged, "because mixed sexes sit together in the audience, and performers are often not modestly dressed. But," she assured, "I don't feel I'm missing out on much." While eighth-century Muslims might have condemned belly dancing and dueling spectacles, the restrictions of today's Islam range from *Swan Lake* to Monday-night football—a broad boycott against even the slightest suggestion of sexuality, violence, or immorality. Yet it would be misleading to suggest that American Muslims are somehow like the Amish, cut off from mainstream society, fixated only on the preservation of their own religious system. Indeed, so long as it doesn't compromise their unambiguous code of conduct, Muslims eat, work, and play alongside the rest of us.

Considering the focus, sacrifice, and high expectations indicative of modern Muslim life, I wondered if Christina's many years of training as a professional ballerina didn't inadvertently prepare her for the demands of her religious performance. She agreed they had, but said that even more significant had been "the perspective" her previous life afforded her current one. "I'm learning how wonderful it is to spend time *at home*," she said, "and realizing what true intimacy is all about." Avoiding what she now considers destructive distractions—rampant consumerism, vanity, popular entertainment, drugs, and alcohol—Christina said her relationships with other people have deepened.

"But even when you're selective, you can never totally control your environment in this information age—it's a real challenge," she admitted. Christina's willingness to face that challenge head-on reminded me of something theologian Huston Smith once wrote: "To be a slave to God is to be freed from other forms of slavery—ones that are degrading, such as slavery to greed, or to anxiety, or to the desire for personal status."[7] Christina did seem unusually secure and happy, possessing an inner quietude that she said came directly from her faith, and from being relieved of the expendable preoccupations that have come to define much of American life. The energy she once spread thinly in dozens of directions, she now pours into the priorities of Islam: God, mosque, family, humanity, and peacefulness.

As I listened to Christina compare lifestyles, I found myself dwelling on the countless hours and dollars that are, every day, forfeited to televisions, computer screens, bathroom mirrors, treadmills, malls, drug dealers, and bars—often at the expense of relationships and obligations. Islam aims to remove from its path whatever might inhibit direct connection to God and between individuals, redefining in nonmaterial terms a desirable life experience built on the temperament of decisive restraint. Universal yearnings are recast by the Qur'an to allow for the one thing America's competitive and consumptive worldview can never afford us: enduring satisfaction.

"It's not always easy to practice with the cluttered, instant world we live in," Christina said, as she enumerated her acts of daily devotion. "In ways big and small, I have to work hard to stay focused, like when I'm praying in my office and suddenly hear the little song coming from my computer telling me I've just received an e-mail; I have to fight against jumping up to see who it's from. But when I stay focused for the five daily prayers, or when I fast, I reconnect to myself and to God, and regain the vital realization that I'm not really in control of everything, though I might feel I am, or want to be. And there is peace in realizing and accepting this."

Christina applauded the promise America holds for its devout Muslim citizens. "Our country's founding documents espouse high morals that reflect our Founders' long-term vision," she said. "And with the equality and opportunities found in this country, changes continually unfold that

make it easier for Muslims to observe their faith as written in the Qur'an."
As examples, she pointed to the nearly seventeen hundred mosques flourishing all around America, the many Muslim schools with compliant dress codes and curriculum, and the necessary *hallal* (religiously sanctioned) restaurants and butchers that can be found in most urban areas.

"I feel like I'm on the cutting edge of a faith that has been in existence for a long time," said Christina, "but is just now coming into its own in this country. The international Muslim community is watching America as *the* experiment in freedom, equality, faith, and cultural intersection."

Long after Boston's rush-hour traffic had dwindled just beyond the walls of the mosque, inside our labor of devotion was just gaining speed. Arabic chants rang out like a school bell calling us back for study. Following Ramadan tradition, the Qur'an was read aloud, as it had been on each of the previous nights, a task normally managed by a mosque's imam or another male congregant who has committed all one hundred and fourteen chapters of the holy book to *memory*. The portions of the Qur'an read aloud multiply throughout Ramadan's thirty days, until, by the final night, its entirety has been digested not once but twice. Gaining momentum with time, families commonly haul sleeping bags and blankets into their mosques for the month's concluding nights, grabbing catnaps between standing-room-only Qur'anic vigils punctuated by rounds of group prayer.

"The last ten days of Ramadan are *exhausting*," confirmed Christina a few nights later when we again sat next to each other for what she said would "probably" be the last night of Ramadan. Each year, the end of the holy period is determined by a confirmed sighting of the moon over Saudi Arabia, giving overcast skies the authority to temporarily extend the observance. Awaiting the official word as twilight fell, everyone in the mosque went about their ritual, business as usual: washing, praying, and ending the day's refrain with figs and water. After sharing another communal meal eaten picnic-style on the floor, we settled in for the extended bedtime story of the Qur'an, picking up where we had left off the night before. In the burned-out listeners I sensed restlessness, an unspoken, heavy-eyed hope that the moon would indeed stand brightly in witness to the closure of this lengthy worldwide ceremony. Between verses, the much-anticipated confirmation arrived via an international phone tree, eliciting a joyful exchange of kisses on hands and cheeks. Like toy tops, the children spun in circles, colliding with one another, unable to contain their excitement about the following day.

As the capper to every Ramadan, *eid* is a festive holiday of presents and sweets celebrated at the end of the month given to sacrifice. With the eve of *eid* officially in motion, the mosque's crowd almost immediately began to thin, the devotional slumber party broken up as sleeping bags were rerolled and taken home for a much-earned good night's sleep in bed. A few women remained in formation, listening as the last of their holy book was read.

I watched one stalwart prepubescent girl wrestle the demon of slumber that threatened to overtake her. She wrapped her scrawny arms around a structural pipe for support, like a 1950s poodle-skirted teenager slumped over her dance partner. While fasting is not required of pregnant or nursing women, the elderly, or the sick, most children begin to join their family and community in fasting, as a religious rite of passage, between the ages of seven and ten.

During a pause in the Qur'an recitation, I asked the young girl, whose parents had emigrated from Pakistan, if this was her first Ramadan observance. She said, quite proudly, that it was her *third,* though she'd never been permitted to stay up so late, which explained her determination to prevail. I asked her why she had made such a grown-up commitment to fast. "For the reward of heaven," she replied, respectfully leaving off the implied "duh." Forcing her eyes open, she recounted the Qur'an's fertile promise that the afterlife is "ten times whatever you wish." Her particular heart's desire may have looked something like an animated version of the Candyland game—chocolate-front property with gingerbread houses roomy enough to accommodate her entire extended family.

In the competition with oneself for the afterlife prize of heaven, the Qur'an bluntly proclaims that there will be winners and losers.[8] The winners—those who worship God and avoid evil—are promised an eternity of whatever pleasures have been so strictly prohibited on earth. The losers—those who ignore God and indulge in wickedness—will, unfortunately, be exiled to "hellfire" where they will writhe for a million nights and as many days. At ten, the girl was emboldened by the realization that the conditions of her afterlife would be solely determined by the fortitude of the life she was now living. No one likes to think they're missing out, especially when it comes to chocolate rivers, fountains of youth, and everlasting glory. This, along with the human appetite for insurance and guarantees, is the incentive upon which Islam most relies.

As I talked more with the drowsy, willful girl, her father popped his head into the room to check on his family. When I'd shared the gist of our exchange with him, he affirmed, as much, I suspected, for his daughter's benefit as for mine: "Paradise lies between hope and fear. We fast and pray to please Allah, and the hope that we have achieved that obligation inspires us to continue." With that, he turned on his heel to answer his own final call to prayer with the men upstairs.

When I finally left the mosque, there were still a handful of women counting a few last votes for God on their fingertips. Once inside the car I had driven to avoid walking Boston's darkened streets alone, I unpinned the head covering I had become adept at folding and fastening, scratching my freed forehead and scalp with relief. As I drove back to my apartment, I dreamed of the next morning with a tiny thrill, anticipating the resumption of my ritual posture at the corner coffee shop: a latte in one hand, a bagel in the other, shoulders squared over the morning paper. I thought of the Muslims who would likewise wake with the kind of appreciation for the ordinary that comes when you go without it. If Islam is all about having things to look forward to in heaven, then its practice of Ramadan is about remembering there is also much to relish right here on earth.

Buddhism

Chapter Thirteen

A round 560 B.C.—centuries before the birth of Jesus of Nazareth—a boy named Siddhartha Gautama was born to a king in what is now Nepal. Painstakingly sheltered from the world and its suffering teeming beyond the walls of his family's privilege, Siddhartha was groomed to be heir to his father's royal legacy. But at the age of twenty-nine, disguising himself as a peasant, Siddhartha fled his palace and its riches, determined to shape for himself a different kind of destiny.

For years, in relentless pursuit of wisdom and inner peace, Siddhartha anonymously explored the religious practices of his Hindu homeland, but found himself dissatisfied with their offerings. Eventually he decided to forge his own path to spiritual ascension, an experiment that culminated in forty days of sequestered, uninterrupted meditation, at the end of which he was symbolically reborn as the Buddha (the word derives from the Sanskrit root budh, denoting both "to wake up" and "to know").

Making a decisive choice to share his discoveries in hopes of lessening the suffering of others, the Buddha spent forty-five years teaching his philosophy and practice, a set of disciplined exercises that did not include the worshiping of a Creator or a pantheon of deities. Instead Siddhartha's methodology was concerned with the attainment of "awakened mind"—commonly known as enlightenment. Revolutionary in a strict caste-system culture, the Buddha proclaimed that inner liberation was accessible to anyone with the right intention and effort.

It wasn't long before people of every age and social rank began to open their throats in chant, bend their knees to bow, and cross their legs to meditate for hours, days, and years on end. They all sought the Buddha's earthly promised land: inner stability and clarity, freedom from unnecessary suffering, and the neutralization of "karma"—the repercussions of one's earthly actions, words, and deeds. The Buddha's techniques of mental discipline and heightened awareness, and his extensive code of moral conduct, became known as "the middle path"—a way of life poised between the ascetic and the indulgent.

Following the natural course of most world religions, time and shifting geography incited rival interpretations of the Buddha's Four Noble Truths about suffering and his Eightfold Path of alleviation. With independent styles and techniques, and varying doctrinal emphases, the various teachers and "schools" that emerged to impart the Buddha's message were given shelter and continuity under one of three primary headings: Mahayana ("great vehicle"), Hinayana ("small vehicle"), and Vajrayana ("indestructible vehicle"). As the Dalai Lama has said regarding the diversity of Buddhism: "Our human mind always likes different approaches. There is a richness in the fact that there are so many different presentations of 'the way.' "[1]

Throughout the nineteenth century, as more Asian meditation masters visited and established schools in Western countries, Americans began earnestly exploring Siddhartha's discourses as preserved in the "sutras" and walking the Buddhist path of liberation. Extracted from its original cultural packaging, American Buddhism has flourished, in many cases engendering a more egalitarian and democratic form of its teachings. Today, nearly every school of Buddhism is practiced in America by converts and immigrant populations alike, constituting roughly two and a half million disciples.

Meditating with Masters

Unable to sleep on my assigned bony futon in a room of snoring strangers, I lay awake, dreading the impending wake-up call. My mind and my glow-in-the-dark watch seemed to be competing in the same relay race, two instruments ticking round and round. In a matter of hours, I would be occupied entirely by exercises designed to quiet the mind, a task that felt more insurmountable with each passing minute.

Finally drifting off to sleep, I was jolted moments later by a loud GONG!—a sound that traveled through me as if it had emanated from inside my chest. In the predawn gloom, I glimpsed a cropped-haired, gray-robed figure clutching a saucer-shaped bell still reverberating from its blow.

Within fifteen minutes we were all—residents and visitors alike—dressed and standing ready in the Cambridge Zen Center's dharma room, a space dedicated to formal Buddhist teaching and meditation. For these Zen practitioners, morning bows—a symbolic gesture of inner awakening—are like the ritual morning cup of coffee for the rest of us.

With as much grace and energy as can be mustered at 5 A.M., everyone around me dropped to their knees onto small cushions, their foreheads brought briefly to rest on the ground, their hands thrust forward, palms up. Maintaining physical fluidity, both hands were then turned over and used to push the body upward again, with a bend at the waist for a culminating half bow, hands clasped over the heart. For devout practitioners, this "full bow" is repeated at least one hundred and eight times each morning, three hundred and sixty-five days a year.

I broke into a sweat as I bowed again and again, my own labored breath the only sound I could hear besides the *swish* of arms and legs in motion. By bow one hundred, I could easily envision letting go of all my attachments and desires—the source of all suffering, says the Buddha—in exchange for a single pair of knee pads. I found myself distracted not only by the strain of my uncooperative muscles, but also by the stoic supervision of the Buddha, whose statue sat, like a miniature well-fed king, on an altar to my right. I must confess that meeting the physical challenge of the morning's first active meditation was as much as I could handle. Its deeper spiritual significance—to convey a willingness to both give and receive spiritual liberation—felt, at least at that hour, beyond my reach.

In a nation born of rebellion against idolatry and monarchy, the submissive connotations of bowing do not come naturally. Not only did the custom feel foreign to my body and my mind, I wasn't sure what or whom I was bowing to. Familiar with this apprehension, one of the monks later assured me that while gestures of appreciation are paid to the Buddha for his invaluable teachings, his personage is not to be worshiped. Rather, the act of bowing, whether directed toward a statue of the Buddha or the foot of a teacher, is intended to honor the bower's *own* "Buddha-nature." By this, he meant the clear-sighted, utterly compassionate potential in each of us that is pristinely reflected in the Buddha's example. As the Cambridge Zen Center's founding master, Seung Sahn, has written: "Small I (ego) is bowing to Big I (our true nature). Then Small I disappears and becomes Big I. This is true bowing."[2]

A system that developed in China in the sixth and seventh centuries, Zen Buddhism, like all Buddhist schools, teaches as its primary practice a form of sitting meditation called *"zazen,"* from *za,* "sitting," and *zen,* "absorption." As is common among Zen masters, Seung Sahn prescribes upwards of four hours of *zazen* per day for the lay monks and nuns who reside in his center. But during retreats, meditation—for *all* attendees— becomes like a triathlon of the mind; *zazen* can go on for more than *twelve* hours a day.

To prepare for my retreat's intensive schedule of not only sitting, but walking, bowing, chanting, eating, and laboring Zen-style, I first took instruction at the center on an "outpatient" basis. Coached mostly by a bookish twenty-something monk named Ben, I put myself through a thirty-day training regimen. I told Ben that it was unlikely I would be able to meditate on my own for more than half an hour a day. He assured me that even twenty minutes of daily or semiregular "concentrated sitting" was, over time, enough to greatly improve anyone's mental stability and quality of life. "Plus," he added, "there is no 'right' way to realization, no one way 'to Zen.'"

In conveying the basic fundamentals, Ben recommended I sit in "full lotus position" (legs crossed with each foot propped up on the opposite thigh). My hands were placed one inside of the other, thumbs arching above my palms to form an oval—the "cosmic *mudra,*" a symbol of the universe—and casually held at the navel. Ben instructed me to keep my eyes "half open" and "soft-focused" on the floor with a "wide perspective." When I asked why I shouldn't close my eyes like other meditators I'd seen, he said, "Open eyes helps cure people from the sickness of being lost in their own world."

Ben suggested I clear my mind and focus only on the rise and fall of my breath. "But don't fight the thoughts that come," he said, recommending that I acknowledge them, like someone passing me on a sidewalk, and then return to the gradual rise and fall of my breath. To help keep my mind from wandering too far, Ben recommended one of Seung Sahn's techniques: to silently repeat the mantra "clear mind" while inhaling, and "don't know" while exhaling. It is a simple chant designed to slowly recondition its speaker to greet life without preconceived notions and judgments, only with curiosity and innocence. Like Christians who are asked to come to their practice of prayer and devotion like children, Buddhists are taught, in the words of Seung Sahn, that "Zen mind is children's mind"—a space and time untouched by the erosion of overintellectualization and the cementing of opinions.

Paradoxically, Seung Sahn also describes the attainment of this childlike awakening as a process of maturation, offering his students the image of a wheel to illustrate the ground any person must cover on the way to spiritual mastery. The first quarter of the seeker's journey, he says, is invariably occupied by attachment "to thinking," which, through diligent practice, progresses into attachment "to emptiness," followed by a period of attachment "to freedom" (otherwise known as nirvana), and finally reaching "no-attachment thinking." This final state is one of pristine perception that is neither overly attached to, nor too detached from, self, others, and the physical world.[3]

To this end, Seung Sahn warns of the dangers of excessively loitering in the echoey halls of emptiness, or of getting too comfortable on the couch of nirvana, or gazing too long into the seductive eyes of detachment, lest one form an attachment to *that*. As Japanese Zen Master Takuan Soho has written, "The mind that does not stop at all is called immovable wisdom."[4] For the Buddhist who never gets stuck, no-attachment thinking is a kind of inner observatory—a state of transparent awakeness from which all actions, words, and thoughts can be seen for exactly what they are, not what our subjective perspectives expect or make them out to be.

A retreat like the one I attended is a haven where time and personal concerns are put on hold. It's an environment ideal for what Seung Sahn calls a "beginner's mind," which is, despite the sound of it, the goal of enlightened mastery. But as a *literal* beginner, I inadvertently became everyone's source of distraction as we completed our morning rounds of bows and sitting meditation, and prepared for our first communal meal. Given the "noble" silence and no-eye-contact policy, I couldn't ask questions about how mealtime worked. So I trailed behind a woman with a shaved head—the hallmark of having taken "refuge" in the Buddha's teachings. Doing as she did, I retrieved a bundle from a shelf near the kitchen and returned to my meditation cushion with a wordless bow to the Buddha-essence buried within me.

Imitating the lay monk and nun to my left and right, I untied the cloth bundle containing a stack of bowls, a spoon, and chopsticks, and arranged them in a constellation around me. Servers carried in big pots of food and kettles of tea and set them down in the middle of the room, adjusting each slightly to the left or the right to create symmetry between them all. After a prayerlike pause, the expressionless servers each lifted a pot and carried it around our rectangular configuration of cushions, silently filling the bowls we held up to them. When it was my turn, I watched passively as my server generously piled, and piled, a towering mound of goo into my oversized bowl. Setting my bowl in front of me, I identified its contents as oatmeal—a food that has never been a personal favorite. Glancing at others' portions, I was mystified as to why I'd been singled out as the one with the appetite of a lumberjack. I wondered how I would slyly slip my leftovers to the garbage disposal or perhaps to a nearby enlightened dog.

The room's tranquil etiquette was split by the loud clack of the *moktak*—a fish-shaped wooden paddle struck by the palm of the hand—and just like the race to bow, the race to eat was on. I sat, stunned, as everyone lifted their bowls, opened their gullets and inhaled their food like frat boys chugging beers. I began to take normal-sized bites of the bland mush, chewing and swallowing at the rate at which I'd always eaten flavorless food. It seemed that within a minute, everyone had emptied and returned their bowls to their designated place on the floor. A monk came by and filled a second bowl with a steaming brown liquid. Once again I was unwittingly dealt a jumbo serving, but figured that at least the tea would help wash down the oatmeal. Our third bowl was filled with plain water, which everyone used to wash out their two already-empty bowls, slurping every last drop of the murky remnants, and restacking the bowls on top of one another. Everyone's focus was then redirected toward the center of the room in silent, panoramic meditation as they waited patiently for this straggler to finish.

I'd read that for most Buddhists, eating is a meditative act, and had anticipated a slowly-chew-your-food-fifty-times-before-swallowing approach. And I later learned that this, indeed, is the norm among a number of Buddhist schools, which sometimes even require the student to fill thirty minutes with the savoring of a single raisin. Digging deeper into my doughy heap, I suddenly understood that my companions and I were riding in Seung Sahn's fast lane of nonattachment. I knew our meditative objective was to wean ourselves from "form and name"—those identifiers we attach to all people and things, including breakfast foods.

It struck me that the only way I was going to get through my impasse of oatmeal was to overcome my thoughts *about it.* In this state of Buddha mind, there is neither bad nor good, neither pleasing nor displeasing, for judgments and preferences do not exist when there is complete and utter dedication to the present—in my case, present bite. In a rather desperate attempt to save—or prove—myself, I closed my eyes and emptied my thoughts along with my bowl. And then, sipping the tea, which at first tasted like the bitter guts of a decomposing tree, I emptied more thoughts, followed by the last drops of liquid.

Re-creating the steps I'd observed, I cleaned the sides of the oatmeal bowl using my third container of water and index finger, and then drank everything that remained—each action imbued with purpose, utilitarian function, and self-sufficiency.

After stacking and rewrapping my bowls in their miniature sarong, I assumed the meditative position, feeling heavy and sick. Rising up from our cushions without a sound or a wandering glance, we returned our bowls to their rightful place on the shelf.

Later, I learned that when the bowls are being filled, the recipients give a subtle twist of the wrist to signal when they've received enough, sign language I put to use for the rest of our meals. But I was grateful for the lesson that came from my ignorance.

After a few days of meditation—hours and hours of it, in many forms—I hit some thick walls. My greatest challenge was maintaining for more than a nanosecond that space in my consciousness called "before thinking." This is Buddha's ultrastable zone of reality, uncluttered by reviews of the past, speculation about the future, and thoughts spurred by physical discomfort. With my "before thinking" oatmeal triumph behind me, it seemed the more I tried to get ahead of my thoughts, the faster they came. Just to make it halfway around Seung Sahn's circle of enlightenment to the understanding of emptiness, sameness, and nothingness, I realized I was going to have to undo decades of tutored study.

Like most Americans, I'd been methodically primed for the pursuit of relationships, higher education, ambition, and acquisition—all in the name of happiness. But life, liberty, and the pursuit of . . . nothingness? Having attempted both, I now sensed that to achieve Buddha's nothingness required even more backbone than to achieve the American Dream's somethingness. My ingrained assumptions, knee-jerk reactions, and opinions about *everything* were keeping me from what Seung Sahn calls "losing your mind"—a way of halting the intellect long enough to perceive Buddhism's ultimate truth: the oneness of existence, or, inversely, the illusion of separation.

While the practice of prayer requires the articulation of thoughts, beliefs, and longings, meditation asks that we simply relax our thoughts and allow things to be as they are. "There is nowhere to go, nothing to achieve, nothing to do except be *here*," reiterated every Buddhist teacher I'd meet in an effort to help me lose my mind. And for maybe a blissful few minutes of every forty-five-minute meditation session, I would simply be *there*. I would be genuinely and acutely aware of *only* the feeling in my body and the conditions of the room in which I sat—the brightness of the light falling on the floor in my sight line, the grain, texture, and color of the wood, and the dryness or moisture in the air—experiencing everything as it actually was, without wandering off down some random mental corridor. It felt like a feat of astounding proportions for a chronic multitasker. When my thoughts would gang up on me, often four at a time, I would sometimes be able to make note of their bullying and simply dismiss them, coming back to an integrated, single-pointed focus. Much of the time, however, I'd catch myself roaming some inner hallway, having no recollection of how and when I'd turned the corner from presence to absence of mind.

Everyone assured me that even master meditators are not free from their psyche's harassment—"monkey mind," as the Buddha called it. However, I still felt at a unique, potentially insurmountable disadvantage. I found myself warning anyone who attempted to encourage me that I had spent the last decade in Hollywood—in the *cradle* of illusion—as if to prepare them for my hardened case. But given Buddhists' impartiality to form and name, my former address seemed immaterial to them. In their eyes my hindrances were the same as everyone else's.

I remained frustrated by my inability to beat my mind at its own game. I wanted to taste the fruits of the Buddha's *bodhi* tree, not just look longingly at them swinging overhead. Yet I seriously wondered if years spent inhaling the smoggy vapor of Los Angeles had contaminated my insides with an acute resistance to the sweet stillness of serenity.

As with any proud, industrious place, Hollywood is dependent upon its populace's unquenchable desires—their urgency to create, prosper, be seen, heard, and acknowledged. It's a formula that feeds on insecurity, comparison, and an enormous wattage of human energy, instilling in willing participants a fear that no matter how much they give of themselves, it's never enough, because someone, somewhere is giving—and thus achieving—*more*. To survive, much less thrive in this phantasmic subculture, most people take to wearing a second skin, a superpersona of invincibility that comes to feel as necessary as medical scrubs in a real-life ER unit. In the name-dropping, form-obsessed capital of the world, which I had navigated for over a decade, it seemed the only time people removed their protective armor in public—revealing even a glimpse of the Buddha's universal, bare self—was alone behind the wheel of their car, shielded by metal and glass.

It was during long hours of commuting that I observed more closely our collective pauses from the demands of expectation and performance. Like department store Santas on break behind the Dumpster, beard in one hand, cigarette in the other, most of us looked lost in regurgitations and projections of then and when, how, and why—so many toys, so little time, and definitely no room for beginner's mind. Being self-aware, as the

Buddha had taught, is a particular challenge for those of us juggling more than one self.

The Buddha says desire—like the desire to be someone or somewhere else—is what separates us from happiness and wholeness and makes us suffer, if only existentially. But I saw no way out of this, having been programmed to never be satisfied, to be ambitious, to never really rest, though I may sleep. I'd left the physical boundaries of Hollywood two years earlier, and yet its impulses still fired in me, making me desire and doubt as if I were still there. So far, the magic meditation serum had not yet worked on this recovering overamped city dweller who, at least for the moment, was hiding out in a place where nobody knew her name. But in my efforts and constant study, I at least found validation for my flailing. "The Buddha has pointed out that the mind, when one starts to try to withdraw it from its evil resorts, is like a fish taken from its native water and lying thrashing on the bank. Here we have it in practice—but everyone finds, or has found, the same problem."[5]

"Start where you are *now*," a new monk implored in another attempt to sever my overidentification with past and place, form and name. Paraphrasing his master's teaching, he said, "Put it down. Whatever you're mentally attached to, hanging on to, harboring—put it down, leave it behind. You cannot progress if there's a part of you that's enjoying the resentment and anger; you can't get well if a part of you secretly enjoys carrying the attention around." He was onto something. I began to see that I was attached to what I saw as my identity: a half-crazed girl from a half-crazed place.

Eager for further focused instruction, I signed up for another retreat—this time with an American-born teacher of Tibetan Buddhism, Lama Surya Das. Surya Das tutored about sixty of us—mostly middle-aged Caucasian "upper-middle path" people, as he joked—in his Dzogchen (pronounced "zochen") tradition. Considered by many to be the consummate path of Tibetan Buddhism, Dzogchen reverses the gradual realization of Seung Sahn's circle by *starting* with a newly enlightened perspective and working backward through a practice of mental purification. Surya Das introduced it to us this way: "Instead of schlepping up a mountain of enlightenment, we swoop down from above and start with the view of things as they *are*— pure reality, and a recognition that we already *are* natural perfection." Simplifying it even further, he said, "It's not as much about Buddha as it is about *you*-dha."

Before becoming a Dzogchen master with a disarming sense of humor, Lama Surya Das was a middle-class, vaguely religious Jewish boy named Jeffrey Miller who grew up on Long Island. Coming of age in the sixties, he had (among other classic experiences from that decade) a close encounter with the Kent State shootings and, like countless others, became disillusioned by the conflicts and contradictions of American society. Deciding the "fight for world peace" was too oxymoronic, and unaware of his own tradition's mysticism, Miller turned to the East in search of *inner* peace.

For a decade he shuttled between India and Asia under the tutelage of a number of Buddhist and Hindu teachers, most of whom were Tibetan monks driven from their homeland by the Chinese government. Settling on the Dzogchen tradition, Miller was eventually recognized as an enlightened master in his own right and enthroned as a lama—a title of authority comparable to priest or rabbi.

Surya Das, with his cut-to-the-chase brand of Buddhism, has good news for fellow Americans hoping to shorten the fermentation process of enlightenment: it can be done in a matter of *years*, not lifetimes. The Buddha himself decreed, at least in theory, that it is possible for realization to occur, without any preparation, in a literal second. Between bites of oatmeal, even. Before meeting Surya Das, I had assumed that was just good old-fashioned—or rather, ancient—advertising.

Not exactly corroborating the Buddha's millisecond claim, Surya Das did insist we "lighten up about enlightenment." He pledged to teach us everything we needed to know about liberation in one week. "You don't need to read a library of books, pilgrimage to distant lands, or retreat for years in a meditation cell—it's simple and right here," he proposed. He spoke from an elevated cushion, encircled by sacred Tibetan bells, bowls, and drums. While his words evoked something like an enlightenment infomercial, what Surya Das imparts cannot ultimately be bought with six easy installments, though he does convey in a matter of days the essence of what took him years to learn from libraries and distant lands.

"Americans have a tendency to overlook the humor inherent in life, especially the humor in what we consider *unpleasant*," Surya Das said one afternoon of the retreat. He insists that humor and laughter allow us the chance to step back from the melodrama of life and observe it objectively, rather than getting swept up in it. Offering the image of a street circus, he suggested that the wanting, trying, doing, forcing, getting, loving, fighting, feeling, failing, and forging that make up daily life should be seen as a magnificent spectacle passing us by—an illusion of grand proportions that, unlike the soul, is impermanent.

As a Westerner and a newcomer to Buddhism, I had long thought of it strictly as an escape hatch—a way of numbing the anxieties and stresses of everyday life that are, after all, not really real. And I found that this is the case for some people, who separate the practice of meditation from its broader foundation of ethics and compassion. Most Buddhists are taught to take what they've accrued in practice and apply it, like a salve, to the suffering of *others*. As Surya Das said to us, "No Buddhist goes away to meditate for the sake of going away; you go away to come back with full hands." Like other religious disciplines, Buddhism teaches its followers to be *in the world, but not of it*. In other words, contribute to its betterment without succumbing to its corruption.

Suggesting we each designate a quiet room in our home as a kind of temporary isolation tank, Surya Das provided three essential meditations to take in with us. The first was reminiscent of the panoramic open-eye Zen method, though without the "clear mind/don't know" mantra. The second was "sky-gazing" or "space-mingling," in which you gaze at a seamless space, such as a cloudless sky. The third was a simple walking meditation— "just walking," he said, "naturally and deliberately."

On each of our days together, we formed a circle with about a yard of space between us to practice this slow-motion walking exercise. Occupying our minds with the minutest movements in our bodies—the gradual lift of the foot, the bend of the knee, the pressure on the heel, then the ball of the foot—we attempted to remain so "presently in the moment" that each increment was a new and unfamiliar event. According to Surya Das, "natural meditations," like the three shared with us, are reliant upon simplicity, authenticity, spontaneity, and complete "awakeness."

Someone in our group raised his hand to ask if meditation masters, like Surya Das, experienced bouts of equanimity and clarity that were longer lasting than the ones he was managing. "The challenges continue no matter how long you practice," Surya Das said. Earlier I'd overheard a psychologist in the group say that, on average, the human mind experiences a new incoming thought about every three seconds, and that the majority of these thoughts aren't even new at all, but redundantly and relentlessly *recy-*

cled. While our steady stream of thoughts cannot be stopped, Surya Das said, we *can* affect our relationship to those thoughts, and that is what allows us to experience suffering and desire in a way that frees us from their strangulating grip.

Somewhere around the third day of the Dzogchen retreat, while "just" gazing out the window at the blueness of the sky, I had a moment of clarity that was more than fleeting. It was a truly restful feeling and yet I felt more awake than ever before. I could suddenly see the value of cultivating this clarity for life beyond the meditation cushion, applied to situations that would normally conjure in me impatience, anger, fear, or defensiveness. I was excited by the tangible possibility of acting with conscious thought, rather than reacting from old emotions. I got a glimpse of being as generously clear with others as the open sky was with me.

Having reached a temporary cease-fire with the forces of my thoughts, I stumbled into an unselfconsciousness that called to mind round four of the peyote medicine circle. I felt a sense of wanting transformation while simultaneously accepting things (including myself) as they are. I was neither clinging too tightly to this desire nor pushing it away, which reminded me of something I'd read in one of Seung Sahn's books: "Aspiration is . . . desire without attachment. If enlightenment comes, good. If enlightenment does not come, good. Actually, this *is* enlightenment."[6]

Then I realized I'd caught myself *thinking* about how well I might be understanding the teachings, instead of simply *doing* them. In the domino effect of the mind, I was then reminded of a private consultation I'd had at the Cambridge Zen Center with one of Seung Sahn's master students, Popsinim Brown. She'd said to me, "Insights are fine, but as soon as you get one, release it; do not hold on to it. Keep coming back to"— *WHACK!* With swift force, she struck the floor between us with a billy club she always carried, like some kind of dharma cop. "Come back to don't-know mind," she charged. "Keep it simple. *This* moment is all we have for certain—stay in it."

Popsinim Brown's teacher, Seung Sahn, has compared this moment-to-moment clarity to a calculator. Describing Buddhist practice as that which brings the practitioner again and again back to "zero," he teaches that by continually clearing our accumulation of mental and emotional calculations (our preoccupation with the past and future), we are guaranteed accuracy in our moment-to-moment perceptions of the present. This accuracy of perception, in turn, prompts appropriate, mindful action, which creates, when exponentially multiplied by the lives of individuals, a more even-keeled world. Formal meditation, the sound of the baton striking the floor, the mantra of "clear mind . . . don't know," and the dong of the dharma bell are all synonymously utilized as a CLEAR button inside the well-trained mind of a Buddhist.

Popsinim Brown was so adamant I understand this, she continued to assault the floor with precise blows whenever she sensed my mind was wandering, or whenever my answers to her riddlelike questions failed to reflect Zen-like clarity. It seemed a curious tactic to try to *stun* someone into spiritual liberation. But then again I had to admit how effective that *WHACK!* was in bringing me back to the moment, and to the realization that if I remained *absolutely* present, her strikes no longer held the element of surprise. This calm readiness for whatever came was ultimately what she hoped I'd take with me into the world. Since my encounter with Popsinim Brown, I've heard stories about Zen masters smacking their *students* instead of the floor, or shrieking in their ear without warning, or even throwing them from second-story windows—all to instill the same rug-pulling, zeroing effect.

Through meditation and the array of Buddhists I met, I came to recognize the peaks and valleys of Hollywood as having been my most indispensable crazy-wise teacher. The place had thrown me from my ledge of complacency, rousing me to flee its palace in search of greater understanding. But now when I think of its palm tree–lined streets, I also realize that the perspective I fled to find would have, given the same intention and effort, been just as easily gained there amid the mansions and poverty, personalized license plates and strategically augmented body parts. Buddhist practice takes its seeker on a circuitous, sometimes harrowing adventure only to arrive back at the point where one began. We wake up and meet and appreciate the courage, heart, intellect, and promise that were, all along, right there.

I've begun to learn to change my thoughts *about* my old city, to experience it no longer as an obstacle to clarity, but rather as a vehicle for it.

It was not unlike a giant vat of oatmeal from which unexpected truths can come.

Hinduism

Chapter Fourteen

Also known as "Sanatana Dharma"—or eternal faith—Hinduism was given its name by the Greek forces that invaded northwestern India under Alexander the Great. Reaching the banks of the Indus River, the soldiers dubbed the people they encountered there "Indoos," or "Hindus," though the religious system dominant among the country's inhabitants existed long before foreigners gave it the name.[1] Predating the records of all other primary world religions, Hindu beliefs and practices evolved gradually out of the widespread cultural worship of a pantheon of deities combined with the development of complex yoga disciplines.

Hinduism regards its gods and goddesses as myriad representations of the one supreme Creator or universal soul, known in Sanskrit as "Brahma." Both a ritualistic and ascetic practice, Hinduism promises to unveil the true spiritual nature of the human being through three pursuits: to know, to embody, and to seek joy.[2] Accommodating individual temperaments and progressive social, emotional, and spiritual development, the Hindu path adapts to each stage of human life—from student, to pleasure seeker, to worldly householder, to sage—converging at samaddhi: complete absorption into the Brahman, or Absolute Truth. This state of oneness (also known as moksha)—the experience of no separation between self and other—is analogous to Buddhism's enlightenment.

Indeed, given the cultural and spiritual springboard Hinduism provided the Buddha, the objectives of the two religious systems are intimately related. Discarding the ceremonialism attached to Hinduism's deities and the limitations of India's caste system, the Buddha simplified and made widely accessible the essence of liberation long sought by the elite among his fellow Hindu countrymen.

Though Hindus visited and settled in the United States throughout the twentieth century, the decade of the 1960s brought with it the first significant wave of emigration to the West. Many gathered together in storefronts and in living rooms for traditional group ceremonies, eventually erecting and consecrating temples all across America—from Houston, to Pittsburgh, to Flint, Michigan.[3] As with Buddhism, many Americans have embraced a more egalitarian form of Hindu beliefs and practices, fostering an environment free of discrimination in which all people can seek the inner elevation of sammadhi. With growing interest and openness, America has drawn to it an influx of Hindu teachers, called "gurus," who help advance students along their path toward infinite being, awareness, and bliss. Today there are more than seven hundred million Hindus worldwide, with an estimated one million residing in the United States.

Worshiping with Devotees

I stared intently at the living room wall, searching for the extra dimensions those around me seemed to effortlessly perceive. Everyone spoke under their breath, as if engaged in quiet, intimate conversation with the collage of photographs that hung there. To my twelve companions, the framed images were a portal into timeless rapture. Gazing through their heavenly window, however, all I saw was an East Indian woman with coffee-colored skin, dark brown gleaming eyes, a contented smiling mouth, and gentle-looking hands frozen in midmotion. But to those seated next to me, this woman was a divinely cast manifestation of God, one capable of transporting them to a more ecstatic place.

Formally known as Mata Amritanandamayi Devi, and more affectionately as Ammachi (the Mother), the woman is considered by many to be a *guru*—an expeller of darkness and messenger of enlightenment. Ammachi leads her multiethnic disciples toward light and knowledge by giving them and teaching them profound love.

Her love is great; Her Love is endless.
Her Love is vaster than the sea.
Oh, Amma, please come and take my hand;
Open my heart, lead me to thee.

Sitting on the floor of the unremarkable living room, Ammachi's devotees began this energetic chant of praise, called a *bhajan,* accompanied by an assortment of instruments. We sang in both English and Sanskrit—I followed along with the aid of printed lyrics—and our voices melded with the organlike bellows of the Indian harmonium and the throbbing of the drums. The haunting, repetitive rhythms of those four lines, combined with the intoxication of trapped incense, were dizzying. It was as if a pulsating harmony were being circulated between us and the images of Ammachi placed all around.

After nearly three more hours of worshipful song, we released a few last *om*s from deep within our bellies, a primal tone believed to represent the universal cosmic vibration, the sound of all creation. For a while we sat in silence, though the music continued to ring, round and round, inside my head. And this, I gathered, was the very objective shared by these Pacific Northwest Hindu faithful—to stir an adoration so lasting as to echo through them for the remainder of the week.

Looking around the room, I felt strangely disconnected from the love written euphorically across each face. The worshipers' half smiles seemed almost smug. But then again, I've always been suspicious of a desire to be anyone's "disciple." The word itself reminds me of an after-school special I once saw on TV in which teenage runaways were lured by a cult leader to his sunny farm and brainwashed to be slavelike followers who blissfully tilled and harvested his fields from dawn till dusk. Watching this program as a teenager, the dangers of giving oneself over to a charismatic stranger were wedged into my psyche.

I wondered if those enchanted by Ammachi weren't also running away from something, perhaps a state of modern malaise, a viral sense of incompletion and emptiness. Or perhaps I was the one who was running, clinging tightly to my own reluctance to give in to anything that seemed too good to be true, even something as basic as unconditional love. Like a long-lost parent, Ammachi's affection appeared to fill psychic voids and heal emotional scars in her followers. And through the rituals of loving her back, Ammachi's disciples came closer to placing less meaning on what is ultimately impermanent, like the kind of cars we drive and the accolades of others. Instead, with Ammachi's help, these individuals pursued a sense of self measured solely by the amount of devotion they were able to give and receive. A life worth living became an epic love story that culminated in oneness with God and—by association—others.

Everyone remained cross-legged on the floor, staring longingly at the photographs of Ammachi, in deep concentration. My eyes drifted down the wall to an altar that bore a precisely placed collection of objects: an urn of water from the Ganges River, peacock feathers, shells, a vase of flowers, incense, tiny brass bells, fresh fruit, three unlit oil wicks, a plate of food, one cup of chocolate kisses, and a garland of pink rose petals—each article a sensual and sacred offering to Ammachi's likeness. Under the altar, atop a tiny pillow, rested a pair of rubber flip-flops once worn by the guru on her petite feet. (The feet themselves were the subject of a photo nearby, a thick snake coiled around one ankle.) Looking like any old pair of thongs to the uninitiated, they were, to these faithful, nothing short of magic slippers, still shimmering with the energy of the divine serpent charmer who had walked in them.

One of the devotees reached around the slippers to retrieve a copper tray onto which she placed the three oil wicks from the altar and a tiny pile of fragrant, incenselike camphor. Lighting each one, the young woman moved the gleaming, smoky tray in circles around the wall dedicated to Ammachi. Once the three flames symbolizing awareness, faith, and gratitude had been exhausted, our abbreviated *puja*—an act of ritualized reverence—was complete. Each devotee then waved the purifying camphor toward them praying as the smoke wreathed their head. Taking my turn, I splashed my face with the pungent swirls, reminded of Gene Begay's sage, the Catholic priest's incense, and the Muslim's ablution. From another tray, I dabbed a pile of ash as I'd seen others do, and pressed my powdery fingerprint just above the intersection of my eyebrows, leaving behind an oval *bindi*, an emblem of awakening the "third eye" as the seat of spiritual sight. Everyone's three eyes looked again toward the images of the guru.

Ammachi was born as Sudhamani in 1953 to a poor family on the west coast of India. Even as a child, she says, she was immersed in God—an all-powerful and impersonal Creator she and other Western-oriented Hindus equate with Brahman, their faith's title for the half-masculine, half-feminine source of all being. "From childhood I had an intense love of the Divine Name," writes Ammachi. "I would repeat the Lord's Name incessantly with every breath and a constant flow of divine thoughts was kept up in my mind, no matter the place where I was or the work I was doing."[4] But the young girl's precocious fixation was not immediately revered. In fact, according to her accounts, her own family shunned her, spurring local villagers to ridicule, stone, and even attempt to starve and poison her.

Undaunted, she remained in a state of "Oneness" with God until a mystical vision endowed her bliss with earthly purpose. Appearing in an orb of brilliant light and calling itself "the Divine Mother," the figure told Sudhamani: "Worship Me by showing mankind the way back to Me."[5] At that moment, Sudhamani was "reborn" as a physical manifestation of the Divine Mother's nurturing energy, a saint with a mission to quell the suffering of humankind, both practically, through social service programs, and spiritually, as a guru named Ammachi.

Children, as the breeze that blows through the trees has a soothing effect on travelers in the hot sun, so too a guru enables us to live in the scorching heat of worldly existence.

—AMMACHI

As a direct route "back" to the Divine Mother—or God—Ammachi teaches her disciples the yoga of devotion known as *bhakti*. Pursued through one of four inner doorways—the intellect (*jnana*), the physical (*karma*), the experimental nature (*raja*), or the emotional (*bhakti*)—yoga enables its practitioner to experience personally what can otherwise remain an abstract teaching. All paths of Hindu yoga—literally translated as "yoke" or "union"—are intended to achieve just that: an interwoven bond between those who practice it and their Creator. The devotional *bhakti* yoga practiced by Ammachi's followers—with its emotional outpouring of chants, offerings, and meditation—is designed to focus all attention on a love that flows through Ammachi from God. Known as "the hugging saint," Ammachi tours the world giving public talks after which throngs of people—both disciples and not—line up to be briefly embraced by her.

I attended one of these love fests in a downtown Seattle hotel, still desiring to understand firsthand what captivates Ammachi's devotees. Sitting on the floor at the foot of a draped stage, I waited with hundreds of others for Ammachi's unveiling. The excitement in the room was uncapped as the curtain of tapestries dropped, revealing the woman from the photographs now wrapped in hot pink, bright green, yellow, and gold silks. Thousands of flower petals were strewn over her and the stage as a collection of harmoniums played what sounded like an anthem to her godliness. We each held in our hand a number we'd been given at the door, telling us in which order our hug would be given.

For hours I watched people crawl, one and sometimes two at a time, across the bed of petals and into Ammachi's arms. When it came my turn, I was struck by the uncommon sweetness of her smile as she unhesitatingly wrapped me in a bear hug, rocking me back and forth, like a baby, for a few brief seconds. Having never been treated this way by a virtual stranger, I had to work consciously to accept Ammachi's gift. I was told that she psychically senses exactly what you need as you approach her and hugs accordingly, healing ailments—both physical and emotional—with her touch, and sometimes a few words. For a world of grown-up children, Ammachi provides a kind of maternal twist on the old-fashioned kissing booth, single servings of comfort worth waiting in line for. I saw many people burst into tears as Ammachi finally reached for them, placing their head against her chest and holding them tight. And the reactions she inspires are ultimately what motivates her mission—to help people overcome their boundaries, customs, judgment, and fear, for the sake of love.

Determined to overcome my biases about why people *worship* this woman who doles out saintly squeezes, I struck up a conversation with one of her devotees sitting next to me. I asked him why his search for oneness with God depended so heavily upon a multitude of figures and props.

"We're human, we need tangibles," he replied. His words rang true. I made a mental grocery list of the objects and imagery that mediate for believers of other faiths: the Native American medicine pipe and animal messengers; the pendulum and personal guides of the Spiritualist; the shofar trumpet and Torah ceremoniously protected inside every Jewish temple; the Christian cross sculpted in wood, stone, marble, and glass, and its Holy Ghost companion; the bread and wine incarnation of the body and blood of Jesus; the Catholic battery of highly specialized saints; the stoic Buddha statue poised in every dharma room. Each of these gives a sense of mass and proportion to elusive ideas like salvation, spirit, guidance, providence, and perfection. To her followers, Ammachi is a *human* talisman of these kinds of divine qualities.

While some people prefer a practice of simplicity, those drawn to Hinduism are more inclined to joyfully relish the detail of ritual, the dramatics of bedazzlement. Placing offerings like fruit, incense, or flowers at the ornamented altars of a guru or one of the many deities that enliven India's cultural heritage, the devotee will sometimes pray for holy merit or practical assistance, such as the improvement of health or finances. But the most elevated intent behind a Hindu's pattern of worship is to perfect unity with the Creator by *practicing* on its earthly representation. Some Ammachi devotees have taken this so far as to carry around and dote on tiny doll replicas of their guru—accurate right down to the body piercings and sari. Watching middle-aged people care for their baby-size Ammachi dolls as if they were literally alive, I was reminded of a foot-tall plastic redhead I used to know named Ginger.

Ginger's most notable attribute was the versatility of her hair—burnished locks that could be lengthened at will with a pull of her ponytail, or instantly bobbed with the push of a button that sucked those enviable tresses into her otherwise empty head. As a six-year-old, I meticulously bathed Ginger, groomed, dressed, fed, entertained, and rested her.

In doing so, I was practicing on Ginger how to care for myself, and for other people, until it simply became a part of my nature. It seemed Ammachi's followers were similarly mastering—or perhaps renewing—attentive love for the animate by practicing on the inanimate. For Ammachi's formal *puja,* her devotees are instructed to bathe, dress, and decorate her likeness using a statue, photograph, or doll, and then chant and dance for its pleasure, even lift spoonfuls of food and drink to its lips. At night, some tuck their guru—and favorite deities—into bed, covering their eyes so that they, too, can sleep soundly.

Witnessing these parallels made me ponder what exactly distinguished my child ritual of play from another person's ritualistic religion. Both developed the habit of devotion, which in its highest form is selfless love. But I still wondered how one went about choosing—as an adult—an object of affection that served as one's signpost to *spiritual* devotion.

For another perspective, I contacted one of America's most renowned Hindu converts, a former Ivy League professor who helped define the counterculture of the 1960s. Joining forces with his Harvard colleague, Timothy Leary, Dr. Richard Alpert set out to examine—some would say *unscientifically*—the potential consciousness-expanding effects of psilocybin, the hallucinogenic component of what are commonly known as "psychedelic" drugs. When their unorthodox project spun outside the bounds drawn by their conservative sponsor, the professors' contracts were terminated, casting them unceremoniously from their ivory tower. Hoping for insight, or maybe just an overdue vacation, Dr. Alpert packed his bags—and his drugs—and traveled east to India.

At the time, his experimentation with psychedelics gave him an unprecedented sensation of boundless freedom, a certainty of oneness with everything, and a much-needed detachment from his ego and earthly possessions. But the drugs were also leaving the doctor of psychology with a case of spiritual indigestion. The sense of higher consciousness was only attainable chemically and episodically and left him feeling moody, if not depressed. "No matter how ingenious my experimental designs were, and how high I got, I came down," he later wrote of his dilemma.[6]

A chance encounter in a Katmandu café led the aimless Dr. Alpert deeper into the remote foothills of the Himalayas, to a saint named Maharaji, meaning "great king." It would be this aged, non-English-speaking man who would rename the professor Baba Ram Dass and give his life a new kind of focus. And it would be Ram Dass who, in turn, would come to call the stranger his beloved guru, prostrating himself before Maharaji as a newfound disciple.

I traveled to northern California to meet the now sixty-something Ram Dass, a seasoned Hindu teacher and author whose bestselling book, inspired by his guru, popularized the phrase *Be here now*. Entering through his propped-open front door, I was greeted first by the wheels of his chair, and then by his gradual smile, both results of a near-fatal stroke that has left him partially paralyzed. He invited me into his primary living space, his bedroom, and asked me to take a seat among piles of books—both scholarly and pop—and the paraphernalia required for his physical therapy.

Each word infused with visible effort, Ram Dass spoke slowly about the daily spiritual practice he continues, no matter what his physical limitations. "I hang out with my guru," he said, describing a day in the life of Ram Dass. "I live in conversation with Maharaji, and his consciousness reflects a higher consciousness in me. We might sit on the porch and talk about the sounds outside, the people and cars passing by, the nature of travel, or just sit quietly and breathe."

With the belief that all matter is reducible to energy, Hindus attest that those attuned to the *divine* laws of nature are capable of splitting their consciousness, existing simultaneously in more places than one, even after they've died. Maharaji "let go of his body" back in 1973, yet many people who never met him while he was alive, have adopted him as their guru, claiming to experience a strong sense of his presence. The way this was described to me by Ram Dass and other practicing Hindus reminded me of the oft-encountered description given by Christians of the presence and power of the Holy Ghost. Like Ammachi's devotees, Ram Dass keeps photographs of Maharaji strategically placed around his home—even in his bathroom—to continually evoke his guru's presence and everything he represents. "My method, if you will, is palling around with this imaginary playmate who is spiritual, wise, compassionate, loving, and sharp," said Dass.

"Having a guru is like having a close friend who drags out from you the highest possible perceptions," he explained. "We have a number of *I*s. We have an I ego, which is the hardware for us to live in this plane. And then we have an I soul that is separate from other people, and, finally, an I God, which is shared by all. Through those three *I*s, my guru awakens in me the I that is the same in all of us."

It is specialized "sight" that is believed to lead people, like Ammachi's devotees and Ram Dass, to their personal guru, the saint who patiently waits, even for millennia, to be seen—indeed, recognized—by each student under his or her charge. This moment of recognition is considered the holiest of reunions, a coalescence of destinies conditioned by karma and readiness that is, in concept, like lovers finding their one true soul mate. And all that can be done to speed up the eventual encounter, says Ram Dass, is diligent preparation, purifying one's intentions, body, and thoughts through yoga, meditation, prayer, selfless service, and study of the Vedas—the authoritative and mystical texts of ancient India. It is believed these disciplines will help develop one's inner stillness and hone one's intuitive senses, which can prove imperative, considering that the appearance of a guru can be as obscure and cryptic as a dream. This fact, warns Ram Dass, can make it difficult to distinguish a real guru from an imposter, or, shall we say, a saint *in training*.

While there are no universal markings or definitive résumés for legitimate gurus—all of whom are considered to be saints by their disciples—one renowned yogi, Paramahansa Yogananda, once described their "common" superhuman qualities as "breathlessness, sleeplessness, cessation of pulse and heartbeat, calm eyes unblinking for hours, and a profound aura of peace."[7] While this description could just as easily pertain to a dead person, the saints of which Yogananda speaks are the ones still very much alive and committed to awakening and enlivening others. According to the accounts of disciples through the ages, a guru's individual karma and disciplined mastery can manifest itself as miraculous healing, psychic phenomena, enlightened transmission or ESP, and the ability to exist for years on earth without a morsel of food or drop of liquid. Called *siddhis,* these special effects–like abilities indicate nothing of guru authenticity, cautioned Ram Dass, unless they're applied responsibly to draw others to *God*. When the traits are appropriately aligned, they are easily noticeable to those they're intended to serve. Ram Dass described his moment of guru recognition as a "homecoming."

Recalling the details, Ram Dass spoke of his first meeting with Maharaji. With a healthy degree of skepticism, he had sat down to talk with, if not test, the man others regarded as holy. Maharaji proceeded to recount Ram Dass's thoughts from the night before when he sat alone under the starlit sky—silent, personal recollections about his mother, the experience of witnessing her death in his parents' East Coast home, and the lingering devastation he felt. These were facts and feelings Ram Dass had not shared with anyone in India. "She died last year," relayed Maharaji to the professor through a translator. "She got very big in the stomach before she died." Maharaji leaned back and closed his eyes as if replaying the death in his mind. "Spleen, she died of spleen."

Face-to-face with Maharaji's knowingness, Ram Dass said he began to feel a wrenching pain in his chest that erupted into a flood of tears. "And I wasn't happy and I wasn't sad," he later wrote of the experience. "It was not that kind of crying. The only thing I could say was it felt like I was home. Like the journey was over. Like I had finished. I had met my guru and he was outwardly the representative to the thing I was looking for inside."[8]

But as a truly enlightened teacher, Maharaji presented himself to the convinced Ram Dass not as an idol to be worshiped. Rather, he presented himself as a mirror and as someone who instructed more by example than by sermon, reflecting back to Ram Dass the essence of what Hindus call the *Atman*—the real self, the eternal life principle.

During his stay in Maharaji's ashram, Ram Dass began practicing karma yoga, in which everyday thoughts and actions are deliberately dedicated to God (in any of its manifest forms), whether one is eating, showering, laboring, or engaged in conversation. The thrust of this practice reminded me of the Arabic phrase *Bismillah*—"In the name of God"—uttered by Muslims throughout the day as a way of consciously dedicating one's actions to one's Creator. Karma yoga is intended to exhaust the ego, bringing the aspirant closer, with every consecrated word and action, to a state of awakened union with God or *Brahma*.

I asked Ram Dass how his stroke had affected his yoga practice. "The stroke has definitely *helped* it," he assured me. In true yogi fashion, he chooses to perceive *everything*—positive and negative, hard and easy—as fuel for spiritual transformation. "In karma yoga one's physical condition, family relationships, and every daily event become grist for the mill when you see it all—and everyone—coming to you as God to teach you something." Ram Dass spoke of a young girl he'd once seen sitting at his guru's feet who said in a most complaining voice, "Oh Maharaji, I have so much suffering." Maharaji looked up and said to the girl, "Suffering takes me to God."

"So, if that's true," posited Ram Dass, "and if I am melding with Maharaji's consciousness, then my stroke should take me to God."

When I inquired what, aside from his guru, had taken him to God *before* his stroke, Ram Dass sang the praises of the muscular monkey deity named Hanuman, in whose heart dwells the whole of humanity. In the Hindu pantheon, there are thousands of deities, some more popular than others. Each one reflects one or more of the Almighty's attributes, intended to help balance and perfect various human temperaments and speak to differing needs. While over the years a number of Hindu deities have captured Ram Dass's interest and respect, he, like most Hindus, developed a *lifelong* bond to one deity in particular.

Ram Dass says Hanuman, who allegorically symbolizes service, sought him out as much as he sought out Hanuman, influencing the last many decades of his humanitarian efforts. Combining his educational background in psychology with his spiritually inspired activism, Ram Dass has counseled the terminally ill and prison inmates, facilitated medical attention for people throughout third world countries, and taken every opportunity to write, lecture, and teach about the importance of compassion and service. As if to refute his old cohort Timothy Leary, who coined the phrase "Turn on, tune in, drop out," Ram Dass wrote, "To drop out is a cop-out."

"But the stroke has made me more quiet and physically stationary," acknowledged Ram Dass, who once jetted around the globe for sold-out speaking tours and hands-on public service. While he's learning to appreciate the extra time to contemplate and write, he says the stroke's most poignant gift has been its lessons in dependence.

"Before the stroke, I wrote a book: *How Can I Help?* Now," explained Ram Dass, "because of my physical condition, I'm forced every day to ask others: *How can you help me?* I wake up, somebody helps me out of bed. I go to the bathroom only if someone helps me get there. I eat only if someone cooks my meal and cuts it for me. I am now experiencing the reverse of the power trip of helping, the luxury of being in a position to give. Before, I felt compassion toward others." He paused as if to pick and arrange, one by one, a bouquet of words to match the images in his head. "Now . . . I see . . . that they . . . are compassionate . . . toward me."

The Buddhist master Lama Surya Das also at one time crossed paths with Ram Dass's guru, Maharaji. During our retreat, he shared with me something he'd once overheard the guru say: "To see God everywhere, you need special eyes. Otherwise you can't handle the shock." With special eyes, one can also look at the incapacitation of stroke and see it as a chance to be closer to God. Or look at a man who spends hours talking to his "imaginary friend" and behold an enlightened man conversing with the holiness at the heart of the universe.

Ram Dass searched for the word *good-bye* as he offered his good hand to me. I, too, searched for words, ones capable of expressing my gratitude for his having agreed to meet with me, given his physical vulnerability and speech impediment. It was clear that he was not so much concerned about upholding his reputation as a powerful public speaker and spiritual trend-setter as he was interested in furthering the understanding of others. Though on the surface our lives hold little in common, I felt a tremendous connection with this man for whom my reach to know seemed as important as his own.

As for Ram Dass's religion, I haven't yet met anyone who fits the description of my own personal guru; I've yet to find a spiritual teacher who feels like "home" or a surrogate mother. But both Buddhism and Hinduism have opened my eyes and made me less judgmental about the idea of being someone's disciple. I now understand the pull to find the kind of person who can perhaps reflect back to me the I God that Ram Dass says is the same in all of us.

Sikhism

Chapter Fifteen

n 1469, twenty-three years before Columbus set out to discover a shorter route to India and instead landed in North America, an Indian man named Guru Nanak established a new route to God that would also eventually find its way to this continent. He'd become disillusioned by what he saw as fanaticism and intolerance among his country's Muslims, and senseless ritualism and caste oppression among Hindus. Guru Nanak combined these faiths with a pragmatism all his own to form the religion of the Sikhs, or "seekers of truth." Integrating simplified worship of the one almighty God with India's guru tradition, Nanak forged a practice grounded in the visceral experience of higher consciousness and a valiant accountability for the well-being of others.

Exactly five hundred years after Sikhism's establishment, Siri Singh Sahib of Sikh Dharma (affectionately known as "Yogi Bhajan") voyaged from his home in India to the United States. As Sikhs in his country commemorated their faith's quincentennial, Yogi Bhajan celebrated Woodstock; what followed would be a fruitful intersection between a disciplined spiritual practice and the idealism and experimental spirit of counterculture Americans.

In response to the inroads Yogi Bhajan managed to make in the United States and Canada, a prominent spiritual authority of the Sikh faith in India ordained him the Chief Religious and Administrative Authority for Sikh

Dharma in the Western Hemisphere. Today, Yogi Bhajan continues teaching yoga, meditation, and natural lifestyle to Sikhs and non-Sikhs alike through the Healthy, Happy, Holy Organization (commonly known as "3HO").

While various forms of yoga—Sikh-related and not—are currently practiced by as many as eighteen million Americans, Yogi Bhajan was the first to bring kundalini yoga to the West. It is said to produce dramatic results quickly, which is why Bhajan has declared this advanced system of spiritual awakening—still shrouded in secrecy in his Indian homeland—the most viable practice for a Western culture hungry for timesaving spiritual evolution. As Mahan Tantric—a title held by only one person in the world at a time—Yogi Bhajan possesses the sole right to teach a particularly potent derivative of kundalini known as "white tantric" yoga.

America is home to about three percent of the world's twenty million Sikhs (pronounced "seeks"), and they are mostly of East Indian origin. 3HO Sikhs, of which there are about ten thousand, are primarily American, Canadian, and European-born converts committed to this ancient traditional approach to health, happiness, and holiness.

Stretching with Yogis

Running late, I drove up the five miles of mountainous unpaved road like an ambulance driver responding to a 911 call. Two people wearing lustrous white turbans that seemed to touch the roof of their SUV drove toward me, on their way down the mountain. As our cars passed, they shot me an unsubtle glare, making me suddenly aware of how much dusty havoc I was wreaking, how much noise my radio was making, and how stressed I'd become in trying to get to a yoga retreat on time. As I glanced in my rearview mirror, just as their car was sucked into the cloud streaming behind me, I caught my own reflection, the pleat between my eyes disturbingly pronounced. Easing up on my right foot and lowering the radio, I sailed more discreetly toward the circuslike tent in the distance.

Upon reaching my destination, I beheld a gathering of nearly one thousand men, women, and children, all cloaked in white. They lay on sheepskin mats, covering the ground like a heap of fresh fallen snow framed in the gold leaf glimmer of the New Mexican desert. I stood at the edge of this purity in blue shorts and a T-shirt, wishing I had remembered to inquire about the dress code. Everyone wore light cotton shifts—cropped at the knee on the men, and at the ankle on the women—with matching ballooning pants that narrowed and bunched at the bottom. Gossamer fabric flowed from the women's white turbaned crowns down their backs like wedding veils, while the men's turbans coiled upward. Both configurations are believed to be literal conduits for vitality, like a lightning rod drawing down electricity from the heavens. Aside from its more esoteric function, the Sikh turban is a statement of pride, distinction, and solidarity—a kind of medal displayed for bravery and service under God's command.

I searched the floor for an available spot among the limbs contorting in all directions. A beacon of noncompliance, I was quickly spotted by a roving monitor, who politely suggested I cover my head in *something* white. With but a tape recorder, Chapstick, and a few dollars in my pockets, I was left to improvise. In a quick scour of an adjoining medic tent, I found an extra-absorbent paper towel, which I tacked with borrowed tape to my hairline. From the curious glances, it was clear that disposable turbans were not likely to be the next Sikh-chic craze.

Now more acceptably garbed from at least the neck up, I was partnered with a man of about twenty, a complete stranger, who would act as my mirror for the next *nine* hours of white tantric yoga. Squeezing between other pairs of people, my partner and I faced each other in a seated position, joining in the mass stretch; my muscles felt as taut as a phony smile. Like many Americans, I had long associated yoga with a dimly lit, New Age-y class at the gym—a roomful of bendy, organic people I always bypassed for a "real" workout on electronically driven machines. The Hindu yoga of devotion—one more emotional than physical—had already broadened my understanding. But I sensed from the seriousness of preparation going on under this sideless tent that I was about to discover a new dimension of this increasingly popular practice.

I scanned the perimeters of the room for the man I'd seen only in photographs—the seventy-something yoga master Yogi Bhajan. But I saw no hint of the imposing Indian figure with the long white beard. Just as I was about to ask my partner to point his teacher out to me, a big-screen TV came to life with Yogi Bhajan's enlarged face jovially welcoming us all. Catching my confused expression and inferring its cause—that our facilitator was not physically present—my partner explained that, even digitized, Yogi Bhajan could transmit, like radiation, "infinite balancing energy" to the place we now sat. This one man's mighty current was said to adjust others' nervous systems and clear emotional and psychological blocks. Defining the ultimate objective of its yoga-centric practice, the introductory 3HO literature reads: "Our concept of highest consciousness is to be 100% sane, to live in a state of unshakable positivity, to understand ourselves in every thought and action, and to live with heart and mind full of compassion and wisdom."[1] I watched intently as Yogi Bhajan's talking head detailed what would be the first of many postures held for either thirty-one or sixty-two minutes. The postures are engineered to awaken and uncoil our "kundalini energy"—a kind of Slinky of invisible, dormant potential believed to be buried at the base of every spine. Bhajan's system of high-intensity yoga outlines the steps his students take to unlock an inner treasure of spiraling magnificence. To activate this raw, untapped energy—under Bhajan's supervision, for it has the unpredictable power of a Pandora's box—is to transform the finite human condition into the infinitude of God.

Easing us into the day's journey toward infinity, Yogi Bhajan offered cursory reminders and demonstrations of proper oxygen intake, like a flight attendant reviewing emergency procedures. Being a first-time user of Bhajan's techniques, I found comfort in my meditation training, having at least learned how to maintain focus by concentrating on the breath. "We consider breath to be a sacrament," my partner slipped in as an aside when the prerecorded tape was paused. His statement made me think of a Buddhist master I had recently met, who had said that the East's "most profound gift" to the West had been "the ancient science and discipline of the breath." Simply coming to think of my breath as malleable, as a tool that should be sharpened and used, was a revelation to me, having subsisted on shallow, stunted half breaths for most of my life.

Knee-to-knee with my well-practiced partner, I felt my breathing fall into sync with his, and eventually the whole crowd's, as we collectively struck our first pose. Sitting with crisscrossed legs, we straightened our spines and threaded our fingers together and arched our hands high above our heads, forming something like the eye of a giant needle. I began forcing out what Yogi Bhajan called "breaths of fire," exaggerated exhalations that made me sound as if I were being repeatedly punched in the gut by an invisible fist. There was no way to track the passage of time, as all two thousand arms remained high in the air. Voices in the crowd shouted encouragement in the form of phrases they'd picked up from Yogi Bhajan. "Keep up to be kept up!" one man hollered over my silent inner groan, my arms shaking from the load of bricks it felt like I was hauling. My partner remained unfazed, offering unflinching supervision to my struggle. Thirty-one minutes later, just as I was about to stop breathing and start screaming, everyone relaxed and shook their arms. Though satisfied with my accomplishment, I knew I was out of my league. That was, after all, just a *warm-up*.

For our second assignment, we sat with our legs held in the air at a sixty-degree angle, arms jetting out toward our partners. I started strong. But somewhere down the line, fiery licks of dusty desert wind threatened to choke me on each inhalation, burrowing under my contacts to form tiny deposits of mud in my watering eyes. I could no longer hold my partner's stoic stare as I had been instructed to do, catching only intermittent murky glimpses of him. I half hoped one of the monitors would peg me as a disruption and send me home. But having staunchly avoided the stigma of "quitter" ever since a particular second-grade Red Rover debacle, I pressed through, finding deep inside myself new reserves of energy I didn't know I had.

Evading the torrid advances of the next round of dust devils, I braved yet another doozy of self-inflicted torture: thirty-one minutes cross-legged with fingers interlocked behind my neck, staring at the tip of my nose while repetitively chanting *"sa-ta-na-ma."* It's a mantra that means "the name of truth," but it didn't take long for my cross-eyed stare to reconfigure the chant into "se-lf-de-feat," taunting me with the probability that I might indeed fail to grasp the allure of this extreme sport of religions. Sensing my tailspin, my partner intensified his stare, refusing even a single blink as he helped will me over the next hurdle. I realized I was fighting against my own body, making it out to be an enemy that needed to be conquered, whereas my partner seemed to relax into each new pose, as if to let it lead him through a dance he imagined in his mind.

Delirious with strain and the sound of a thousand chanting voices, I entered into a trancelike state. I could no longer hear my own voice, or feel my own body: I was drowned out by the multitude, or absorbed into it, or through it, like a trapdoor. I suddenly felt a floating sensation, dispassionately observing myself and my partner from a distance, finally and mercifully liberated from the burn of physical pain. I felt as if I'd left my physical body behind and was able to glide around the room and look at other pairs of people whose muscles and expressions revealed determination but, like my partner's, seemed immune to the kind of spasmodic stress mine had known. Most conspicuously, the diverse faces all bore the complexion of a child's—utterly flawless, eerily timeless. The women's features were void of makeup, free of the need to alter what was real and God-given. I inspected each brow for the furrow that proves we belong to a place of inordinate effort and worry, but found none among these people in white, so tranquilly steadfast in their position.

I must have spent a good deal of time hovering because the minutes, without resistance, breezed by. Deciding my magic carpet ride was the secret to yoga mastery, I later learned that it was but an amateurish trick, a technique for temporary relief. The ultimate intent of white tantric yoga, I was told, is not so much to escape from the physical self and the sensations to which it is bound, but to cleanse and expand the self until it unites with God and everything in existence. Like a canvas stretching over a four-cornered frame, it is believed, the accomplished yogi becomes one with the perfect balance, love, grace, and purpose that is the four-corner essence of the Creator. "As Yogi Bhajan says, if you can't see God in all, you can't see God *at all*," said my partner, assuming our next position: flat-footed squatting, hands held together at our chest. We looked like rows of praying ducks.

Half an hour later, my partner rose up easily as the bell chimed, indicating the conclusion of our first series of postures and a welcome fifteen-minute break. He offered his hand to help me up so that I might join him and the others at the nearby rehydration table, but I suggested he go ahead without me. "I'll be right behind you," I peeped before rolling over onto my side and into a fetal position. From behind the slow blinking shutters of my eyes, I surveyed a dreamy, arid landscape of ghostly figures holding watermelon slices and Day-Glo drinks. Feeling tendons and blood vessels I never before knew existed, I fully understood why Yogi Bhajan's yoga is not wildly popular. While exertion and catharsis are central to other practices, the Sikhs under Yogi Bhajan's care expressed them more tenaciously, meticulously, and excruciatingly than any other lay members of a religion I had yet encountered. It seemed theirs was an attraction to the radiant adrenaline surge that comes from pushing one's body and mind—and in their case, soul—to their outer limits. But as Yogi Bhajan would later argue, his practice amounts to much more than the momentary buzz that comes from industrial-strength yoga.

A few months after my desert induction, I dressed more appropriately and traveled to a town outside of Boston for another day of slightly less tormenting kundalini yoga, which Yogi Bhajan again oversaw from a comfortable distance. I finally managed to encounter him in the flesh, however, when it was conveyed to me through a chain of assistants that my months-pending request for an interview had been granted.

As I pulled my car into a long, tree-lined driveway, I was startled by the size and beauty of the home at its end—the permanent residence of two of Yogi Bhajan's students and the temporary guest quarters of their preeminent teacher. Escorted into the impeccably clean, exquisitely furnished living room, I was left alone for over an hour. I got the distinct impression that a prolonged wait is simply protocol for an audience with the *yogini*.

Loosely wrapped in flowing fabrics of orange and gold, he finally made his entrance, attendants cloaked in the predictable white trailing alongside him. Reaching the oversized chair across from me, the stout man waited patiently as pillows were fluffed and a sheepskin rug straightened before lifting up his arms to indicate his readiness to be lowered into the prepared nest. Another man propped his beloved holy man's feet on an ottoman and set a glass of water at his side.

Despite all the ceremonial pomp, Yogi Bhajan—like Guru Nanak five hundred years before him—insists that he is *personally* not to be worshiped, "even as an *intermediary* to God," he declared, distinguishing his faith from his homeland's Hinduism. "I have not come to gather disciples," he assured me. "I have come to create teachers ten times greater than I." Though Yogi Bhajan's words seemed to contradict his royal treatment, I wondered if he regarded it as an unavoidable upshot of his effectiveness as a teacher who instills in his students the virtues of service and generosity. When I asked him how he viewed his role as a spiritual guide, he said, "I'm just a technical know-how man."

It is exactly the precision with which Yogi Bhajan manages his holy craft that his followers say has in turn *earned* him their devotion and respect, along with its titles of guru, master, and even messiah. Yogi Bhajan says that he is careful to redirect this focused affection to the ancient holy book of God, the *Guru Branth Sahib*, a collection of sacred wisdom, primarily in the form of poems and hymns. All Sikhs regard their scripture as the only complete and incorruptible embodiment of "guru" capable of leading them to the ultimate Author of divinity. A recitation from the *Guru Branth Sahib*, along with devotional music and a dharma talk given by a resident teacher (or Yogi Bhajan, if he happens to be in town), makes up the programming for 3HO Sunday services.

Given their intense reverence for scripture, God, *and* guru, I asked Yogi Bhajan where exactly he and his students place their faith. "In experience," he said definitively in his heavy East Indian accent. "Everyone has their own experience of infinity. The teachings of Guru Nanak are a way to help it. For us, [guru] lineage means nothing. If this glass is empty, it can't take away my thirst. If it is full, it can quench my thirst. Sikh way of life is the way of the student. It's simple. It's Aquarius religion."

Not readily seeing the simplicity in his answer, I was left to wonder once again if my mind was simply too Western to grasp the subtleties of an entirely different style of thought. Or did the emperor have no clothes? Seeking clarity, I asked Yogi Bhajan if he could expand upon experience and Sikhism being "Aquarius religion."

"Piscean religion is 'I want to learn, take me where I can learn [information],'" he explained. "Aquarius religion is 'I have learned, give me experience.'" Yogi Bhajan went on to suggest that the aftermath of the Age of Enlightenment has cleared the way for a new age of *experiential* enlightenment, having exhausted the all-cognitive "Piscean" approach to religion that he says Americans have long clung to. Offering me a crash course in the astrological foundations of his prognosis, Yogi Bhajan explained that "in 1991, the axle of earth changed to .9, bringing us to twenty-one years, the cusp." Everyone in the room but me nodded their heads in silent agreement, like mathematicians concurring on mental calculations. "In another fourteen years it'll change completely, and everything will change with it: your mental wavelength, your communications, your magnetic field, and the biorhythms of the heavens—everything and everybody is going to change whether they like it or not. We are entering the Age of Aquarius. Now is the time for people to go beyond information and learn for *themselves*—feel it, experience it, and then keep going."

Going back to my original question—disregarding for the moment earthly axles and cosmic cusps—I asked Yogi Bhajan if his objective was indeed to strengthen his followers' belief in God.

"I don't *believe* in God," he intoned defiantly. "Believing is a second-hand choice—a low-grade mammal's personal defunctness. I *trust* in God, I *dwell* in God. Either you trust or you don't trust," he concluded. His words echoed Gene Begay's equally stubborn assertion that "belief" is a lame disservice to a Creator who wants to be *known* and *trusted* with certainty. I loved this notion of dwelling in God and the fearlessness that such an intention required—a strength of dedication I felt I had in me, though I wasn't yet sure exactly how, and with whom, to express it.

As their way of expressing their trust pact with God, Sikhs, upon initiation, make five formal lifelong vows. First, to carry a dagger called *kirpan,* once worn by their forebears for physical self-defense, now a ceremonial symbol of spiritual valor. Second, never to cut their hair—considered the primary channel of energy into the body. Third, to wear a small wooden comb as a reminder of the importance of cleanliness. Four, to wear a metal bracelet as a reminder that one's hands should remain always in service to

God. Fifth, and finally, to sport "scientifically designed underwear" both for the biological benefit of balancing the body's levels of calcium and magnesium, and as a sign of chastity for those who are yet unwed.

Aside from the five vows—and a requisite abstention from alcohol, meat, and tobacco—what else, I asked Yogi Bhajan, was required to live the "healthy, happy, holy" way?

"It is *grace* we should be focused on," he said, reclining his head as an attendant massaged his feet with fragrant oil. "Grace is when you are not on sale and you shall never change your word. Come what may—time, weather, God, angels, heavens, earth changes—if your commitment does not change, then you understand happiness. Each time you make that sacrifice, for the sake of others or all, that is happiness. But people here [in America] are into *themselves*—that is the worst. And others are searching to be on sale—that is second worst. And then cold depression sets in, absolute disharmony and unhappiness, quarrels, diversions, and perversions." Pausing, Yogi Bhajan closed his eyes and said, "Man is a prisoner of his rib cage. He cannot be rescued unless he grows."

We sat in silence for a moment. Then the man anointing Yogi Bhajan's feet spoke up, adding that Sikh practice "gets you in control of yourself so you're not affected or overwhelmed by the events of the day and others' thoughts of you." It seemed these words were intended to help translate Yogi Bhajan's more abstract language, and the man went on to explain further that the rib cage metaphor was the equivalent of being unable to see beyond the subjectivity and needs of one's *self*. With this practice, he said, "you become *consistent* in who you are, and capable of taking care of much more than just yourself." In the Sikh worldview, the natural tendency to be self-absorbed is crushed by an honorable—even heroic—way of communal life. Called *sat sangat,* Sikh communities form the intersection between spiritual growth and the mundane realities of the physical world. Emphasizing the distinction between self and community, the anointer said, "It is specifically through the latter that one finds God, or universal consciousness." It seemed to explain why Sikhs wear their spiritual affiliation literally on their sleeve—and every other part of their body—as if to say *I'm here to help.*

I asked Yogi Bhajan if he had to adapt his Eastern teachings of selflessness in order to penetrate Western individualism. "There is a little more work involved in teaching Westerners," he acknowledged. "They are window-shoppers, you know. They like to have many things. They don't want to be nailed down to one. So they need help sharpening their sensory system, and that takes a little more time."

It was a pointed comment, I thought, perhaps directed at me. From the beginning of my explorations into practice, I worried that I would be perceived as just that, a window-shopper. But I didn't see myself that way, as a casual browser among other people's valued wares. Instead, I hoped to do exactly what Yogi Bhajan had described: "sharpen my sensory system" by observing how others strive for a state of grace. Maybe it would prepare me to discover my own.

Yogi Bhajan detailed what he recognized as other typical American weak spots. "Rising before dawn to meditate on the primal word of God, and passing time alone," he said without hesitation, having obviously given this some previous thought. "You Americans trade wisdom for blind reach, for *goals*—what a polite word for something so nasty," he added. "You know if you take *E-G-O* and *G-O-D*, and drop the *E* and *D*, what remains in the center is *GO-GO*. That defines about ninety-nine percent of Western people's lives—passion, commotion, and survival."

Again I was cornered, wondering if Yogi Bhajan had right away pegged me as one of those go-go girls. Was it the faint red lines in the whites of my eyes that gave me away? I wondered. Or was it a lack of poise—what Bhajan calls "imperial divinity"—that tipped him off? He never directly asked me if I felt I was one of those people who forever turn in the addictive spin cycle of *just keeping up*, but I knew he had his suspicions.

"None of us is a commoner," he decreed from his rustic throne. Since asceticism is not a tenet of Sikhism, Bhajan encourages his followers not only to infuse their character with the qualities of benevolent nobility, but to embrace the physical comforts that typically come with it. Following his lead, Bhajan's disciples are socially conscientious, politically active environmentally concerned vegetarians who carry leather Coach bags, live in big houses, and drive souped-up sport utility vehicles. But the faith's devotees are not apologetic for what they say is "realistically integrative" with their family life, professional life, and American life. "God is not found on mountaintops. He lives in cozy homes," Yogi Bhajan is fond of repeating. I thought about how, to the contrary, Ram Dass had connected with God, literally, on a mountaintop amid people who had no real material possessions. It was interesting to me how people came to the same truths and internal experiences through vastly different means.

Yogi Bhajan has a master's degree in economics, a Ph.D. in psychology, a record of service in the Indian government, a wife, three children, an international following, and the responsibility of overseeing a number of successful Sikh-run businesses. He is not unaccustomed to the balancing act of a capitalistic spiritual existence, one he seems to manage with ease. I asked him if he found any inherent conflict in practicing capitalism as voraciously as Sikhism. "You *have* to be capitalistic to be Sikh," he declared, "because you have to be in a position to give. If you don't have abundance, how can you share? What are you going to share if you are a beggar yourself? We are made of God, and in the name of God we produce." Like other disciplines I've come across, Sikhism overturns America's compartmentalization of self, family, work, recreation, and religion so that one can indeed *dwell,* as Bhajan had said, in their faith.

Isolating the first article of his 3HO motto for the sake of discussion, I asked Yogi Bhajan about the physical health aspect of his full-immersion practice. He proceeded to rattle off a list of daily dietary supplements he and his followers swear by: one banana a day "for alkaline," eaten specifically at four in the afternoon, one raw onion to stave off cancer, a pear for the processing of "excess tissue and stone growth," an apple "to keep the doctor away," a lump of garlic for the nervous system, a tablespoon of raisins ("particularly for women"), and ginger "to suck out the poison in the body." Pausing for a few seconds, he detained me in his radar, as if I'd been elected to represent the entire population of non-Sikhs. "So what out of all this can you not do?" he asked. "Everybody has nine holes. One should watch *carefully* what comes in and goes by these holes." He caught me counting. "Nine!" he shouted.

Highlighting the Sikh ritual that sounded least bearable to me, Yogi Bhajan added, "And one must rise before four A.M. to begin the day with a cold shower. If you do this, you will not get cancer or other mammalian diseases," he promised, "because your capillaries will be flushed and your circulation will be perfect." In addition, this predawn physical sacrifice awakens (some would say startles) the body and mind into remembrance of God and the lionhearted commitment to serve others. As Guru Nanak's only official commandment, Sikhs are compelled to keep this early-morning remembrance of God in their hearts, continually reciting "His Name" throughout the day. "Not to do these things," Yogi Bhajan assured me, "means choosing to live like a dead rat—simple as that."

Though Yogi Bhajan has a way of making his life's choices sound effortless and plainly sensible, I admitted to him that I didn't think I'd last very long on his spartan regimen. He shot me a look of pity, which morphed into indifference. Then, as if to make one last attempt for the sake of diplomacy, he demonstrated a basic meditation that he felt confident would at least "improve" the lives of people like me. Focusing his eyes on the tip of his nose, he repeated "*sa-ta-na-ma*" with measured breaths, a "simple, high-frequency" exercise he said would help me get in touch with my "true spiritual identity." "Do this every day for eleven minutes," he said, uncrossing his eyes. "Not ten minutes, not twelve—*eleven*. Just that is enough to change a person from depressed to empowered in just forty days." He returned his head to its reclined position. "If somebody cannot spare eleven minutes, the hell with it," he concluded with finality.

Standing on wobbly legs after my first day of white tantric yoga, I downed cups of Gatorade on top of that parched New Mexican mountain. Meeting the eye of a woman standing next to me, I noticed that she, like everyone else in our vicinity, had no furrow in her brow and no lines on her face. I blurted out that I needed to know, once and for all, if her spiritual practice was truly the reason she and her kundalini comrades looked so good and seemed so confidently peaceful.

The woman chuckled (though it might have been my tattered paper turban more than my question that inspired that response). She introduced herself as Tara and described for me the tenor of her days "pre–Yogi Bhajan," when she lived a more "typical American life" in an Arizona city where she and her husband owned and operated a small business together. Tara assured me that during those years she and her husband were plenty familiar with stress and anxiety and had acquired the lines and signs to prove it. But—and she seemed as surprised by this as anyone—those indentations had indeed slowly faded "as a direct result of Yogi Bhajan's approach to life." Tara explained that knowing nothing about Yogi Bhajan, she and her husband had gone to hear him give a public lecture about yoga and his Sikh path. Within a year, the pair had formally converted, moved closer to a 3HO community, and reprogrammed their alarm clock for just shy of four A.M. As part of their new identity, they'd also taken jobs at one of the many 3HO-run businesses, manufacturing and distributing the popular Yogi tea.

Tara spoke of her practice's effectiveness in filtering the "white noise" of twenty-first-century life. After adopting Yogi Bhajan's practice, she almost immediately felt it diminish the inner and outer "static" she'd nearly gotten used to, enabling her to have and communicate "one clear thought at a time" with a consistency she had never before known. To Bhajan, this state of being equates with spiritual liberation—ultimate emancipation from the rib cage—for God does not have to compete for attention in a mind that remains lucid in the center of chaos. To Tara, it means "plainly evident quality of life improvements," the reason "more people than you might expect" are attracted to the stringent 3HO path.

During our meeting, Yogi Bhajan had also emphasized the indicators underlying our basic human experience. "Some people are in the streets, others in mansions," he'd said. "Some dine in zero-star restaurants, some one-star, two-star, five-star. The important questions remain: Do you digest your food or not? Do you sleep well or not? Are you for sale or not? Do you have the capacity to give or not?" In the mind of Yogi Bhajan, the answers to questions like these are, at the end of the day, what separate those of us who are genuinely healthy, happy, and holy from those who are not.

Despite keeping me waiting, and despite his seeming disdain for many of my "American" tendencies, Yogi Bhajan sat with me for hours. At the end of our talk he requested that a piece of chocolate cake be cut and carried to me, his guest. His insistence that I eat reminded me of a few mothers and grandmothers I know, and gave me a window into the maternal, nurturing side of this sarcastic, slogan-slinging man. As I forked up my first bite, I told Yogi Bhajan that I found his prescribed routine easier to consider now that I knew it included homemade chocolate cake. "Once in a while a little cake is good for you," he said with a stern jaw.

As I dutifully consumed every last crumb, one of Yogi Bhajan's many assistants leaned toward his ear, whispering something about a "four o'clock appointment with a holy man." Without a word, Bhajan raised up his arms like an infant asking to be held, the two people closest to him responding accordingly with a gentle hoist. Fitting him with shoes and a shawl, his attendants, and their attendants, led him toward the door. Following behind the entourage, I watched as they loaded Yogi Bhajan into an idling Range Rover. Assuming his quick escape meant that he was too rushed for good-byes, or that he never gave them, I stood behind the large cluster of turbaned heads, taking in the scene. Rolling down his window, Yogi Bhajan scanned the crowd, stopping on me, and with a raised, regally jeweled finger summoned me forward.

Self-conscious about making him late for his appointment, I hurriedly thanked him for agreeing to meet with me and made a move to step out of the way. Nabbing my hand, he placed it inside his, as if intending to leave me with one final sacred nugget. "We're only late for a *movie,* my child," he whispered. "And thank you for your questions, the pleasure was all mine." With a wink of an eye and a squeeze of the hand, he released me, directing the devotee behind the wheel to step on it. I watched as the faces of the *yogi* and his faithful passengers—all lit with an unworldly beauty—sped away, full, like life, of amusing contradictions.

Suddenly I was alone again. In the absence of their guru, the dozen or so people who had mysteriously appeared, as if drawn out of the house's woodwork, retreated almost instantly. In the calm after the storm, I walked to my car, flashing on Tara and her determination to ward off the corrosion of white noise that clutters the human airwaves. I knew that if I were ever going to sustain the kind of clarity and quietude I had thus far only studied in others, real changes in myself and my life were unavoidable.

But I still wasn't sure exactly which changes to make, or even which direction to take. In some ways, I was more confused than ever about how to assimilate all the information and experiences I'd thus far gathered. I wondered if my hesitation meant that a part of me wasn't quite ready for the sorts of sacrifices I'd seen people of many faiths embrace. After all, there are certain things about being a go-go girl that I relish, like staying up late, sleeping in, drinking coffee, and occasionally lingering in a hot shower. And while there were aspects of Bhajan's path I was open to trying—like his forty-day prescription of eleven-minute cross-eyed meditation—something didn't feel right about selecting only a small piece of a practice that was inarguably an intricate *way of life.* Looking at Bhajan's path in the context of Gene Begay's metaphor that religion is like a language, it seemed to me that the 3HO practice, like all the other practices I'd encountered, should be left intact as a system, not pilfered for its most useful or easily digestible phrases.

I decided it was time to turn my attention to someone who challenged this idea, who'd taken traditional notions of God and devotion, and turned them on their ear.

The New Age

Chapter Sixteen

A random review of any nonfiction bestseller list reveals three equally pervasive American obsessions: getting rich, getting skinny, and getting spiritual. Over the last few decades, in the spirituality category in particular, people have devoured books by the likes of Carlos Castaneda, Richard Bach, Robert Pirsig, Dan Millman, James Redfield, and Marianne Williamson, among dozens of others, as literature of inspiration, if not modern scripture.

Fill-in-the-blank workbooks, paid speaking engagements, and weekend workshops are all part of a lucrative circuit of spiritual guidance. Offering user-friendly systems for putting a book's message into practice, these New Age messengers (most of whom dislike that nebulous term) have together built a new, more transient house of worship for Americans. So many have come and gone in the past forty years that it may seem odd to consider one of current popularity in the same context with millennia-old faiths. But the tremendous attention and energy devoted to these self-invented gurus forces the question of what kind of impact, if any, their prophecies will have on future configurations of American faith.

A heavyweight among America's pop prophets, Neale Donald Walsch hails from Portland, Oregon. Before achieving worldwide fame as "the man who converses with God," he quietly struggled to keep a job, a relationship—

a life—intact. His sketchy past is the very selling point of his message: that if a man like him can seize a private audience with God and dramatically alter his life, anyone can. Around this hopeful assurance of divine accessibility, Walsch has assembled a miniempire of bestselling books and a grueling schedule of public-speaking engagements, reaching millions of readers in the United States and abroad.

Godding with a Bestselling Author

Slipping through the door just as the first night's workshop was beginning, I encountered over a hundred people of varying ages and ethnicities, arranged in two giant circles. They rotated in opposite directions, one inside of the other, to the dramatic tinkling of live piano music. Then suddenly the man behind the keys stopped playing, and in a weird variation on a game of musical chairs, everyone paired up with the person closest to them from the other circle. The workshop's main attraction—Neale Donald Walsch—wouldn't be arriving until the next morning, so in his absence, the guy playing the piano had been appointed to the task of orientation.

"Okay," he announced from his polished white bench, "now take turns sharing with your partner your expectations for this weekend, and your intentions for what you hope to get out of the workshop." Not quite ready to jump into "sharing" after my five-hour navigation through snarls of Massachusetts traffic, I tried to back discreetly out of the room. A man posted near the door stopped me, asking if I wanted to be his "partner." Too slow with an excuse, I acquiesced.

Attractive and in his midthirties, the man explained that he had volunteered to help facilitate the weekend's workshop as part of his residency program at the center. What was once a secluded Catholic monastery had been converted into a yoga hub that also hosted weekend workshops such as this one. Curious about what he "hoped to get out of the workshop," I asked the man how familiar he was with Walsch's conversations with God. "Well," he answered, "they changed my life."

"Really?" I returned, surprised by such an instant testimonial.

"I was a different man one year ago," he said. "Dealing drugs and working in insurance, you could say I was pretty unhappy."

"And then you read Walsch's books and got happy?" I asked.

"Pretty much," he said, perhaps sensitive to the tone of incredulity in my voice. "I read Walsch's first volume," he explained, "and it simply made me realize that it was time to change my life. So I relocated to Boston, went to massage school, and just recently came here to live at the yoga center for concentrated instruction. A year ago," he said with a chuckle, "I didn't even know what yoga was. Incredible things have happened to me since I read that book."

I, too, had read Walsch's first book, and the others that followed it, finding them insightful in a commonsense sort of way and refreshingly candid, though they hadn't caused me to move or change careers. But over the course of the weekend, I encountered dozens of people who, upon reading *Conversations with God,* transformed their lives as radically as the drug-dealer-turned-yogi. Among them there was a feeling of having been literally born again, given a second chance to establish a new kind of relationship with God, one more intimate and relevant to modern American life.

While the world's religions tout the promises and miracles of ancient prophets, sages, deities, and the almighty Creator, Walsch emphasizes that you yourself are your own best savior. In his own former incarnation, Walsch battled low self-esteem, a disappointing career path, bouts of poverty, and five failed marriages that produced nine children. Mired in what was for him a routine state of despair and frustration, Walsch found himself alone one night, angrily drafting a complaint on a legal pad addressed to none other than God. Walsch demanded to know what he could possibly have done "to deserve a life of such continuing struggle," certain he'd been dealt more than one man's fair share of disappointment. Much to his surprise, says Walsch, the pen he held in his hand began to move of its own accord, drafting a response to his question.

He watched as a series of words strung themselves together, as if his pad were a Ouija board. "Do you really want an answer . . . or are you just venting?" the letters spelled out, claiming the gender-neutral authorship of "God." Walsch did indeed want answers, and answers he got. That night and on many to follow, he received responses to a flood of inquiries on topics ranging from why there are disasters and death, to what can be done to help the environment, to what Walsch should do with his abundant sexual energy. Gradually, Walsch compiled the pragmatic prose into a volume he says was reproduced exactly as it was originally written to him—a casual Q&A session between a man attempting to retrieve the fulfilling life he had always expected to live, and the God willing to help him, not just for the sake of this one man, but for the others God said would one day overhear their conversations.

Conversations with God gives its readers the license to create their own blueprint for a spiritual overhaul. It offers instructions for drafting dream profiles of new and improved self-actualized lives. "The whole point of the conversation, in case anyone missed it," explained Walsch as he settled in for the first morning's lecture, "is that we shouldn't be placing our authority for any spiritual truth anywhere outside of ourselves." Walsch says that God, from the beginning of human creation, intended our fate to be left in our *own* industrious hands, which He equipped with capacities nearly as vast as Her own (Walsch's books interchange the feminine and masculine pronoun to refer to God).

To help us make the most of what's at our disposal and become "totally aware of who we are and the potential we each embody," Walsch offers an informal system of practice, beginning with a stock of self-inquiries, awareness meditations, and mental cues for proactive solutions to everyday challenges. He also offers the "tool" of *affirmative* prayer, such as this one—a revamping of the traditional Christian Lord's Prayer:

> *My Children, who are in Heaven, hallowed is your name.*
> *Your kingdom is come, and*
> *your will is done, on Earth as it is in Heaven.*
> *You are given this day your*
> *daily bread, and you are forgiven your debts, and your*
> *trespasses, exactly to the degree that you have*
> *forgiven those who trespass against you.*
> *Lead your Self not into temptation, but deliver your*
> *Self from the evils you have created.*
> *For thine is the Kingdom, and the Power, and the Glory, forever. Amen.*[1]

Over a lunch of wholesome food, I asked Walsch why he thought his spiritual system had become so instantly and enormously popular. "For the same reason that Jesus became so instantly popular," he answered. "Not that I want to compare *Conversations with God* to Jesus in any other way, but in this way the comparison, I think, is apt: Jesus spoke to the people of his time in the language and the idioms of his time; he was very easy to understand, he spoke in parables and stories and riddles, and he was a person of great humor, much more than most people are aware." Walsch hopes his own laid-back, straightforward dialogues with God will demystify the two great mysteries that institutionalized religions have long "cornered and complicated." First, he wants to instigate a *direct* relationship between individuals and God. Second, he wants to instill a sense of the "limitless" possibility in each of us, no matter what the transgressions of our past.

"Jesus hung out with thieves and murderers and prostitutes," Walsch continued, "not placing himself *out* of the company of those he was most urgently trying to reach. He saw good in everyone, and he palled around with people that gurus don't pal around with. I think *Conversations with God* as a book does the same thing. It makes the same kinds of friends."

Walsch's own self-acknowledged life blunders have prepared him for the kinds of sticky questions his diverse friends now fire at *him*. And Walsch happily offers himself as a campfire around which people feel comfortable sharing stories and making confessions. One young man raised his hand to ask Walsch's advice, sharing his wife's recent request for a sexually "open relationship," and the stomachache he'd had ever since. Walsch, drawing upon his many attempts at partnership, and his own past promiscuity, said one is often required to compromise when "authentic" love exists between two people "who want for their lover whatever he or she wants for him- or herself." Walsch explained that this kind of partnership can only succeed with perfect trust and clear communication, an everyday practice of honest, full disclosure he calls "transparency." But, warned Walsch, one should never agree to anything that irretrievably compromises one's own deepest individual needs, desires, and visions. "Or else you will experience the boomerang effect of blame and regret," two emotions that, along with guilt, God wishes humanity would transcend. After the five-minute exchange with Walsch, the man concluded that he probably could not, then, in good conscience compromise enough to remain in his marriage.

After witnessing a number of these efforts to lay the *Conversations with God* principles over the intricacies, obstacles, and phobias of people's lives, I became curious about what in Walsch's past had most prepared him for this unique responsibility he confidently shoulders. When we next spoke during an extended intermission, Walsch shared with me a particular chapter from his life that hadn't been covered in his trilogy of books or publisher's press package—a year that he says provided him with the "liberal education" he now brings to his job as God's camp counselor. Before the release of his first book, Walsch, who says he's always been "intuitively sensitive," worked in a rented office space in downtown Portland as a for-hire psychic. Driving to work one day, Walsch was hit by another car, leaving him with a severe neck injury and the inability to sense the fortunes of others and therefore earn money to pay his bills—medical and otherwise. Still recovering from his accident and unemployed, Walsch walked outside one day to get into his mangled car—his one earthly possession—only to discover it had been stolen.

"That was the day," Walsch said, shaking his head, "I dropped to my knees on the cement—if people had seen me, they would have taken me to a little rubber room, because I just fell to my knees and cursed God with the worst obscenities, banging my fists against the cement." His girlfriend at the time, in whose apartment he was living, quickly tired of Walsch's self-termed "drama," landing him on the street without anyone to turn to for more than a few nights of a borrowed couch. Desperate, Walsch managed to gather up enough change to cover a bus fare to the home of one of his ex-wives—the mother of three of his children—hoping for a warm reception and a place to sleep until he "got on his feet." Instead he was handed a small tent and a Coleman stove—wedding gifts to the once-upon-a-time couple.

Walsch lived the next rainy northwest year in that tent, part of an underground society of homeless men who inhabit abandoned cars amid a dense forest near an Oregon campground. Collecting cans that messy travelers left behind, Walsch pulled in twenty-five dollars a week. "We'd have bonfires and big parties in the woods, eating our sardines or whatever we could afford, pooling our resources," he reminisced. He also recalled the many less romantic nights he lay awake, wondering what his life had come to. But it is the men who exist on the outskirts of contemporary American life, the ones Walsch bonded with over all-night bonfires, who he says taught him the best of what he knows about friendship, interdependence, humble pride, and survival.

Standing with Walsch in our bucolic retreat setting, I felt I had a better context for the nothing-to-lose edge that defines him as much as his freshly showered Grizzly Adams appearance. When we came back from break, Walsch was fired up to share more of his blessed advice. "The most important question we can ever ask ourselves," he said, "is, *Is this who I am?*" Walsch likened his pithy mantra to the seminal "who meditation" of

Eastern mystics—a repetitive mantra of self-inquiry which reminds us that while our flesh gives us the impression that we are a multitude of discrete selves, we are actually One. Though this is also Walsch's core message, he isn't much interested in teaching it through formal practices found in ancient traditions, East or West. Instead he suggests a few easy-to-remember thoughts to keep in one's mind throughout the day, such as "Is this who I *choose* to be?" Conjugating his favorite noun into a verb, Walsch above all advocates the practice of "godding." He uses the word to describe the active pursuit of the best version of the person we choose to be.

When Walsch and I spoke at the end of the day, I suggested that his philosophy and its practices could be interpreted as religion minus the hard parts. Walsch disagreed, citing his cardinal tenet of personal responsibility and its insistence on cause and effect. "Being accountable is the greatest challenge there is, which is why most people avoid doing it," he said.

I liked the fact that Walsch's self-governing worldview tried to get at the essence of religiosity without becoming a religion in the traditional sense. Balancing his free-form approach to conscientious self-fulfillment, Walsch recasts the ethical doctrine of utilitarianism—choosing action aimed at producing the greatest good for the greatest number of people. Walsch suggests a litmus test that weighs the impact on the human race if *everyone* were to make the same choice. If the result would net disaster—warns the voice of God—then it is advisable *not* to exercise one's godding in that particular way.[2]

Spinning his John F. Kennedy–spirited maxim, "Ask not what your spirituality can do for you, but what you can do because of your spirituality," Walsch never wavered in his insistence that our liberty to self-help is ultimately meant to liberate and uplift all of humankind. In his constant reiteration of this tenet, Walsch painted a shiny new coat over the "personal empowerment" movement and its tendency toward self-absorption. "Whatever it is you feel you're lacking in your life—be it love, money, clarity, time, friendship—give that freely to five or ten people," Walsch instructed. "I promise you will begin to notice it appearing abundantly in your own life, like magic." Walsch calls this wand of a practice "sourcing," a kind of chain-letter twist on the foundational Christian creed *Do unto others as you would have them do unto you.* "You must divorce yourself from the need for results," implored Walsch, "and just act with choice and intention to give." There seemed to be an ominous tone in Walsch's voice when he spoke of the reciprocal imperative in his foundational practices of "godding" and "sourcing."

I remembered reading somewhere in his books about the timeliness of his dialogues with God, and asked Walsch about this. "God has made it very clear that we are at a critical juncture, a cusp," he said. "One wrong move and the game is over. That hasn't been true before. In days past, we were capable of rudimentary battles; we could destroy whole villages, even whole nations. But not until recent time have we had the ability to end all life on this planet within seventy-two hours or less. Not only that, outside of nuclear power, we've gotten to the point where we can end life on this planet in other slower, less dramatic, but no less effective ways, like the destruction of our rain forests. With this we threaten to make it literally impossible for the oxygen factory on planet Earth to produce sufficient material for us to breathe. For these sorts of reasons, God is choosing now to say in very plain terms, *'Let's talk.'*"

After hearing Walsch talk *about* his talks with God, it became clear just how unique it is that so many people have adopted *Conversations with God* as not only modern scripture but a virtual diagram for life. While I found Walsch's anti-institutionalism attractive, I felt that his system of practice— essentially, trying to be a decent, fulfilled person—was one I'd already been *practicing* for some time.

Nouveau theology or just popular reading, Walsch has captured the interest of not only Americans, but the citizenry of the world, as *Conversations with God* surpasses translation into thirty languages. "There's no doubt in my mind that people everywhere are finished with dogma," a worn-out Walsch declared from the bed on which he reclined after the workshop had ended. "People are finished with religious movements of every kind that place on them artificial constraints, and that require them to operate within artificial constructions that have no resemblance to the reality about God and life that lives within the human heart. What many religions have long asked us to do is to deny the yearnings and the truths in our own heart in order to be pious or worthy or acceptable in the eyes of God. What *Conversations with God* says is quite the opposite—that, in fact, you are not to deny the yearnings of your soul, nor the passions of your mind or your body, nor the truths of your heart to find God. The only way to find God is to honor what is within us," he said, nearly gasping from exhaustion, "because *God* is the one who placed those yearnings and truths there."

With his validation of natural *and* philanthropic urges, and his appealing promise that God never intended for our lives to be a relentless struggle, Walsch has, at least for the time being, secured a position of celebrity for himself. It is a fact he sometimes revels in, and other times deflects. I asked Walsch about the attention swirling around him—the countless strangers wanting autographs, hoping for a picture, vying for a tidbit of his wisdom. He admitted that his ego has at times gotten the best of him, but joked that if anyone ever tried *too* hard to make him into a "legitimate guru," he'd simply invite them to stay in his home for a few days. "That would be a quick antidote," he promised. But still, Walsch's dilemma threatens to stump even his most trusted "Is this who I *choose* to be?" inquiry. Actively involved in coordinating *Conversations with God* study groups and developing training programs to further a virtual grassroots ministry, Walsch's teachings are inching dangerously close to becoming institutionalized—the very thing he and his books rail against. "It's human nature," he admitted when I questioned him on this. "Someone will eventually make a religion out of a religion that says 'Don't make a religion.'" So, hoping to beat those someones to the punch for the sake of quality control, Walsch feels compelled to succumb to *some* structure.

Fielding with closed eyes the questions I tossed at him from across the room, Walsch seemed to need to rest in peace. He had, after all, endured many months on the road, trying to keep up with his wildly popular workshops. Wrapping up our talk, I commented that while lay people of nearly every faith speak to God through prayer or song, not many religious institutions validate the *literal* possibility of God talking *back*. I asked Walsch, who seemed willing to answer a parting question, how he handled the inevitable detractors. "Many people cannot accept the *Conversations with God* premise," he agreed, "because if God is revealing Itself to us at all times, we then must involve ourselves in listening. The idea that God stopped talking to us thousands of years ago has allowed us to step aside from the space of responsibility to hear—to listen."

But the flip side, added Walsch, is that a greater number of people have approached him to say: "What's the big deal? God and I talk all the time." This oft-encountered affirmation from the Joe Lights of the world exposes what Walsch calls "the only error" in his series of books, which boasts as its subtitle: *An Uncommon Dialogue.* "It turns out," said Walsch, "there's nothing uncommon about it."

Self-Help

Chapter Seventeen

n the 1920s, a man known as "Bill" pursued his dreams of power and wealth as a Wall Street stockbroker, intoxicated by speculation until that fateful day in 1929 when freewheeling capitalism suddenly capsized. While some of Bill's colleagues chose to end their lives quickly, stepping through the windows of their high-rise offices, Bill opted for a more gradual suicide in the form of a drinking habit he'd acquired during his more celebratory days. The gratifying praise of his associates—the sounds of success Bill had long relied upon to measure his internal net worth—were gone. Their replacement came in the sounds universally heard from inside a dimly lit bar. "No words can tell of the loneliness and despair I found in that bitter morass of self-pity," Bill later wrote of that time in his life. "Quicksand stretched around me in all directions. I had met my match. I had been overwhelmed. Alcohol was my master."[1]

Determined to quit drinking, Bill was admitted to a hospital rehabilitation program, dried out, and discharged as "recovered." It wasn't long, however, before he awoke hung over again, a roller-coaster ride he reenacted until he stood, finally and hopelessly, on the brink of death. With impeccable timing, an old drinking buddy of Bill's knocked on his front door—not to partake of a nightcap as Bill had presumed, but to share his new and sobering faith in God.

"God comes to most men gradually, but His impact on me was sudden and profound," Bill marveled when he later recounted his friend's visit and the *literally lifesaving faith he left behind.*[2] *Based on his own experience, Bill became convinced that addiction was more than a physical or even a psychological condition. It was, he concluded, a spiritual crisis, one that called for a remedy of unearthly proportions. Adapting and expanding upon principles espoused by a Christianity-based organization called the Oxford Group, Bill set out to develop his own step-by-step, nondogmatic approach to sobriety founded on a fundamental belief in a "Higher Power." Bill hoped the graduated process by which his own life was being restored would similarly relieve fellow alcoholics, who in turn could share the program with even more people.*[3]

By the mid-1930s, Bill and a handful of newly sober believers had established the first Alcoholics Anonymous support group meetings in Akron, Ohio, and New York City. These discreet rented spaces became safe havens for the founding members of A.A. as they worked to refine the twelve steps to recovery. These pioneers of sobriety wasted no time in compiling Alcoholics Anonymous—*a text more informally referred to as "the Big Book." Providing instruction and personalized testimony, the Big Book has, over the last six decades, sold more than twenty million English-language copies, and continues to be read out loud, every day, in A.A. meetings all around the world.*

From the founders' initial trials emerged a nondenominational organization with self-governing satellite groups that impose no membership dues or requirements for admission other than a desire to stop drinking. As one founder writes, "You are an A.A. member if you say so . . . no matter . . . how grave your emotional complications—even your crimes—we still cannot deny you A.A."[4] *And no matter how many slips, binges, or absences, one and all are invariably welcomed back. "We are average Americans," says the Big Book, in describing the organization's members. "All sections of this country and many of its occupations are represented, as well as many political, economic, social, and religious backgrounds. We are people who normally would not mix. But there exists among us a fellowship."*[5]

Since its inception, the basic formula of recovery developed by A.A. has been replicated time and again to address an array of some two hundred addictions, ranging from gambling, to overeating, to sexual compulsion. Support groups for family and friends with addicted loved ones have also been created. Today, A.A. comprises over a hundred thousand registered groups worldwide, though exactly how many people its twelve steps have positively affected—for a period of time or a lifetime—is impossible to calculate due to the program's tradition of anonymity.

Recovering with a Friend

Everyone succumbs, on occasion, to temptation, whether in the form of a lover, a double-chocolate brownie, or a pair of shoes they just can't live without. But there are those among us who don't just possess desires—desire possesses them.

I had long thought of Alcoholics Anonymous as a recovery program that equipped people with twelve ways to take *control* of their addictions, and thus take back their lives. But in looking closer, I found that, in fact, A.A. teaches its members just the reverse: admission of powerlessness. "Most of us have been unwilling to admit we were real alcoholics," says the Big Book. "No person likes to think he is bodily and mentally different from his fellows. Therefore, it is not surprising that our drinking careers have been characterized by countless vain attempts to prove we could drink like other people. . . . [But] we alcoholics are men and women who have lost the ability to control our drinking. . . . We are like men who have lost their legs; they never grow new ones."[6]

It is among a roomful of people who understand this disability that each new member takes the first, ineluctable step of publicly acknowledging the often painfully protected secret of their addiction. Thus begins a lifelong process of surrendering to a Higher Power a faith they once placed solely and destructively in themselves. "If a mere code of morals or a better philosophy of life were sufficient to overcome alcoholism, many of us would have recovered long ago," says the Big Book. "But after a while we had to face the fact that we must find a spiritual basis of life—or else."[7]

I became aware of this spiritual dimension of A.A. through an old friend who had long been as attached to his methamphetamine and vermouth as he was to his atheism. My longtime Los Angeles neighbor, David's apartment was connected to mine by one uninsulated wall. Sometimes our living arrangement was quite peaceful, when, like a traveling salesman, David would disappear for days at a time. But his return was always as predictable as the sleepless nights that followed. Our flimsy partition was unable to buffer the aching, hacking sounds of a binge's dead end, tar-clogged lungs, physical exhaustion, and regret exacting their unsympathetic toll on a human body. But what rumbled loudest through the plaster was David's contempt—an upheaval of blame and resentment for the parents who failed him, the society that scorned his gay "lifestyle," the God of his youth who disdained "his sort," and the immune deficiency disease that stalked him. Having never been the violent type, David turned fear and anger inward.

Sometimes I tried to confront David; other times I tried to soothe him, wishing I could pry him away from his ever-present despair and denial. But like everyone else in his life, I was unsuccessful. Eventually outgrowing my narrow and noisy rental, I moved up the street, continuing to observe David's ever more excessive sprees and downward spirals from a distance. When I later moved away from Los Angeles and hugged David good-bye, I privately wondered if he would still be alive when I next had the chance to knock on his door.

Many months later I received an e-mail from him, announcing that he was not only alive, he was sober. Even more shocking, he was attributing this achievement to *God*. In his message he explained that at the end of one of his weeklong "episodes" he had woken up in yet another strange hospital bed. Only this time, there was a conspicuous lack of visitors and get-well cards. And for some reason, he said, he was able to step "outside of himself" and see clearly that this was a matter of life and death, and that he wanted to fight for life.

"For so many years I had been trying to slowly kill myself *and* stay awake for every moment of what was left of my life," David said with uncharacteristic candor, when we spoke briefly on the phone. "I figured I'd go out with a bang by exercising, in a pathetic way, this control over my life—a life that otherwise felt out of my hands. But alone in that hospital room, I took an honest look at myself and was forced to acknowledge that the control I was certain I possessed was just an illusion.

"I have spent the better part of my life indulging in anything that would keep me from having to honestly reconcile the world I was living in with any sort of fairness, or anything greater than myself," David acknowledged when we continued our conversation a few months later, this time in person. That evening we celebrated his sixth month of sobriety with the clink of soda cans.

"I worked *so* hard at being an atheist," he said, a veteran surveying the washed-out beachhead he'd once painstakingly defended. "You have to work very, very hard to deny the existence of God. I was able to do it for a long time because I was a 'thinking person,' and, after all"—he smirked—"it's not responsible of an intellectual to believe in God." But with a renewed desire to live—and the imperatives of A.A. so clearly laid out before him—believing is exactly what David set out to do.

Studying David's face, I saw that it reflected the internal changes he had undergone. His once pocked, pale gauntness and darting eyes had been replaced by healthy pink cheeks and a gaze that held mine with a new willingness to be seen and known. But what was most gripping about David's retooled demeanor was the way and speed with which he had become downright spiritual. This sudden top-to-bottom alteration had not come by the means I might have expected, such as through a liberal parish, or a conveniently located meditation center, or even a laid-back guru. Rather, his metamorphosis had been administered by a recovery program determined to make him physically well by rehabilitating his spirit.

While A.A insists its program can be effective with or without spiritual conversion, a remarkable number of members find that their sobriety depends upon it. Following the instruction of A.A.'s third step, every member chooses how they want to define their Higher Power. Die-hard atheists might decide to vest their faith in secular humanism, or find their deity in nature—in the expansiveness of an ocean or the quiet strength of a mountain, perhaps. Or they may simply place their faith in fellow A.A. members, whose collective fortitude and insight is greater than that of any individual. But many long-term members, most of whom were previously irreligious or at least on sabbatical, look to "God" as their Higher Power, a wisdom to which they must now defer.

David began to craft his personally defined relationship with God under the guidance of his A.A. sponsor—a more senior member who volunteers to be on call twenty-four hours a day, seven days a week, for one-on-one support. Overcoming the negative religious experiences of his past, David reimagined the despotic God with which he'd been raised, envisioning for himself a new source of divinity that inspired his trust. "I made a list of

God's desired qualities," recalled David as we drove to the West Holly-wood church where he daily attends an A.A. meeting: "loves me for who I am, wants the best for me, speaks to me through all people and all things, and is not wrathful or patriarchal." I told David that it sounded as if he had managed to pull the best of every religious tradition's definition of *Higher Power* under his one concise roof.

As we pulled into the church parking lot, I asked David what his first A.A. meeting was like. "I just sat there thinking *These people are onto me*," he said. "And then I realized they were onto me because they *are* me—they have the same self-obsession and powerlessness over drugs and/or alcohol as I do." Making our way to the church entrance, we joined about two dozen of those people, who, like grifters, can readily spot each other's scams and disguises.

Abuzz with chatter, this extended A.A. family clustered around the church stoop catching up from when last they spoke, which, for most of those present, was exactly twenty-four hours earlier. The unhesitating handshakes, reassuring shoulder squeezes, and inexhaustible willingness to lend an ear reminded me of my college days, when cataloging every minute detail of many friends' lives never felt burdensome. This casual camaraderie seemed as important to these men and women as the more structured one-hour meeting that followed.

David and I took two seats among the rows of metal folding chairs fac-ing a podium. This informal soapbox would accommodate the spontaneous thoughts, confessions, and encouragement of many of those present. That night's "visiting speaker"—a rotating volunteer who oversees each meet-ing—called ours to order by reciting A.A.'s preamble: "Alcoholics Anony-mous is a fellowship of men and women who share their experience, strength and hope with each other that they may solve their common problem and help others to recover from alcoholism. . . ." All out-of-towners, first-timers, and those returning with less than thirty days of sobri ety were welcomed and asked to stand and state their name as well as "the nature of their disease." As each person stood to give their first name only—honoring the rule of A.A. anonymity—the rest of us pitched back a personalized and boisterous hello.

Flipping open an old cigar box, one veteran member began awarding the highly coveted colored poker chips to those who had been sober for milestones of thirty, sixty, and ninety days, or six or nine months. To those who made their way to the front of the room, the plastic chip, like a communion wafer, represented rebirth and renewal—a very tangible form of salvation. Hearing his name on the roll call, David lunged forward to claim his six-month marker with the blushing grin of a schoolboy.

Reaching under his chair, the chip guy pulled out a miniature cake topped by a single candle, which he lit as he led the room in a classic rendition of "Happy Birthday," slowly shuffling toward a tearful middle-aged man who very apparently had a wish to make on this the eve of his first year of sobriety.

Reclaiming the podium, the evening's guest speaker contextualized A.A.'s success by relaying her own story: the partying in college that led to daytime drinking, the drinking on the job that led to blackouts, the stealing from family that led to a humiliating web of lies and guilt, a thwarted career, and a brush with death. It all finally led to a first day of sobriety, and another, and another . . . until today.

After others randomly stood to confide their stories and most recent struggles—a method of self-preservation through self-exposure—another reflective section was read aloud from the pages of their Big Book. "Our book is meant to be suggestive only," wrote the founders of A.A. to future generations in recovery. "We realize we know only a little. God will constantly disclose more to you and to us. . . .

"Abandon yourself to God as you understand God. Admit your faults to Him and to your fellows. Clear away the wreckage of your past. Give freely of what you find and join us. We shall be with you in the Fellowship of the Spirit, and you will surely meet some of us as you trudge the Road of Happy Destiny.

"May God bless you and keep you—until then."[8]

Bringing closure to our meeting with the recurrent A.A. theme of humility and willingness, we all stood to recite the traditional version of the Lord's Prayer:

> *Our Father who art in heaven, hallowed be Thy name.*
> *Thy Kingdom come, Thy will be done on earth as it is in heaven.*
> *Give us this day our daily bread.*
> *And forgive us our trespasses as we forgive those who trespass against us.*
> *And lead us not into temptation, but deliver us from evil.*
> *For Yours is the Kingdom, and the Power, and the Glory forever. Amen.*[9]

As David drove us back to his apartment, he told me his sobriety depended on two things: service to others in need—particularly other addicts—and the maintenance of his "spiritual condition" through a practice A.A. calls a "fearless and searching moral inventory."

"As an addict," David confided, "I never examined my motives. . . . Now, I try to be constantly aware of what I'm doing and why, watching my reactions and self-centeredness, because it's what separates me from God and other people. I have to take constant inventory in order to continually discover what God's will is over my own." Through a careful itemization of past words or deeds that have negatively affected another person, David and others in A.A. actively try to make amends for the suffering they've caused, giving unqualified apologies to those they feel they've harmed through the years. Following A.A.'s guiding tenets of truth, open-mindedness, and surrender, members try to move closer to the kind of transparent, objective reality sought through denominational faiths, particularly those of Eastern origin.

A.A. has its own way of practicing present-moment awareness, akin to Zen Master Seung Sahn's metaphor of the CLEAR button on a calculator. Maintaining sobriety *one day at a time,* recovering alcoholics constantly return to zero, every morning reiterating their effort to reorient their lives and proceed with conscious intent. The A.A. motto is not unlike a mantra: "spiritual progress rather than spiritual perfection"; and David told me he repeats this silently to himself throughout the day.

After six months of learning not how to conquer but how to *manage* his addictive tendencies through steps like admission of powerlessness, surrender to a Higher Power, life inventory, and restitution, David reached the twelfth and final step: *"Having had a spiritual awakening as the result of these steps, we tried to carry this message to alcoholics, and to practice these principles in all our affairs."* A.A. members say that by imparting their steps and offering support to other alcoholics, they all but guarantee their own sobriety; the dutiful messenger is gifted, again and again, with his own message, a uniquely beneficial example of the "sourcing" that Neale Donald Walsch had extolled.

The eleventh step offers A.A. members a way to help sustain on a daily basis their newly acquired equilibrium: *"Sought through prayer and meditation to improve our conscious contact with God as we understood Him, praying only for knowledge of His will for us and the power to carry that out."* As one of the program's founders writes, "It has been well said, that 'almost the only scoffers at prayer are those who never tried it enough.' Those of us who have come to make regular use of prayer would no more do without it than we would refuse air, food, or sunshine."[10]

Knowing David's history of spiritual and philosophical anarchy, I was curious about how he was negotiating these conventional practices. "People make such a stink—probably not just in A.A.—about the *right* and *wrong* way to meditate and pray," he protested. "How I go about them is simple—I clear my mind to make room for God, deleting any thought or plan that would impose my own will, asking to be shown *God's* way." Defining *God's way* as "that which alleviates all sense of isolation and aloneness," David says he asks that he be shown the choices and actions that will "usefully" connect him to himself, the people in his life, and the world at large.

David and I sat in my old apartment; he now rents both and has removed the wall that once stood between us. Against a panoramic backdrop of downtown Los Angeles, David spoke of, and then marveled at, his new sense of kinship with all that glimmers beyond his picture window. It was in the room where we sat that I had encountered my grandmother after her death, a premature passing caused largely by the effects of alcoholism. I could remember so vividly what it was like to feel the sensation of meeting my grandmother for the first time—a virtual stranger to me who had all along been dwelling beneath the addiction. Sitting with David, I experienced the same sensation, relieved and also in awe of the fact that, unlike my grandmother, he had found the courage and the faith to uncover himself while still alive. Dispelling the common notion that people cannot fundamentally change, David was, one day at a time, exhibiting the human capacity to do just that. In this way, he had become for me the best kind of spiritual teacher.

"It says in the Big Book," he interjected into our silence, "we are not a glum lot; we are meant to be happy, joyous, and free. If we're seeking out God's will, being sober, and being a worker among workers, this is what we can be."

Chapter Eighteen

According to the *40th Anniversary Scientology Catalogue*, the most popular self-help book of all time is L. Ron Hubbard's **Dianetics: The Modern Science of Mental Health**, *published in 1950, with more than eighteen million copies sold to date.[1] Forming the foundation of Scientology,* Dianetics *explores the influence that past events have over our current physical, emotional, and psychological well-being. The book's premise states that our minds have two primary components—one "analytical," the other "reactive." Through a series of cues and drills, Hubbard intended to isolate and effectively neutralize the reactive, unconscious part of the brain that records and stores internal, unfiltered responses to every moment of our lives. Hubbard believed it possible to virtually uproot the source of any physical or psychological ailment while strengthening all analytical, rational faculties. He even claimed to have healed himself of near blindness and a crippled leg using his set of procedures, inspiring him to invent and patent the Electropsychometer (abbreviated as E-Meter), an instrument purportedly capable of measuring the activity of the unconscious mind.*

After the successful publication of Dianetics, *Hubbard began to found his religion. Authoring a complex creation story and belief system replete with its own vocabulary, ethical code, and curriculum, Hubbard unveiled a methodology whereby people could access their full potential as spiritual beings. In 1955*

Hubbard opened the doors to his first Church of Scientology, broadening the definition of religion in America with a flamboyant futurism. However, it wasn't until 1993, seven years after Hubbard's death, that Scientology's twenty-five-year legal battle with the Internal Revenue Service for recognition as a religious organization was finally resolved, formally inducting Scientology into the tax-exempt hall of faith.

Today, the church estimates that eight million people worldwide regularly participate in some form of Scientology, whether through its classes, one-on-one "auditing" sessions, volunteer programs, or Sunday services held in many of its nearly four hundred churches and missions around the globe. Membership figures specific to the United States are not available.

Crossing the Bridge
with Scientologists

For more than a decade I drove past the towering neon sign on Hollywood Boulevard—three stories of glowing letters reaching for the sky to proclaim SCIENTOLOGY. Sandwiched between Frederick's of Hollywood and McDonald's golden arches, the founding Dianetics Center is its own landmark of near-legendary status. Having long beheld its premises at a speed of at least twenty miles per hour, I decided to stop and find out what Scientology was all about.

"Tired of having problems? Tired of being ill? Tired of being human? Dianetics and Scientology contain the bright new effective answers to life's problems," entices a typical Scientology brochure.[2] The organization offers solutions to everything from acute allergies and addiction, to psychosomatic illness and phobias, to failing marriages, a lagging memory, a low I.Q., even an overdrawn bank account. Lafayette Ron Hubbard's utopian vision includes a civilization healed of crime, drugs, insanity, war, and everyday doldrums. All of this, and more, Hubbard encapsulated in the term *Scientology,* which he defined as "knowing how to know."

Naturally I was curious about how all of this promise was translated into practice. Like most people, I had surface impressions of Scientology, like its knack for attracting celebrities and its reputation for defensive secrecy. And with a quick Web search, it's easy to find reams of complaints lodged by disgruntled ex-members, concerned families, cult-watch centers, and even whole countries, such as Spain, France, Belgium, and Germany—all passionately denouncing the methods and motives behind Hubbard's work. Before he died, Hubbard famously returned his critics' fire, labeling them all "merchants of chaos" who conspire to maintain the status quo of widespread poverty, crime, mental illness, and war as a way of keeping the masses emotionally and mentally enslaved. Obsessed with coining new terminology, Hubbard even created a special acronym for his detractors: SP, for "suppressive person"—an individual who is part of the "roughly two percent of the population [who] cannot tolerate that Scientology is successful at improving conditions around the world."[3]

As a linchpin to his plan for spiritual emancipation, Hubbard dreamed up the Scientology Celebrity Center of Los Angeles, the first of thirteen such sites nationwide. Another Los Angeles monument, this iron-gated château is shrouded in the members-only mystique of an exclusive country club at whose entrance one can see smartly dressed valet parkers helping sports figures, business executives, and, of course, movie stars out of their cars. In one of its promotional videos, the actress Jenna Elfman explains that the Celebrity Center is "the only true safe space for us as artists."

Hubbard's affection for artists—or more precisely, celebrities—was explained to me by a Scientology employee. Called a Registrar, this person's sole professional mission is to sign up individuals for the classes and sessions offered by the church, keeping members moving across Hubbard's "bridge to total freedom."

"L. Ron always said," the Registrar recalled as we sat together in her office, "a culture is only as great as its dreams. And L. Ron believed those dreams are dreamed by *artists,* so when we in Scientology help raise the tone of an artist, the tone of all of society is uplifted."

"Tone?" I queried.

"It's like awareness," she clarified.

I was meeting with the Registrar because I had recently completed Scientology's standard personality test, called the Oxford Capacity Analysis, a kind of assessment exam that helps a Registrar pitch a tailored program to both prospective and active Scientologists. After responding to about a hundred multiple-choice questions, such as "Do you feel comfortable talking to strangers at a party?" my computer printout results were ready for review.

An enthusiastic fast-talking Bostonian, the Registrar skimmed the pages of my evaluation, interpreting them. "You're very active and communicative," she began. "And you did score in the ninetieth percentile for overall happiness, *but* I see that you lack empathy. You're not well understood by others and/or you have a hard time understanding where others are coming from. You're not very appreciative, and you tend to assume the negative over the positive. And on stability," she continued as I tried to keep up with my handwritten notes, "you scored only in the sixtieth percentile. But your most pressing issue," she concernedly concluded, dragging her index finger across my chart, "is your lack of responsibility, which, as you can see, dips down into the 'unacceptable state.'"

When the woman finally paused for breath, I asked her if I could have a closer look at the stapled report. "Oh, no, I'm sorry, this goes in your file," she said cheerily, slipping the paper into a manila folder and placing it out of my reach.

I was stunned, and then indignant. I explained that being new to Scientology, I was disturbed by this KGB-style treatment of my personal file. "Well, you see, that's your tendency to assume the negative," she said. After listening to her describe which particular classes she felt I should take, I explained that I was already scheduled to begin an intensive Scientology course in "auditing" and had been told to take her test as a procedural precursor. "Well then, I hope to see you again when you finish your course so we can talk some more," she said, as if our next meeting was something we could both look forward to.

Given the choice of either attending a Hubbard class or pairing up with a Scientology "minister" for one-on-one counseling, I opted for the latter. I hoped, among other things, that these private sessions would reveal the essence of Hubbard's philosophy and practice. Without the budget to afford Scientology's going prices—my intensive three-month course would have cost about five thousand dollars—a minister-in-training named Therman agreed to take my case pro bono.

Derived from the Latin root *auditio*—"one who listens"—Scientology's practice of auditing is essentially a hybrid of confession and talk therapy. Through precisely worded questions and carefully monitored answers, Hubbard believed, one could attain mental clarity and emotional transcendence—a system he claimed was even more effective than modern psychiatry. In fact, Hubbard went so far as to condemn psychiatrists and their prescription pads. As my Scientology auditor—also referred to as a minister—expounded: "Psychiatrists mask underlying causes by prescribing drugs, and they *evaluate* people, which diminishes their 'beingness.'"

Despite Therman's uncanny resemblance to the outrageous Salvador Dalí (right down to the ink-black handlebar mustache), he was shy and soft-spoken. Prior to pursuing a career in Scientology, Therman had been a milk-truck driver, delivering his dairy goods the old-fashioned way in a rural town a few hours outside of Boston. After dabbling in Scientology and attributing profound personal changes to its program, Therman and his girlfriend packed up and headed for the city. There they work side-by-side as Scientology employees by day so that they can be its sponsored students at night.

I met with Therman after hours in the five-story converted brownstone, a once-elegant structure that now housed dozens of uninspired office spaces offset by boldly colored science fiction posters publicizing Hubbard's *other* career as a novelist. In one of these rooms—starkly furnished with a metal desk, two rickety chairs, a framed photograph of L. Ron Hubbard, a *Bridge to Total Freedom* poster, one box of Kleenex, and a mind-reading E-Meter—Therman and I would, week after week, repeat the same routine.

At our initial meeting, Therman prepared me for what was to come, drilling me on the extensive lexicon of Scientology that would prove central to our subsequent sessions. He stressed the importance of *thoroughly* understanding "the complete meaning" of each of Hubbard's words; "otherwise the effectiveness of the technology could be compromised." If at any point I experienced doubt or confusion about Hubbard's acronyms and special terminology, I was to interrupt our session so we could review the vocabulary test.

Practicing my fluency, I asked Therman what "all the RDs, TRs, and hatting had personally given him as a once-aberrated man." In other words, how had all his Scientology practice improved his life? "It's given me practical, useful knowledge," he said, drawing two metal cylinders from a briefcase and attaching them to the E-Meter's dangling cables. "Like learning how to shingle a house, Scientology teaches you how to more effectively operate in the world with greater affinity. Most of the practical data is transmitted through the classes, while auditing clears you of 'stops' "—anything that compromises a person's potential. "Plus the process of auditing can be quite a spiritual experience, so you get the best of both worlds."

I followed Therman's instruction and gripped the two metal cylinders lightly, one in each hand, making sure the pads of my fingers made full contact with their smooth surface. Therman's job was to survey the E-Meter—considered a "religious artifact" in the Church of Scientology—and record its measurements as well as my verbal responses to his questions, noting the instances when my words failed to match the E-Meter's more accurate extrapolations. Later this "data" would be double-checked by my "case supervisor," an individual whose identity was not revealed to me.

Offering me an E-Meter demonstration, Therman turned the board around (it is normally kept obscured from the parishioner's view), allowing me to observe my own "electropsychic" signals. The E-Meter needle, which sways between a positive and a negative "charge," indicates trauma or "enturbulence" lurking somewhere beneath the surface of whatever thought or memory is *consciously* taking place at that particular moment. But with each of my thoughts, the needle tilted only *slightly* to the left or the right, like an unconvincing battery diagnostic, giving Therman the suspicion that I'd been fitted with the wrong-size cans. Dipping back into his briefcase, he produced an alternate pair, as well as a squirt of lotion he asked me to rub into my hands to improve conductivity. Satisfied with my strengthened signal, he turned the board to once again face him, ready to begin.

"What we'll be doing is a 'PC disability rundown,'" Therman explained. PC is the Hubbard-approved acronym for "PreClear"—an individual whose reactive mind has not yet been deactivated and is therefore in need of auditing in order to reach "Clear." Clear is Hubbard's equivalent of spiritual mastery, an exalted state that enables those who attain it to see everything—themselves, events, others, the world—with pure objectivity and compassion.

When one "goes Clear"—usually after thousands of hours of auditing, which cost tens of thousands of dollars—one becomes an O.T. ("operating Thetan"), an individual who has "become refamiliarized with his native capabilities" as an embodied spirit.[4]

Not surprisingly, Hubbard was the first Scientologist to go Clear and achieve O.T. status. According to his and others' accounts, this endowed him with unerring control over his life's conditions, total accountability, flawless communication skills, an evolved ethical standard, and—as with cartoon action figures and the saints of India—extrasensory abilities that enabled him to manipulate at will matter, energy, space, and time.

When pressed for an example of O.T. powers, one Scientology spokesperson shared with me a collaboration he says his church is currently engaged in with the Central Intelligence Agency. Calling it "the remote spy millennium project," he said certain advanced Scientologists have been demonstrating for our government their ability to "astrally project" themselves from the room in which they sit to any destination around the world, allowing for a risk-free collection of top secret data. The spokesperson assured me that if the project moves forward, it will conform to Scientology's high ethical standards, spying only if such activity would result in the betterment and preservation of *all* of humankind.

Setting my sights a little lower than secret agent, I plodded along with Therman. At the top of each session, I would answer a preliminary series of questions to test my "current state of physical being," though Therman was more interested in the E-Meter's silent responses than my verbal ones. If it was mechanically indicated that my vital signs were low, or that I had not eaten or slept enough, or was deficient in certain vitamins, or had taken any medication, including aspirin, I would be considered unfit to audit, and be sent home. This occurred only once, when the E-Meter indicated that my banana-on-the-run was not sufficient nourishment to sustain our Saturday-morning appointment.

With an otherwise clean bill of health issued by the E-Meter, Therman would proceed with his instruction that I "locate" an incident when I "took" the emotion of acute anxiety, fear, inadequacy, or danger. After analyzing the E-Meter's results, Therman had theorized during our intro-ductory session that some traumatizing childhood events must be the cause of at least some of the lagging percentages my personality test had revealed. Since I had never met anyone who had made it through childhood without trauma, I couldn't disagree with his—via Hubbard's—hypothesis.

Sitting across from Therman with closed eyes, I would dredge up men-tal images of my yesterdays, one by one, at first going back just a few weeks until progressively reaching further and further into my toddler years. Frag-ments of my life that I'd all but forgotten resurfaced, like the time I dialed my adoptive father's number in the middle of the night, desperate to hear that the physical distance between us hadn't made him stop loving me. I remembered the time I watched with horror as my dog, Shags, was mur-dered in my front yard by another, larger dog—my first experience of death and my powerlessness to stop it. And then, traveling even further back to the age of four—the look on my biological father's face as he ner-vously drove me back to my mother's house many states away while I lay next to him delirious with a fever. I was asked to relive each unpleasant remembrance again and again in vivid detail using my "perceptics"—senses of sight, sound, smell, taste, and touch. In the process, Therman came to know my archive of memories as well as I did, given the Scientology prem-ise that it is the *repetitiveness* of reviewing these experiences that neutralizes their "charge."

After reviewing, ad nauseam, a single scene from the story of my life, I would open my eyes and shake off the trancelike state that comes when you so completely transport your mind's eye to another place and time. Based on the needle's response, Therman would either indicate that I still showed "charge" and must once again recount the memory, or he would direct me to search my "time track" for an earlier, related event until we would, at last, arrive at an "engram." Engrams lock the mind into a distorted thought pattern. To isolate an engram—and decode its "postulate"—is to wipe out the root source of its particular mental plague.

Complicating—or at least drawing out—the scavenger hunt for charged memories and the engrams to which they attach, is Hubbard's supposition that we've all been reincarnating for some seventy-six trillion years. Downplaying the element of reincarnation, Therman insisted that to simply clear the *one life* I was now living would, in and of itself, be of measurable benefit. "Though a past life could slip through at any time," he warned, as I tried to imagine the kinds of traumatic scenarios I might have found myself in even just one trillion years ago.

Intrigued, I pursued Scientology's tenet of reincarnation through an official spokesperson, who provided me with what he called "corroborated evidence." Children, he said, have been walking off the street into Scientology Centers, demanding they be given their "old jobs" back. According to this insider employee, these youths have clear memories of their last life as contracted employees of Scientology—the small-print terms of which are said to stipulate a *multiple* life commitment. Because of the copious files it keeps on every member—even after he or she has died—the church has apparently been able to, at least internally, verify these far-out claims as accurate. "Of course, we can't give these children their jobs back *right away*," the spokesperson chuckled, as if child labor laws were the only thing standing in the way. But he said the church does allow these reincarnated members—for a fee and with their parents' permission, of course—to take classes and be audited, picking up right where they had left off in their last life.

Like people who explore spiritual experience through conventional worship, Scientologists of all ages look to their practice as a means to clarity, truth, wisdom, and happiness. While I personally did not spend enough time, or enough money, to reach the state of Clear, my auditing sessions were sometimes cathartic. They reminded me of forgotten events that explained certain impulses or proclivities, like my visceral fear of German shepherds and my knee-jerk preference for just about any underdog. But I

can't say my excavated memories offered convincing evidence of the anti-
social tendencies disclosed by my Scientology-administered personality
test. In fact, more than any personal insight, the methodical and monoto-
nous reliving of my past left me feeling listless, if not anesthetized. Memories—both painful and pleasing—that once kept times, places, and people
alive in me became worn and deadened. But according to Scientologists,
that was just a necessary part of *the process.*

"Name something in this room that you can have," cajoled Therman after
one particularly draining session. I stared silently at him in my state of
despondency trying to figure out what new scripted game we were playing.
When he repeated his directive, I warily scanned the room for a prize to
claim.

"The box of Kleenex," I finally uttered, opting for something of practical use.

"What else?" he pushed, as if the tissues had already been promised to
another parishioner.

I hesitated, then went for the sepia-toned photograph of Hubbard
hanging over Therman's shoulder.

"Good," he encouraged. "What else?"

This went on until I named every object not bolted to the floor as
something I could "have," an exercise aptly titled Havingness. Therman
later explained that this Hubbard drill is "run" on PreClears as a way of off-
setting the possible side effects of emptying oneself of one's most intimate—and often disturbing—history. (It didn't make me feel better.)
Heading home after some sessions, I felt as I imagined one might after
being exorcised: desperate for a hearty meal and a long night's rest, and forever vulnerable to the minister—and the church—that had orchestrated,
and notated, the entire ordeal.

Still, at a time when we all seem to be in desperate need of being heard
over the din of white noise that surrounds us, Scientology ministers offer
something for which people thirst. But after three months of being expertly
listened to, I felt plenty quenched, ready to do some focused listening of
my own. After months of badgering, the president of Scientology had
finally agreed to meet with me in his office overlooking Hollywood Boulevard, just down the road from that towering neon sign.

My expectations for this one-on-one encounter were admittedly low. I had read enough of Hubbard's "scripture"—a canon that reportedly consists of more than thirty-five million words—to know that his religious overview included instruction on how a Scientologist should respond to virtually every question a non-Scientologist might ask, especially an investigative one. Hubbard even went so far as to formulate a Dissemination Course that exhaustively covers the topic, one of the few classes the church offers free of charge to anyone wishing to arm themselves with bulletproof answers to questions like: Is Scientology a cult? Who was L. Ron Hubbard? Did he make a lot of money from Scientology?[5]

Escorted to his hunter green corporate executive–like office, I was greeted by Rev. Jentzsch's affable handshake and an invitation to take a seat in front of his stately, immaculate desk, as he resumed his place behind it. For a while we cordially chatted about my travels and the faiths I had so far explored, Rev. Jentzsch expressing great interest in my "findings." With one eye on the sand in our hourglass, I redirected the conversation, asking Rev. Jentzsch what had personally attracted him to Scientology some twenty years earlier. "Of course, of course, that's why you're here," he acknowledged, like a politician who secretly hoped the press conference would end without those pesky questions.

With effortless transition, Rev. Jentzsch explained his attraction to Scientology by comparing it with the faith of his childhood. "I was raised Mormon," he began. "When I was young my father had certain abilities. He could lay his hands on people and heal them. But with the technology of counseling we have in Scientology, we can help an individual achieve freedom from *emotional* traumas," he said, pointing to what he felt was an even more profound form of healing. "By reducing trauma, we release the abilities of the human spirit."

Rev. Jentzsch went on to praise the pragmatism of Scientology with his own analogy. "If you're drowning and you have faith that you're going to swim, but no one ever *taught* you to swim, that's not very practical. Having been a lifeguard, [I learned] you have to have some idea of what you're doing in the water," he declared. Scientologists consider the lessons they offer to be a more sensible life vest than a blind belief in supernatural assistance symbolized by a cross hanging around one's neck or a saint taped to one's dashboard. Why wouldn't you want to save *yourself*? Rev. Jentzsch indirectly asked.

"With Scientology, you don't have to believe it at all," he went on to explain. "You just engage in the doingness of its practice, and you will inevitably experience the '*wins*'"—a Scientology term that means personal *benefits*. Illustrating how "doing" Scientology can also be of benefit to others, Reverend Jentzsch shared an experience he'd had on a recent bumpy flight. "The woman in back of me started screaming," he said in recalling the turbulent ride. "I turned around and gave her what Scientologists call 'location,' instructing her to look over there, look over here, back and forth, until she began to calm down. When she continued to insist that flying was dangerous, I walked her through the specifics of what was happening. 'We're going through a pocket of less dense air, and there's been a storm, so we've got some rising heat, but we'll come through that, and then we're going to land and it's going to be okay.' Well, that is how a Scientologist operates."

Confident that a levelheaded non-Scientologist could calm a nervous flier with equal success, and noticing the parallels between "location" and Buddhism's practice of present-moment mindfulness, I asked Rev. Jentzsch if he considered Hubbard's training and techniques to be truly groundbreaking. "I think everybody has the instinct to help another human being," he conceded, "but I believe the *precision* of what we have, and its workability, is more powerful and immediately effective than anything else out there." Like my memories, everything Rev. Jentzsch said felt as if it had been repeated dozens of times before, until emptied of real meaning or emotion. In concluding his assessment of Scientology, however, he added a personal touch through the words of "an Evangelical friend."

"What's so positive and interesting about Scientology," Rev. Jentzsch's Christian colleague had said, "is that Mr. Hubbard gave people a way of achieving a certain amount of heaven while still on earth. They don't have to wait to see whether they collect when they die."

Cashing in their heavenly chips early, Scientologists are also exempt from the traditional, time-consuming rituals of earthly piety, except for that occasional service in memory of L. Ron Hubbard. During my stint as a Scientology parishioner, I attended a few "graduation ceremonies"—gatherings of Scientologists who have successfully completed an increment of auditing or one of Hubbard's classes, and stand to publicly declare the "wins" that Rev. Jentzsch had mentioned. In one ceremony, a young woman walked to the front of the room with a guitar in hand and sang a beautiful folk song, explaining afterward that her auditing had completely cured her of paralyzing stage fright. In another testimonial, a Mexican immigrant credited his Scientology class with a newly acquired ability to read and write in English. "I even know what a gerund is," he joked triumphantly, as he shared his plans to open an auto repair business. The man's optimism and sense of possibility were contagious, and I cheered for him as loudly as everyone else, following his grin all the way back to his seat.

After the last graduate had been praised with group validation, everyone stood to offer one final gesture of appreciation to the man who made it all possible. Facing a large portrait of their founder, all clapped with vigor, except me. While the practice of acknowledging a founder and teacher—alive or deceased—is not uncommon among the world's religions, the sudden outburst of reverence for the color-enhanced Hubbard seemed awkward, if not a little creepy. And yet I had met a number of people at this and other Scientology functions who credited Hubbard with a sense of liberation, enlightenment, and purpose that was no less real to them than that expressed by Christians, Jews, Buddhists, Hindus, or Muslims. I wondered if in a hundred years it would no longer seem strange to give Hubbard a standing ovation, just as it has become less controversial to praise the likes of Joseph Smith and his Mormon followers, and Mary Baker Eddy and hers. Or perhaps my reluctance to clap for Hubbard will still be felt by many, even in the future. Whatever the case, I knew that if Hubbard were still alive, he'd probably say my hesitation was a simple "aberration" stemming from my suppressive personality—an inability to feel unqualified appreciation for the religion that is, according to his own words, "doing more to help society than any other group."[6]

I had made an earnest effort to get at the individual and collective "good" that Hubbard's practice was doing. I had subjected myself to his E-Meter, talked to a variety of Scientologists from all organizational levels, and read thousands of Hubbard's own words. But endeavoring to get an outsider's perspective on this very insider faith was like trying to check the pulse of Siamese twins by monitoring only one of their wrists—I never felt confident that what I was hearing or reading was the full story. The further I followed Scientology's maze, the more disoriented I became, a result I began to suspect wasn't that far from the intent of this man who spent the better part of his career borrowing, deconstructing, refurbishing, and combining his era's scientific, religious, and philosophical theories.

Rev. Jentzsch had suggested that before leaving the inner sanctum of Clearness, I visit the Hubbard Life Exhibit downstairs from his office to get a better sense of Hubbard "as a person." After saying good-bye, Rev. Jentzsch handed me over to a private tour guide, who offered to store my heavy bag behind the lobby's information desk, under the supervision of two young women.

Inside the museum-quality exhibit, a recorded voice described a paneled collage of Hubbard's world travels. From Mongolian bandits, to the Tlingit Indians of Alaska, to lamas in the remote western hills of China and the last spiral magician of Kublai Khan, Hubbard had brushed shoulders and brainstormed with some of the most impressive spiritual masters our globe has to offer. "Mr. Hubbard was even made a blood brother by a Blackfoot Indian shaman when he was just a boy," remarked my twenty-something guide. Cataloging no less than twenty-nine occupations Hubbard had "mastered," including expeditionist, seaman, horticulturist, aviator, photographer, writer, composer, filmmaker, husband, and father, the promo-temple enshrined its host in Midas-like power.

For the next few hours, I wandered the corridors and partitioned rooms crowded with images and information. I gazed through display cases at Hubbard's trade tools and inventions, watched a star-studded short film praising his drug and alcohol purification programs, and was bedazzled by a giant wall of gilded proclamations signed by government officials—a national plethora of Dianetics Months and L. Ron Hubbard Days. At every turn was the subliminal message *Take advantage of all that Scientology has to offer, and you, too, will be as clear, creative, and multifaceted as its prodigal founder.*

Returning to the comparatively prosaic reality of the center's lobby, I headed to the information desk to retrieve my belongings. One of the women stationed there foraged around for my stuff, while another one picked up the phone to make a call. Rev. Jentzsch suddenly reappeared, making awkward small talk about the exhibit's highlights, his cheeks gradually turning pink the way skin tone does before an uncomfortable confrontation.

"Um," he said, clearing his throat, "the girls behind the desk said that the recorder in your bag was left on while you were in the exhibit—I guess to secretly record their conversations." Stunned, I simply stared back at him. "See, we've had a lot of *incidents* lately," he went on to explain, briefing me on recent visitors—journalistic and not—who'd been caught smuggling in James Bond–style microscopic cameras and microphones, hoping for some kind of scoop. As Rev. Jentzsch described how one woman planted a camera in her hair bun, I wondered if I was the pawn in some-one's practical joke. The scenario just seemed too absurd and—given Sci-entology's reputation—too clichéd to be believed.

Realizing he was serious, I explained to Rev. Jentzsch that I distinctly remembered turning off my recorder at the end of our interview. To assuage his unrelenting concern, I offered to rewind the tape so he could hear for himself—an offer I assumed he would decline. To my surprise he suggested we sit on a nearby bench where he donned my headphones and listened intently to his own voice, followed by a few long minutes of a blank tape's white noise. Satisfied, he stood up, muttering something about "the girls" making "a mistake," and offered me another handshake good-bye, as if his shakedown was ordinary protocol.

As Rev. Jentzsch and I went our separate ways, I of course couldn't help imagining what those women behind the desk feared they'd divulged on my tape, information so vital—or perhaps *unspiritual*—that their presi-dent was willing to risk humiliation for its recovery. Or maybe it was just the general paranoia that must naturally pervade a religious practice based on the importance of airing out the dirty laundry of the mind.

Pushing through the doors of the church headquarters, back onto Hol-lywood Boulevard, I proceeded to walk over the stars embedded in the ground, their glimmer in varying stages of decay. I thought of would-be Scientologists lured to the Dianetics doors by the inferred promise that through them they would find fame and fortune, or at least stand very near to it, like a second cousin to Tom Cruise, Lisa Marie Presley, or Isaac Hayes. Passing by rows of souvenir shops, I decided that Hubbard's dream of replacing crime, insanity, addiction, and war with his own variation of clarity and oneness was a mission I could appreciate, even applaud. But his secret celebrity weapon in achieving this vision seemed emblematic of the distortion he attempted to isolate in the human mind—a billboard-size engram of his, and our culture's, scrambled priorities.

Treading over a few last stars before turning the corner onto the less glamorous Cahuenga Boulevard, I realized why Scientology wasn't for me. Strangely enough, as I mulled this over, Rabbi Grossman—the Orthodox rabbi from Memphis—popped into my head, along with his declaration that there are simply some things we as humans are not meant to control, or even to know. My exposure to Scientology had taken the rabbi's words into a whole new realm. I decided that no matter how high-tech or infallible the gadgetry, or how precise the inquiry, sometimes life's ancient riddles, the ones we all contend with—celebrity and civilian alike—defy quantification and captivity. And this natural law of the uncontainable seems to be what separates those of us who are forever in suspicious pursuit of life's slippery truth from those who live in wonder at the mystery whose tail I increasingly hope will never be caught.

Neopaganism

Chapter Nineteen

n the 1960s, pockets of feminist women and men began to revive practices
that belonged to a gender-inclusive, nature-based "Old Religion" inspired by
pre-Christian pagan worship, European folklore, and mythology.

The origins of America's neopagan movement—known variously as
"witchcraft," "the Craft," "Wicca," and "the Goddess religion"—are often
debated, even among its own diverse members. Some claim their practices are
inherited family traditions that have been secretly preserved for generations,
while others look to an eighteenth-century Englishman named Gerald Gard-
ner, whose writings about the Craft have been widely adopted and adapted.
And still others credit ancient civilizations of Siberia, parts of Europe, and the
Middle East, as well as other agrarian peoples of oral tradition, such as the
Irish and Scottish, and our own multifaceted Native Americans. "If you go far
enough back," writes National Public Radio commentator Margot Adler, in
Drawing Down the Moon, *"all our ancestors practiced religions that had*
neither creeds nor dogmas, neither prophets nor holy books. These religions were
based on the celebrations of the seasonal cycles of nature. They were based on
what people did, as opposed to what people believed."

To retrieve these ancient practices, the mostly urban pioneers of the neopagan
movement formed congregations called "covens" or "groves," ideally made up
of thirteen members, while some chose to practice independently as "solitaires."

Modern Craft rituals—both in the 1960s and today—vary widely, a reflection of the Craft's commitment to independence, intuition, and empirical knowledge. While one coven may be influenced by the Greek goddess–centric Dianic tradition, another might draw from the more masculine wizardry of the Irish and Welsh Druids, or perhaps find archetypal balance in the "faerie" tradition. The common philosophic thread that runs through all is summarized by Margot Adler: "The world is holy. Nature is holy. The body is holy. Sexuality is holy. The mind is holy. The imagination is holy . . . [and] Divinity . . . is as much within you as without."[1]

While the neopagan movement has continued to flourish in America since it first gained momentum in the mid-twentieth century, no definitive membership statistics are available owing to its decentralized leadership structure and a continued concern over witch hysteria and discrimination. It is not uncommon, for example, for witches—particularly those residing in rural areas—to be unaware of those around them who share their faith and ritual practices. With a mission to connect and protect, a number of federally recognized organizations like Covenant of the Goddess (CoG) have been formed to administer clergy credentials, provide legal counsel for freedom of religion cases, and facilitate annual retreats for our nation's broad community of witches.

Casting Spells with Witches

Cruising at an altitude of thirty thousand feet, I gazed out my oval window, rapt in the fantasy of skipping across the meringue of cloud beneath me. I suddenly realized how long it had been since I indulged such imaginings. A frequent flier since the age of seven, I have logged countless hours observing the mating rituals of clouds, their blending and separating and newly hatched puffs left behind in jet streams to fend for themselves. Throughout my childhood, my other favorite part of every plane ride was the descent, those isolated minutes before landing when life below is suddenly visible— model-train-set scenery laid across a strangely perfect patchwork of greens and browns.

Now, watching the clouds part to reveal the land hidden beneath them, I felt old and removed from the childlike thrill of plane and amusement park rides. I searched my memory for a clue as to the moment when flying had gone from stomach-fluttering excitement to tedious chore. While my last rooftop jump as Wonder Woman was still fresh in my mind, and I could remember being the husband in plenty of games of house, the maître d' in a string of faux restaurants, and the air guitarist for all sorts of killer bands, the desire to do such things seemed to belong to a lifetime ago.

When I got off the plane in the Las Vegas airport, the first sound I heard was the *clink* of secular tithing—coins dropped into the coffers of the great god of chance. I knew the place and its trappings all too well, not as a weekend devotee, but as a reluctant resident of some twelve years earlier.

Ironically my mother and I had been out shopping for my senior homecoming dress in my high school hometown of Albuquerque when she announced our upcoming move. I was confronted once again by my mother's faith in change as she explained that two states away there was a job offer too good to pass up. Early the morning after my homecoming dance, I resentfully piled my last Hefty bag of clothing into the trunk of my car, said good-bye to our cul-de-sac, and followed my mother's taillights west.

We pulled into our new city just as the sun was retreating. Enormous themed edifices jutted into the dusky sky—neighboring casinos engaged in an absurd high-stakes game of keeping up with the Joneses. From Las Vegas Boulevard, we turned left at the pink towers of Circus Circus and followed Rainbow Avenue to its end: a fluorescent 7-Eleven and a terminally brown apartment complex in which we had leased a one-bedroom apartment, sight unseen. With our old furniture in exile—too bulky for our new close quarters—we rented a plaid love seat, a card table, four folding chairs, and one queen mattress, which came wrapped in plastic.

For a while my mother and I pretended to appreciate the novelty of our simplified existence on the lip of this electric place. Growing up together, we had always sung when times were tough. Helen Reddy's "You and Me Against the World," Sonny and Cher's "I've Got You Babe," and Simon and Garfunkel's "Like a Bridge Over Troubled Waters": our standards had provided nearly two decades of a united front. But we both quietly knew that our time together was running out.

Of its many drab corners, it's our apartment's kitchen nook with its card table and folding chairs that I most remember, being the view from which I observed the watershed ceremony of self-sovereignty: my eighteenth birthday. Coming home after another day as an alienated transfer student, I found a note taped to the refrigerator. Still making first impressions on the job, my mother, in anticipation of working late, had dropped off a birthday "surprise" during her lunch hour for me to share with "a few friends" after school. Without friends or any other reason to hesitate, I followed the note's clues to the freezer, carefully opening the box I found there so as not to dent its sugary insides. I lit the candles and watched the flames tango, taking their bows, one by one, into chilled icing. On the last flicker, I sneaked in a wish, picked off the streams of hardened wax, and ate my mint chocolate chip cake until all evidence of it—and the day it marked—had disappeared.

Somewhere around the halfway point, I was unquestionably full but could not keep the fork from its mechanical return to my mouth. I suddenly became conscious of the bottomless hole I was trying to fill, a void of girlish insecurity that I had expected this day—in all its womanly potency—to seal up. After all, I was technically "of age," newly fitted with independence, legally free to move as I pleased. And yet as I looked around, I wasn't sure which route of self-determination to take. Even more disorienting, I wasn't certain what this sudden state of womanhood *entailed.* After all, my mother's generation was in the midst of redefining these realms of identity for all of us. Though I'd been given pointers and taken plenty of observational notes, none of it felt as if it belonged to me. It would be many more birthdays, and at least as many wishes, before I would come to understand and revel in what it means to be a woman.

Twelve years into that process, I had been drawn back to my old Las Vegas haunt for a weeklong retreat with a few hundred witches. They'd be flying in from all over the country to convene at an off-the-beaten-path hotel and casino.

As a way to cut down on rooming expenses, I'd been randomly paired with a witch from upstate New York named Cindy. She and I became acquainted over ninety-five-cent breakfast specials in the casino's diner. Eyeing our garish surroundings, Cindy assured me that witches normally congregate *outdoors,* under a roofless moonlit sky. But despite the uninspired site choice, her excitement was nearly uncontainable. This was her first Covenant of the Goddess retreat as a relatively new Craft initiate at the age of forty. "There will be a lot of *amazing* people here," Cindy assured me, revealing a little uncertainty about her own prowess as a junior witch. Proud of the Craft's tradition of political, environmental, and social activism, Cindy was looking to gain leadership skills in these and other areas. She hoped she might one day serve as an exemplary high priestess to her local coven.

Cindy and I followed a trail of witches (at a gender ratio of about three to one in favor of women) into the Temptation Room—an oversized meeting hall plainly marked by a beveled plaque set above its door. I couldn't help but wonder if we'd been assigned the room for the sheer amusement of hotel management, considering the less hedonistic names over the doors of the adjacent rooms, which held a nursing conference and a Christian Calvary meeting. The witches seemed unfazed, breezing through the entrance and searching out old friends with screams of delight. I roamed the room, introducing myself to those who were less extroverted: a few computer programmers and middle-aged homemakers, a horticulturist, two psychotherapists, a handful of excessively pierced college students, and one transsexual in transition. Some referred to themselves as "pagan" or "Wiccan," while others wore "witch" as a badge of honor. "A lot of people think we witches worship the devil," remarked one unhesitant spokesperson, a grandmother of three from Ohio. "But we don't even acknowledge evil or the devil's *existence,*" she huffed. Mainstream witches must constantly struggle to distinguish their faith from the more sinister Satanism, or "black" witchery. "It's a terrible shame that some people's misinformed *ideas* about us have kept a lot of us good witches in the closet," she said.

Following the woman's sight line, I spied a brooding man in a button-down oxford shirt standing alone and looking as if he'd like to keep it that way. Wandering in his direction, I noticed a pentagram dangling conspicuously over his pinstripes. If there was anyone in the room who had at least *experimented* with black magic, I wondered if it might be the guy dressed against type. Mustering up gumption, I invaded his space with an introduction and a little witchy chitchat before asking if he'd ever dabbled in the dark side. "I did when I was younger, but I never inhaled," he said with a mischievous grin. Warming up to the idea of talking to someone, he acknowledged that it was his first CoG retreat and he wasn't particularly comfortable around "new people." He had been practicing for many years as a "solitaire" in the Bay Area, and was now flirting with the idea of coming out of the grandmother's closet to explore a more communal practice.

He caught me eyeing his pentagram as he spoke, and asked if I was familiar with its meaning. "Only what I've gleaned from movies and cheesy TV shows about the occult," I admitted. Fingering its five points, he explained that four of them represented the directions—east, west, north, and south—while the fifth embodied the *Spirit,* a broad Craft term encompassing the notions of Creator, divinity, ultimate reality, governing intelligence, and protective guide.

In parting, I asked whether he called himself a pagan or a witch. "Neither, I'm Jewitch," he said, flashing another coy smile before taking an unobtrusive seat in the back of the room.

Grabbing a quick cup of coffee before the morning's proceedings began, I poured cream alongside one of CoG's cofounders—an energetic, no-nonsense woman in her fifties. Seizing the moment, I asked her how she would characterize herself as a modern witch. Without so much as a pause or a break in her forward stride, she said, "A witch is someone who honors the earth and all of life; experiences the divine from within, not without, yet acknowledges the divinity in all; takes responsibility for all actions and choices; honors the feminine as well as the masculine, the seasons as well as the moon, and engages in ceremony to fortify these beliefs." I watched as she carried her vim, vigor, and piping hot coffee up the platform stairs to welcome her fellow witches to their annual retreat.

In olden times, long before there were casinos and 7-Elevens, humans went to great lengths to connect to the cosmic mysteries and seasonal cycles that either sustained or destroyed them. But now, for many of us who don't live in rural areas, our most common encounter with the earth and its cycles occurs in the produce section of our local supermarket. While modern witches shop at well-stocked stores like the rest of us, they also tend to grow at least some of their own food as a way of preserving their ancestrally–bound relationship to the natural world and its rhythms.

I sat through eight long hours of coven updates and argumentative voting on administrative agendas (yes, even witches succumb to bureaucracy). With a "twinkle" of hands, the representative members came to a silent, democratic consensus on everything from budget proposals, to the induction of pending covens, to organizational positions on current First Amendment issues. At the end of the day, everyone seemed anxious to eat dinner and return for our first group ritual. As the roomful of witches stood to stretch before hitting the all-you-can-eat buffet lines, a few parting announcements were made. "Please do not forget to keep all swords and daggers concealed while walking through the casino," implored the woman I'd met at the coffee table. She added, "Unfortunately, due to our location, sky clad will not be permitted at tonight's ritual, or any others during this week. Enjoy your dinner." I leaned over to the grandmother from Ohio for some translation. "It's when one wears nothing but the sky, dear," she whispered. She explained that some witches prefer imaginative costumes to nudity, though dress code—or lack thereof—is never mandated.

Witchcraft descends from agrarian traditions believed to have included ritual orgies as a symbolic means of promoting fertile crops and successful hunts. A few of the witches were quick to distinguish historical fact from modern fiction when I inquired about sky-clad boundaries. "While we are comfortable with our sexuality and sensuality, we *don't* condone orgies," said the woman sitting across from me at the communal dinner table. "Except for the brief exception of the late 1960s," added the eavesdropping witch next to her with a laugh. In the contemporary Craft, sky clad is an ancient tradition preserved as a statement of liberation, and a means for celebrating the natural beauty of the human body.

I traced my steps back to the Temptation Room, fully clothed and unarmed as directed. Joining a half-formed circle, I noticed some new faces in the crowd—locals and tourists who'd gotten wind of the witches' convention and come to see what all the hubbub was about. While Wiccan witches, as an unwritten policy, do not proselytize, they do sometimes open their ceremonies to the general public in an effort to dispel stereotypes of bat tails bubbling in cauldrons. Now numbering well over two hundred, we joined hands to "cast" an enormous lopsided circle intended to ward off the mundane world just outside our double doors.

A high priestess in a tie-dyed dress entered the circle to direct our collective attention to the four directions, starting at the east and working her way clockwise as she called forth the "guardians" and their "elements" of air, fire, water, and earth. With each invocation, it was believed she was raising a "cone" of protective and positive energy around us, an elevated vibration that would induce a more holy state of being. Planting her bare feet in the final direction—the north-ish side of our circle—the priestess raised her phallic wand, called an *anthema,* to proclaim, as she had for the others, "Hail, guardians of the watchtowers of the north, powers of earth—"

A muffled ring suddenly echoed from the bag of sacred props resting at her feet.

"—we seek your presence and protection at this rite," she bellowed in an effort to overpower the intermittent distraction. After four rings, the persistent caller hung up and dialed again. With a wince and a sigh, she passed her scepter to the nearest sorceress, rifled through her bag, and answered her cell phone with gritted teeth. "I'm in the middle of a *ritual,*" she seethed at the anonymous caller. And with that, whatever shred of suspended reality we had mobilized dropped bluntly to the casino's paisley carpet.

Hoping to rescue us from the absurdity of our surroundings and the awkwardness of holding a stranger's sweaty hand just a little too long, the relief witch hurriedly beckoned four men and four women to the center of our circle. Standing back-to-back with palms meeting, the appointed women were ringed by their male counterparts, and a chorus of masculine voices addressed "the Goddess"—the female aspect of the Creator. "Great Mother of us all," they beseeched in unison, "we ask for your presence within the circle and within us. We meet to honor you and unite with you. Bless us with your abundant love. Blessed be." The four women then encircled the men, entreating "the God" with his equally infinite attributes to join His Goddess consort.

Acknowledging masculine and feminine components of the Deity, most witches believe that each offers something unique to their ceremonial life. Known generally as "the lifegiving force," the feminine aspect of the Divine is balanced by the "Horned God" of Paleolithic times, who is acknowledged as "the death force."[2] Untamed, expressive, and strong without being violent, patriarchal, or unnecessarily destructive, the masculine polarity is described by one preeminent witch as "the force of limitation that is the necessary balance to unbridled creation."[3] In circle formation, witches believe that the symmetry of Spirit literally channels itself into the presiding priestess and/or priest to convey divine wisdom to the rest of the coven.

With invitations out to our two honored Guests, the four elemental energies, and a lineup of watchtower guardians, the list was complete, our circle formally "opened," and our "spiral ritual" set to unwind. As one reverberating voice, we rhythmically chanted, over and over again, the simple charm: "We are the power in everyone; we are the dance of the moon and sun; we are the hope that will not die; we are the turning of the tide." With interlaced hands our line began to move, folding in and out and over and under itself, like weaving locks of a giant's braid. While there was an air of earnestness to our ceremonial dance, the veteran witches setting the tone for the rest of us swaggered and crooned with the kind of childlike playfulness I had pondered during my plane ride. I chuckled at my cobwebbed preconceptions about witchcraft, suddenly thrust into my first Wiccan ritual, which felt more like an episode of *Sesame Street* than it did adult programming. I began to understand that modern witches seek deeper states of consciousness and intuitive insight as much through fun and frivolity as through contemplative reflection.

Paying close attention to the sprightly footwork of the witches on either side of me, I careened around the room, the intensity and speed of our steps increasing with each new turn of verse. After the first few rounds, I, and others with not-long legs, were running to keep up, yanked to the left and to the right like rag dolls as we ducked our heads under arms and arched our arms over heads, some of us badly botching the moves. Blurred faces and body parts whizzed and whirled past my eyes, laughing and singing mouths skewed. Our unbreakable human chain was meant to represent the Craft's theme of oneness in motion, though not *gracefully* carried out at every turn. Both of my big toes throbbed, having been inadvertently stomped on by a witch's cowboy boot. Breathing through the pain, I noticed that the oxygen in the room was becoming depleted—a hazard of indoor ritualizing. Eventually most of us resorted to panting the mantra— ". . . we are the dance . . . moon and sun . . . will not die"—some witches reaching ecstatic levels of giddiness. Through the tiny keyhole of the non-rational mind, the witches hoped to unlock a deeper cosmic self, the ego-less spirit essence that people of every religious creed seek to find. It is by recovering the raw imagination and creative energies of the child deep within that witches believe they are brought closer to truth and self-realization, a more integrated state of being attained by coloring outside the bounds of linear-minded labels, conventions, and limitations.

Skipping with wild abandon to keep up, I saw ahead of me a pair of locked hands forming two sides of a small bridge under which I guess I was supposed to duck, as in a child's game of London Bridge. The hands belonged to two men, one in a kilt, the other in black vinyl, whose eyebrows raised with rhapsodic glee as they charged toward me. Just as we reached one another, however, their arms accidentally collapsed and caught me by the neck for a slow-motion second. Just as I thought I might slither unconscious to the floor, I and my unwitting assailants—whose faces were contorted with apologetic horror—were swept away in opposite directions, caught in the undertow of our human swell.

Amid sighs of relief—not just my own—our frenzied song and dance began to slow. At last we resumed our egg-shaped circle, the tie-dyed priestess reclaiming her place at its center. Facing each direction in reverse order, she offered our collective appreciation to the guardians and elements for their "presence and protection," delivering a special thank-you to "the God and the Goddess" who had, it was believed, danced right along with us. "The circle is open, yet unbroken," the woman solemnly declared. "May the peace of the Goddess go in our hearts. Merry meet and merry part, and merry meet again. Blessed be." With that, we rejoined the world of cell phones, slot machines, and smoky hotel bars.

The next day, after observing another round of internal witch affairs—proposals, deliberation, and more voting—I attended an afternoon workshop on spell casting. Spells, also known as "charms"—are an essential component of any witch's practice and every group ritual. Using an easel board and dry-erase markers, two sassy sisters first spelled out their Wiccan philosophy before sharing a few magic formulas from their "Book of Shadows"—a customized diary of secret spells, dream interpretations, and personal writings. On the board were scribbled words and phrases like "integrity;" "accountability;" "power *to*," "not power *over*;" and "threefold" (a karmalike tenet whereby the "positive and negative thoughts and deeds imbued in a witch's spell" create returns, like a boomerang, with three times the punch). As one strapping man in suspenders confirmed from the back of the room: "You gotta eat what you cook!"

Nodding in agreement with his outburst, the sisters went on to say that every spell must measure up to the Wiccan yardstick: *harm no one; do as you please.* "A lot of people are drawn to the Craft because they feel out of control and want to exercise power over others," said one of the sisters. "They need to be adjusted to understanding that the Craft is not about imposing your will upon *others* for self-serving purposes."

"The integrity with which you live will either bolster or diminish your magic," added her sibling.

Whether attempting to heal emotional or psychological wounds, find true love, change jobs, increase happiness, or right social inequity, witches cast spells as a way of influencing outcomes. Their hope is to mold the reality they believe is never predetermined or fixed, but rather, like a free-flowing stream, in constant motion. No matter which particular "family" tradition it is articulated through, the Craft is a faith of collaboration between human will and Divine willingness.

"If you want to fall in love," one of the sisters offered as an example, "don't name a specific person you want to *make* love you. Name the qualities you desire, and let the Goddess draw someone to you." For the actual spell "work" involved in attracting love, the sisters recommended techniques to awaken physical and intuitive senses, from lighting red and orange candles symbolizing passion and friendship, to inhaling the scent of rose oil, to calling upon the deities associated with love, such as Aphrodite. The sisters suggested we write down the qualities we desired on a piece of paper, and place it (folded four times) in a pouch surrounded by our most beloved personal objects. Despite their specificity, they encouraged any alterations or additions we might be "inspired to make" to this and other spells, explaining that the physical objects—be they candles, flowers, herbs, oils, or a lock of hair—were but representations of the "*invisible* power" we each possessed as "cocreators."

Once internal and external forces have been aroused and aligned, a "charm"—similar in concept to a prayer—is verbalized to cement the intent of the spell caster. "Then you must go about your life emanating through yourself the very qualities you dream to find in another," reasoned the sisters. This mystical interplay between human effort and Divine support is seen as the only hope for humankind and for the planet, itself regarded as a living, breathing, sacred organism.

After the spell seminar, I sat and talked with Elana, a precocious thirteen-year-old from Palo Alto who had come to the retreat with her Wiccan parents. Having conducted circle rites since the age of four, Elana wanted to make sure I knew that spells can be effected simply by "focusing one's mind and inner energies on the desired outcome, without the use of any paper and pouches and scented oils." Deities, like Aphrodite or Athena, can provide that focus, she explained, "if we concentrate on their likeness and qualities, like a meditation. For example, I might bring Athena into my spell for a healing, but what I'm really doing is drawing this power of healing out of myself. You don't do ritual and walk away expecting it to happen; you do ritual to help *you* make it happen. There's that useful saying," she added, unknowingly quoting one of America's founding mystics, Benjamin Franklin, from his *Poor Richard's Almanac,* "'God helps those who help themselves.' Well, *that's* the Craft," she said.

"The blessing of coven practice [group rituals] is that it helps people help themselves," Elana continued, offering the example of a spell she and her coven had recently cast on behalf of a member in dire need of employment. "Everyone who had a job took a quarter in their hands and 'charged' it by focusing their energy on abundance and working," she recounted. "With their quarters in hand they formed a circle around the woman." Those in Elana's coven who were unemployed formed a second, outer circle. "Holding hands, we borrowed a very inventive charm," she said, adding that "any" coupling of words can be used as a charm so long as it conveys the right intent. "So we repeated 'Hi-ho, hi-ho, it's off to work we go' about two dozen times." Then Elana and her coven "charged the energy" around a cake and a carafe of wine to spread the wealth from their spell of abundance. "May you never hunger, blessed be," each witch proclaimed as he or she fed cake to another, followed by a sip of wine and the incantation "May you never thirst, blessed be." After that night's ritual, explained Elana, the coven member continued her active job search and, as if by magic, soon found one.

Listening to Elana and others detail their rituals, it occurred to me that I had, while living in Los Angeles, been part of a kind of informal coven. I don't remember exactly how our first outdoor circular assembly came about or who found the deserted hillside plateau we eventually commandeered. The group of women who gathered there were completely untutored—unlike these witches, our circles were not patterned from a secret family tradition, nor did they follow the instruction of a high priestess or priest.

We met every few months at sunset, sometimes on the eve of a new moon or for a seasonal equinox or solstice. Together we would clear away brush and debris and begin building a sort of altar using swaths of fabric, freshly cut flowers, tree boughs, shells, candles, found objects, photographs, instruments, incense, and our own private keepsakes. Around this candlelit created space—this communal canvas—we would circle, women of disparate places and ages drawn together for a particular kind of communion that was lacking in our busy everyday lives. Without interruption, we took turns speaking, praying, reciting, or singing whatever was on our mind or weighing on our heart. Recurrent themes like hibernation, death, germination, birth, fear, fierceness, and forgiveness invariably arose, often reflective of the season despite our perpetually mild climate. With all generations—maiden, mother, and crone, to use the Wiccan terms—represented in our circles, we were reminded, again and again, of what we share as women. It was in this space, surrounded by old friends and strangers alike, encircled in their compassion and wisdom, that I felt as safe and free as I ever have to be strong, weak, silly, serious, off-key, off-kilter, and long-winded.

Knowing what I do now, it's difficult to imagine that in all those years it never occurred to me that an observer might be inclined to call us witches. At the same time, my week with card-carrying pagans made it clear that my earlier dabbling didn't exactly qualify as true Wiccan practice. Like all spiritual traditions, authentic witchcraft is a discipline, an integrative way of life that extends beyond a seasonal ritual, an occasional spell, or a vote for the Green Party.

"Witchcraft is a minute-to-minute thing for me," said Elana on the last night of the retreat, as we stood outside the door of a costume party that was not yet in full swing. "My practice gives me a strong sense of who I am and my self-worth." We were both momentarily distracted by new arrivals who'd managed to outwit the sky-clad ban by painting their naked bodies silver from head to toe—metallic breasts and butts silhouetted in the dim light. "Being a witch allows me to be attuned to, accept, and appreciate my mind and my body when a lot of girls my age are feeling insane and starving themselves," Elana continued, as if inspired by the shimmering spectacle. "In helping me better know myself, the Craft has prepared me to make spur-of-the-moment decisions without violating who I am."

Following the sounds of disco and the glint of the rented mirror ball, Elana and I joined the silver women and countless others in costume on the dance floor for the final night of uninhibited strutting and crooning. While Craft ritual can be as weighty and esoteric as the next religion, the witches I met never turned down the chance to take themselves lightly.

Slipping quietly out of my room the next morning, I saw no familiar faces in the hallways or lobby. I'd finally found a religious order that deemed the sacred hour to be well past the rooster's crow, and not a minute before a strong cup of coffee. Turning in my key at the front desk, I headed for the casino's exit, which, perhaps intentionally, was not easy to locate among the zoo of machines squawking and barking to be fed.

It seemed somehow fitting that my exploration of early-twenty-first-century American faith would coincidentally begin, and end, inside a casino. It was a surreal exaggeration of the material desires and distractions of modern life, a deceiving, climate-controlled place without clocks or windows where hours and days are intentionally undifferentiated from one another. I passed by rows of bleary-eyed slot players who wore debit cards on stretchy leashes around their necks, plugging themselves into their slot machine of choice with a swipe of their card. Wending my way around more banks of animated boxes, I felt starved for things not programmed or manufactured. I'd spent a week observing the practice of a faith supremely connected to the natural world and its cycles and elements, but hadn't inhaled fresh air, or seen the sun or moon more than once or twice, and then, only by accident. Following a sliver of natural light streaming across the floor, I finally made my escape into the blue-skied desert.

I arrived at the airport just in time to catch my canceled flight. Scavenging overpriced junk food, I planted myself at a random gate to wait for the next plane to Boston. "This is the last call for Flight 2014 to Los Angeles," blared the speaker overhead. As I watched the last passenger hurry down the gateway, I resisted the urge to follow behind, to land on familiar ground and be surrounded by the people who'd been part of those hillside gatherings in my twenties. Now thirty, I prayed I would never forget what I had learned in their midst—about the woman I am, and the one I still hope to become. It was because of those moonlit, makeshift ceremonies that I realized it's okay to have your cake and eat it too, though it tastes even better when shared with people who reflect back to you all that you might not see in yourself. Elana, in all her thirteen years of experience and with her coven's support, seemed already to grasp this, laying claim to her identity and making it all her own.

I watched the mouth of the gate close and Flight 2014 pull away. Though all the reasons weren't yet clear to me, bearing east—returning to a new love in a city far from home—felt like the right choice of direction.

As disorienting as being pulled in two directions can be, limbo often defines our lives more than anything else. We seek meaning from uncertainty, and stability in the rhythm of change. If I have gleaned anything from observing the spiritual practices of others over these last few years, it is that only faith can alchemize the unknown, only trust can walk us safely home, to God, to truth, or to our true godly selves.

. . . And thou who thinkest to seek Me,
know that thy seeking and yearning shall avail thee not
unless thou knowest the Mystery:
that if that which thou seekest thou findest not within thee,
thou wilt never find it without.

For behold, I have been with thee from the beginning;
and I am that which is attained at the end of desire.

— DOREEN VALIENTE, "CHARGE OF THE STAR GODDESS"

Epilogue

It has been nearly four years since I left Los Angeles one January morning, my car overstuffed with all my personal belongings. After a decade in the city, I had experienced earthquakes, mud slides, windstorms, and brushfires, not to mention less natural disasters, so it hardly surprised me when the day of my departure was marked by a flood of biblical proportions. I was inaugurating a pilgrimage I hardly had the words to explain to the friends who sent me on my way, their good luck charms dangling from my rearview mirror as I navigated the sheets of rain layering Fairfax Avenue. The creeping procession of orange-red brake lights that I trailed behind felt funereal. I was, after all, paying my last respects to intersections, storefronts, and landmarks that would no longer define my sense of home and self.

I did not know exactly where I was headed, which direction the stretch of road would ultimately lead. I knew only, as we sometimes do, that not to go—though it would be the easier choice—would mean to ignore tugging feelings and whispering signs, like the owl that attacked Gene Begay in his dream, uprooting him and sending him home. I, too, felt the pull of something dreamy and magnetic, compelling me *away* from my embankment of comfort, security, and routine to investigate how people of faith *live* what they believe.

By definition, religion is something that "binds." I had for some time assumed that if something profound—something divine, or of God—was meant to be a central part of my life, it would find its way and bind itself to me. Now I understand that grace does not necessarily come to those who wait; the binding must be proactive. One cannot just exercise faith in pro-

nounced moments of fear, anxiety, desperation, or despair; its very meaning compels us to make it a part of our everyday life, an ongoing process of
choosing what goes on inside of us. To have faith void of routine physical
expression, discipline, and sacrifice—whether in the form of prayer, meditation, work, worship, charity, song, fast, or food—is like taking pictures
without film in the camera; there's no tangible or enduring reflection of
what we fleetingly observe. Whether expressing gratitude or reverence;
merging with an ideal; seeking perspective; sanctifying time; creating a
sense of belonging, cleansing, meaning, and purpose; or honoring life and
its changes, it seems the composition of ritual is not nearly as important as
the consistency and intention with which it is enacted.

Over the last few years, friends and strangers alike have asked me *which*
religious practice(s) I've been most personally drawn to. In a sense, I've
been possessed by them all, their doctrines and devotions inhabiting me like
noisy tenants in a high-rise building. Even in sleep, I relive the experiences
and conversations of each chapter—words, symbols, and ceremony churn-
ing in me day and night. The process of experiencing, distilling, and writing
about others' practices has itself been a spiritual discipline, a monkish existence bringing me back, again and again, to mindfulness, to contemplation
of individual and universal inspiration and aspiration, to self-reflection, to
my computer's keyboard. My writing tools became ritual objects, as sanctifying to me as others inside the medicine circle, around the Sabbath table,
behind the auditing desk, in the dharma room, at the foot of the altar, or
during the Eucharist. The act of conveying what I've heard, seen, and felt
over these last few years has been a rite of passage for me, a daily struggle
with self-doubt and discomfort in examining myself through the lives and
choices of others.

As with any long journey, my topography, both internal and external,
has changed since I began. I fell in love and married in the midst of writing
this book, and my days and nights are now filled with exercises in giving,
accepting, and forgiveness, moments of heightened awareness and ecstasy
linked with the mundane, but no less sacred. And from this love has sprung
a little boy whose birth was my own deliverance, a realization that mother-
hood organically encompasses all that the world's religious practices
attempt to induce in a believer. As is undoubtedly the case for many new
parents, never did I grasp the notion of being one with another being as
when my husband and I watched our son draw his first breaths of inde-

pendent existence. In that moment and ever since, I have possessed the sensations and certainty of beholding the divine in a way I had vicariously experienced through those with indisputable religious faith. Like many people I met who described their spiritual discovery as a sudden sense of home, I found mine the night I gave birth.

And now this child is my seven-pound, eleven-ounce—and counting— meditation bell of mindfulness, the enduring spiritual experience Ram Dass and others headed east to find, the enterprise of selfless surrender monks and nuns seek in their vow of celibacy. My child-centered practice comes with a regimented discipline all its own. A variation of Lama Surya Das's technique, my daily meditation is what I've come to call "skin-gazing"— single-pointed focus on my son's bare body, or any particular limb that happens to be exposed. I do this meditation while he eats or sleeps, and sometimes while I hold him as he cries. A variation of Yogi Bhajan's white tantric yoga, the only remedy for those late-night colicky episodes is deep knee-bending squats, a repetitive, strenuous act of submission—particularly for the perpetually sleep-deprived—that can extend far longer than sixty-two minutes. And substituting for hymns to the Lord, hypnotic Hindu chants to Krishna, and Wiccan odes to the moon, my mantras have become "This old man . . . ," and "We all live in a yellow submarine. . . ." The intention behind these improvised, simple melodies has become the "magic serum" I searched for in Buddhism, the antidote to the acutely preoccupied, self-absorbed mind. As my husband and I rise through the night to feed, rock, and change diapers, we sometimes sleepily acknowledge the twinge of resentment, and then the wave of gratitude I imagine adherents of all faiths experience in the necessary inconvenience of giving oneself over completely to service to another, to love.

I recently read, in one of the new parent operating manuals, that until the age of about seven months, babies have no clue that they are separate entities from their parents. Around that eighth month of human development, the process of individuation begins to take hold, bringing with it the need to learn "object permanence"—the realization that out of sight does not necessarily mean out of existence. The notion of the self intensifies with age, our sense of you and me, us and them, growing as fast and strong as teeth and bones. It is this innate progression that religions attempt to interrupt and, in a sense, reverse. Through ritual practice, people strive to reclaim—if only for blissful seconds at a time—the sense of oneness and trust that came so effortlessly to us during our first six months of life. While every religion offers a code of ethics, a forum for fellowship, methods of exhausting the ego, and the promise of an afterlife, the core of every practice I encountered endeavors to bring us back to what we experienced before we "knew" anything.

When it is placed directly in front of us, piercing the mist accumulated in adulthood, we all seem to instinctively recall our ephemeral, uncomplicated connection. This fact sank into me the first day I took my son out into the world so I could run a few quick errands. While I pushed him in his stroller, strangers' faces beamed as they held open store doors and generously offered assistance and kind words. Having been in a bubble of isolation since giving birth three weeks earlier, my first reaction was to wonder what had so dramatically changed in the world while I was away. Why did everyone suddenly seem to have stepped from the streets of Mayberry to the ones surrounding my local strip mall? And then I realized that the world hadn't changed, *I* had, by virtue of my traveling companion. Hard-faced strangers were stopping in their tracks for the chance to exchange a coo or a tiny shake with this new earthly arrival. Indulging their gestures, my son indiscriminately coiled his miniature hand around each extended index finger, as if to gladly recharge it with the mojo of untainted purity pumping through his veins. Satisfied, and without a word to me—the mere adult porter for this wide-eyed pint of perfection—each stranger would smile contentedly and continue on their way, a brief and dreamy zap of remembrance and recognition tucked somewhere inside of them.

After witnessing a number of these unsolicited exchanges, I imagined what it would be like if it were *me* these total strangers looked upon when they flashed their smiles so easily and sincerely to say "Aren't you just the cutest, most precious thing" before going on about their day. Of course, at first this sort of trend would be startling, even disconcerting. But in time, we would adapt, as we do to all things, greeting one another as adults with the openness, trust, and fundamental acceptance genetically encoded in each of us. Though it sounds like a parody of our society, this is exactly what every religion asks that we do.

The practices belonging to the world's rich traditions collectively require that they be tested in the company of others. Ultimately, both our ancient and newfangled traditions challenge us to come out of our sanctuaries, down from our hillsides of solitude, and up from our knees to see from the vantage point of crowded streets and homes what exactly we've mastered. As one Muslim man said to me, "Praying and fasting are important, but true religion is in our dealings with one another." If the people I spent time with are any indication, most come to find that their acts of communion and heightened states of awareness are, like parenting, a lifelong process. High points, low points, and everything in between, the divinely minded person of the twenty-first century shares with all people of faith, down through the ages, the realization that their practice is not a point of arrival so much as a port of constant departure. Forever in transit, what we do to express our devotion becomes moments of remembrance that arm us for the hours and days of forgetfulness that surround them.

After vagabonding for the last few years, collecting impressions of people in faithful locomotion, I have settled with my family into a small mountain town about an hour or two from my old friends in Los Angeles. It is a fertile town, lush with orchards and unfilled spaces, where people are generally as gracious to me as they are to my child. Not long ago, I sent a letter to John Stoltzfoos, the Amish farmer, describing the plot of land I finally must care for, the patience I'm finding so that I may watch things grow, and how I might just get those laboring calluses after all. Looking around my home, I am surrounded by reminders of what I now know I must do to feel good: breathe deeply, stay aware of my thoughts and actions, be proactive, not reactive, and remain grateful, loving, and giving.

Looking ahead, I realize that as our child grows, so must my mastery of all that I have learned while loving him. As he claims his independence—beginning his own journey into separation and his own lifelong return to connection—I will have to find other ways to recall with consistency what I've found so immediately and evidently in his baby-essence. It is the same, often ineffable experience that others I met found in a medicine pipe, a peyote plant, a statue, a sunrise, holy water, a sacred book, at a dinner table, behind or in front of a pulpit, through charity, or in a turn of a phrase. If by my own future efforts—whether formal or informal—the qualities of mindfulness, clarity, peace, and generosity ever become second nature and unconditional, then I think I will have once and for all absorbed what Zoroaster, Buddha, Moses, Jesus, Muhammad, Confucius, Lao-tzu, Guru Nanak, Gandhi, Henry David Thoreau, the saints, sages, writers, wise crones, and all who have been overlooked by history books were trying to show and tell us.

"*Painted cakes do not satisfy hunger,*" remarks Ram Dass at the end of *Be Here Now*. And while more than thirty years have passed between that book and this one, dried ink and secondhand experience still cannot fill up a soul hungering to awaken, or a mind desiring to *know,* more so than believe. Choosing a religious or spiritual path is a profound exercise in freedom, an idealistic yet sublime right more widely and varyingly afforded us as Americans than any other people in the world. Don't take my word for it. Go taste it for yourself.

Notes

chapter one

1. Interview with Lac Courte Oreilles medicine man Gene Begay.
2. Basil Johnston, *Ojibway Ceremonies* (Toronto: McClelland and Stewart, 1982), 33.

chapter two

1. Aldous Huxley, *The Doors of Perception and Heaven and Hell* (New York: Harper & Row, 1954), 70.

chapter three

1. Donald B. Kraybill, *The Riddle of Amish Culture* (Baltimore: Johns Hopkins University Press, 1989), 4.
2. John A. Hostetler, *Amish Society*, 4th ed. (Baltimore: Johns Hopkins University Press, 1993), 52.
3. Ibid., 14.
4. Ibid., 10.
5. Ibid., 227.
6. Ibid., 228.
7. Ibid., 27.
8. Colossians 2:8.
9. Romans 12:2.

chapter four

1. Mayeul De Dreuille, *From East to West: A History of Monasticism* (New York: Crossroad, 1999), 59.

2.   Matthew Bunson, *Our Sunday Visitor's Encyclopedia of Catholic History* (Huntington, Ind.: Our Sunday Visitor, 1995).

3.   Anthony C. Meisel and M. L. Del Mastro, introduction to *The Rule of St. Benedict* (New York: Image Books, Doubleday, 1975), 93.

4.   1 John 4:20.

5.   George H. Gallup, Jr., and Jim Castelli, *The People's Religion* (New York: Macmillan Publishing, 1989), 252.

6.   Mark 8:35.

7.   Meisel and Del Mastro, *The Rule,* 61.

8.   Interview with Rev. Peter Gomes.

9.   Thomas Merton, *Thoughts in Solitude,* 25th ed. (New York: Noonday Press, 1997), 67.

chapter five

1.   James 1:5.

chapter six

1.   George H. Gallup, Jr., *Religion in America 1996* (Princeton, N.J.: The Princeton Religion Research Center, n.d.), 36–37.

2.   Mary Baker Eddy, *Science and Health with Key to the Scriptures* (Boston: First Church of Christ, Scientist, 1994), 368.

3.   Matthew 18:3.

4.   Matthew 5:48.

5.   Corinthians 6:2.

6.   Eddy, *Science and Health,* 382.

7.   Luke 17:21.

chapter seven

1.   Huston Smith, *The World's Religions: Our Great Wisdom Traditions,* rev. ed. (San Francisco: HarperCollins, 1991), 157.

2.   Fred B. Craddock, *Overhearing the Gospel* (Nashville: Parthenon Press, 1978).

chapter eight

1.   William F. Schulz, The Unitarian Universalist Pocket Guide, 2d ed. (Boston: Unitarian Universalist Association, 1993), 15.

2.   John A. Buehrens and Forrest Church, *A Chosen Faith: An Introduction to Unitarian Universalism*, rev. ed. (Boston: Beacon Press, 1998), 41.

3.   Ibid., 92.

4.   Ibid., 49.

5.   William F. Schulz, *Finding Time and Other Delicacies* (Boston: Unitarian Universalist Association, 1992), 127, 129.

6.   Walt Whitman, *Leaves of Grass* 3rd ed. (Boston, Thayer and Eldridge, 1861), 57.

chapter nine

1.   *The Centennial Book: An Abbreviated Account of the Organization and Its Auxiliaries, 1883–1993* (New York: National Spiritualist Association of Churches of the United States of America, 1994), 215.

2.   Ibid., 228–29.

chapter ten

1.   Meredith Sprunger, *An Introduction to Judaism,* http://www.urantia book.org/archive/readers/601_judaism.htm.

2.   Exodus 31:16.

3.   Exodus 20:11.

4.   *Gates of Repentance: The New Union Prayerbook for the Days of Awe* (New York: Central Conference of American Rabbis, 1984), 103.

5.   Abraham Joshua Heschel, *Man's Quest for God: Studies in Prayer and Symbolism* (Santa Fe: Aurora Press, 1998), 50.

6.   George H. Gallup, Jr., *Religion in America 1996* (Princeton, N.J.: The Princeton Religion Research Center, n.d.), 9.

chapter eleven

1.   George H. Gallup, Jr., *Religion in America 1996* (Princeton, N.J.: The Princeton Religion Research Center, n.d.), 25.

2.   Ibid., 39.

3.   An interview by Marvin Barrett, *Parabola: Myth, Tradition, and the Search for Meaning,* "Inviting Hell into Heaven," May 1999, "Prayer and Meditation," 65.

chapter twelve

1.   Qur'an 49:13.
2.   Qur'an 16:36.
3.   Sayyid Abul A'la Maududi, *Towards Understanding Islam* (Delhi: Markazi Maktaba Islami, 1996), 101.
4.   "Targets in Sudan and Afghanistan," *Boston Globe,* August 21, 1998, A-1.
5.   Ibid., A-15.
6.   Deborah Sontag, "Suicide Bomber Kills 5; in Israeli Retaliation, Jets Kill 12," *New York Times,* May 19, 2001.
7.   Huston Smith, *The World's Religions: Our Great Wisdom Traditions,* rev. ed. (San Francisco: HarperCollins, 1991), 240.
8.   Qur'an 14:14.

chapter thirteen

1.   Benjamin Shield and Richard Carlson, *For the Love of God* (San Rafael: New World Library, 1990), 5.
2.   Stephen Mitchell, *Dropping Ashes on the Buddha: The Teaching of Zen Master Seung Sahn* (New York: Grove Press, 1976), 58.
3.   Ibid., 6.
4.   Samuel Bercholz and Sherab Chodzin Kohn, *Entering the Stream: An Introduction to the Buddha and His Teachings* (Boston: Shambhala, 1993), 223.
5.   Ibid., 138.
6.   Mitchell, *Dropping Ashes,* 91.

chapter fourteen

1.   Paramahansa Yogananda, *Autobiography of a Yogi,* 12th ed. (Los Angeles: Self-Realization Fellowship, 1993), 392.
2.   Huston Smith, *The World's Religions: Our Great Wisdom Traditions,* rev. ed. (San Francisco: HarperCollins, 1991), 20.
3.   Diana L. Eck, *Darsan: Seeing the Divine Image in India,* 3rd ed. (New York: Columbia University Press, 1998), 77.
4.   *Ammachi's Life Story: The Early Years,* http:www.ammachi.org/ammachi/1-life.htm.
5.   *Sudhamani becomes "Mother,"* ibid.
6.   Ram Dass, *Be Here Now* (Kingsport: Kingsport Press, 1971), 11.
7.   Yogananda, *Autobiography,* 380.
8.   Dass, *Be Here Now,* 27.

chapter fifteen

1.   "What is 3HO (Healthy, Happy, Holy Organization)?" handout distributed by the 3HO Foundation.

chapter sixteen

1.   Neale Donald Walsch, *Conversations with God: An Uncommon Dialogue, Book 3* (Charlottesville: Hampton Roads, 1998), 366.
2.   Ibid., 153.

chapter seventeen

1.   *Alcoholics Anonymous,* 3rd ed. (New York: Alcoholics Anonymous World Services, 1976), 8.
2.   Ibid., 14.
3.   Ibid.
4.   *Twelve Steps and Twelve Traditions* (New York: A.A. Grapevine and Alcoholics Anonymous World Services, 1965), 139.
5.   *Alcoholics Anonymous,* 17.
6.   Ibid., 30.
7.   Ibid., 44, 45.
8.   Ibid., 164.
9.   Matthew 6:9–13.
10.   *Twelve Steps,* 97.

chapter eighteen

1.   40th Anniversary Catalogue (Church of Scientology Int'l., 1994), 15. Updated: *The Church of Scientology,* http://www.whatisScientology.org.
2.   *Scientology: The Route to Total Freedom, Training and Processing Services of the Church of Scientology,* (Church of Scientology Int'l., 1993).
3.   L. Ron Hubbard, *What Is Scientology* (Los Angeles: Bridge Publications, 1998), 557.
4.   Ibid., 778.
5.   Ibid., 523.
6.   Ibid., 557.

chapter nineteen

1.   Margot Adler, *Drawing Down the Moon: Witches, Druids, Goddess-Worshippers, and Other Pagans in America Today* (New York: Penguin Books, 1986), ix.

2.   Starhawk, *Spiral Dance: A Rebirth of the Ancient Religion of the Great Goddess* (San Francisco: HarperCollins, 1999), 50–51.

3.   Ibid., 51.

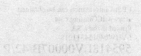

CPSIA information can be obtained
at www.ICGtesting.com
Printed in the USA
LVHW040154311018
595418LV00007B/42/P